# Stories of Beginning Teachers

*First-Year Challenges and Beyond*

NOTRE DAME ADVANCES IN EDUCATION

*Michael Pressley, General Editor*

# STORIES OF BEGINNING TEACHERS

*First-Year Challenges and Beyond*

*Alysia D. Roehrig*

*Michael Pressley*

*Denise A. Talotta*

UNIVERSITY OF NOTRE DAME PRESS
NOTRE DAME, INDIANA

Manufactured in the United States of America

Published for the Notre Dame Alliance for Catholic Education by the
University of Notre Dame Press.

The Notre Dame Alliance for Catholic Education thanks the
Lilly Endowment for its generous support in the publication of this book.

*Library of Congress Cataloging-in-Publication Data*
Roehrig, Alysia D., 1975-
 Stories of beginning teachers : first year challenges and beyond /
Alysia D. Roehrig, Michael Pressley, and Denise A. Talotta.
    p. cm. — (The Notre Dame Alliance for Catholic Education
series)
Includes bibliographical references (p.  ) and index.
 ISBN 0-268-01776-X (Cloth : alk. paper) — ISBN 0-268-01777-8
(Paperback : alk. paper)
 1. First-year teachers—Indiana—Case studies. 2. Teachers—Training
of—Indiana—Case studies. I. Pressley, Michael. II. Talotta, Denise A.
III. Title. IV. Series.
LB2844.1.N4 R62 2002
371.1–dc21
                          2001005495

∞  This book is printed on acid-free paper.

# Contents

# Preface

WHEN THIS PROJECT BEGAN, co-author Michael Pressley had just accepted an appointment to direct Notre Dame's teacher education effort. Alysia Roehrig and Denise Talotta had just entered graduate school. Roehrig decided during her first year that she would focus much of her attention on the challenges beginning teachers face in learning the profession. During Talotta's second year of graduate school, she joined the team, mainly to document the challenges confronted by more experienced teachers, which could be used as benchmarks against which to measure those reported by the beginning teachers.

The project received funding from the University of Notre Dame throughout its life of three years, in the form of provost's discretionary funds assigned to the chaired professorship held by Pressley and with occasional contributions from Americorps and the Alliance for Catholic Education (ACE), which sponsors teacher training at Notre Dame. The project was intended to inform and evaluate, in part, the local Notre Dame teacher education effort, which was then in its infancy. More importantly, however, we felt this work would provide a window on challenges faced by many beginning teachers. The Notre Dame teacher education program has undergone many revisions, a number motivated in part by challenges reported in the surveys and interviews reviewed in this volume. A full report of the evolution of the Notre Dame teacher education program is now being written and should be published shortly.

There are many to thank when carrying out a project of this magnitude. We appreciate the participation of the ACE teachers who gave so much of their time to the research. The mentor teachers were extremely helpful, providing information about challenges all teachers confronted in the school settings served by the beginning teachers in this study. We thank them for the data they provided. Then, there were the various research assistants employed over the course of the project, including Joanna Fee and Kate Borkowski.

Pressley and Roehrig worked very closely on all of the teacher data. First, there were a lot of data to code and decide how (and whether) to use. Second, there were competing categories of teaching challenges in the literature that we reviewed. Although all of these informed our data scoring, none of them determined it. In the chapters ahead, we detail the unique scoring scheme we developed for this study. The mentor data and analyses associated with them were devised by Denise Talotta and generally carried out by her, although she interacted with the first two authors to align her study as closely as possible to the work with the beginning teachers.

Coming to understand the challenges of beginning teaching is an important step in devising ways to prepare teachers in training and to provide support for beginning teachers once they enter the field. Thus, a main motivation for writing this book is to provide information to teacher educators and providers of in-service about the challenges faced by beginning teachers so that they can plan their efforts with these in mind. There is great motivation for teacher educators to be thinking hard about how their programs can help young teachers meet the demands they face, for no approach to teacher education has been identified to date that is particularly effective in preparing beginning teachers for the challenges of the school world (e.g., Brock, 1988; Rapp, 1986).

The book has a broader audience than teacher educators in departments and schools of education, however. It is intended to inform everyone in education—especially those teachers and administrators who mentor young colleagues—about the particular challenges faced by new teachers,. Such information is in great demand, with many, many schools now offering formal mentoring programs to beginning teachers, sometimes as part of the formal certification process. The popularity of mentoring is likely to increase, for beginning teachers who experience it generally report that it helps their teaching a lot (Lewis et al., 1999).

This book also is intended to inform prospective teachers and beginning teachers themselves about the profession they aspire to join, with our belief being that a young teacher who is at least informed about the potential challenges ahead is in a better position to prepare for them. For example, we think that if we can get the young people in our own program to read this book before they begin their first summer of coursework, they will be much more motivated in their classes, for they will understand better the challenges they will face in a very short time. Our students will better understand why a young teacher needs to know about content-specific pedagogy, student motivation, student learning, human development, classroom organization, classroom management, assessment techniques, ethical considerations, the social organization of classrooms, and the administration of schools.

In short, we think that the more known about the challenges of beginning teaching, the more likely those challenges can be confronted and overcome by teacher educators, supportive mentors, and young teachers themselves. This is critical, for it has been recognized for a very long time that the more a young teacher is challenged during the first year, the less likely the individual is to remain in teaching (Taylor & Dale, 1971). Early career understanding of the challenges of teaching is important for another reason, however. Many of the challenges of the beginning teacher do not go away with years of experience. Awareness of them should alert the young teacher to what she or he needs to know and needs to learn to have a successful career as a teacher (Adams, Hutchinson, & Martray, 1980; Dollase, 1992; Fuller, 1969; Koontz, 1963; Lee, 1974; Martin, 1991; Stegall, 1966; Thomas & Kiley, 1994).

At two points in this research, Alysia Roehrig assumed a disproportionate share of the responsibility. In spring 1998, Michael Pressley was diagnosed with a cancer that required extensive treatment. Most of that semester, Roehrig carried on alone. Near the very end of the project, in August 2000, as the write-up was being completed, Pressley was again diagnosed with cancer, which put him out of action for much of the last three months of manuscript preparation. At a minimum, he was distracted. To intensify matters, Roehrig was also Pressley's editorial assistant for the *Journal of Educational Psychology,* of which Pressley is editor. During the illnesses, Roehrig's responsibilities broadened considerably with respect to the *Journal* and with respect to managing Pressley's professional affairs in general. Hence, he personally extends thanks to Roehrig for her many services above and beyond the call of duty during the period when this book was written.

In the end the authors feel gratified about this project, which generated several very large data sets that arrived at many converging findings across data analytic approaches and various ways of classifying teachers. The volume provides a certainly compelling case that beginning teaching is challenging, filled with many little problems and some big ones. These findings should guide future teacher education efforts, providing many indications of just what our students need to know and need to know how to do in order to minimize their difficulties during the beginning years of teaching.

## REFERENCES

Adams, R. D., Hutchinson, S., & Martray, C. (1980). *A developmental study of teacher concerns across time.* Paper presented at the Annual Meeting of the American Educational Research Association, Boston, MA. (ERIC Document Reproduction Service No. ED 189 181).

Brock, B. L. (1988). *First year teachers in Catholic schools: A study and analysis of perceptions of undergraduate preparation, entry level assistance, and problems, and development of a model of assistance* (Doctoral dissertation, University of Nebraska–Lincoln, 1988). *Dissertation Abstracts International, 50-01A,* 117.

Dollase, R. H. (1992). *Voices of beginning teachers: Visions and realities.* New York: Teachers College Press.

Fuller, F. F. (1969). Concerns of teachers: A developmental conceptualization. *American Educational Research Journal, 6,* 207–226.

Koontz, J. E. (1963). *Problems of Arkansas secondary school teachers in certain selected schools* (Doctoral dissertation, University of Arkansas, 1963). *Dissertation Abstracts International, 24A,* 1493.

Lee, C. S. (1974). *An investigation of the frequency, bothersomeness, and seriousness of classroom problems as perceived by first and fifth year secondary teachers* (Doctoral dissertation, University of South Carolina, 1974). *Dissertation Abstracts International, 35-10A,* 6576.

Lewis, L., Parsad, B., Carey, N., Bartfai, N., Farris, E., Smerdon, B., & Greene, B. (1999). *Teacher quality: A report on teacher preparation and qualifications of public school teachers* (NCES Publication No. 1999080). Washington, DC: U.S. Department of Education.

Martin, G. J. (1991). *Teachers' perceptions of their first year of teaching* (Doctoral dissertation, Claremont Graduate School, 1991). *Dissertation Abstracts International, 52-03A,* 885.

Rapp, P. R. (1986). *A study of problems confronting first-year teachers with recommendations for their remedies* (Doctoral dissertation, University of North Carolina at Chapel Hill, 1986). *Dissertation Abstracts International, 48-02A,* 367.

Stegall, H. H. (1966). *A study of the induction of new teachers and the problems encountered by the new teachers in the public schools of Jefferson*

*County, Alabama* (Doctoral dissertation, University of Alabama, 1966). *Dissertation Abstracts International, 27A,* 2808.

Taylor, J. K., & Dale, I. R. (1971). *A survey of teachers in their first year of service.* Bristol: University of Bristol, Institute of Education.

Thomas, B., & Kiley, M. A. (1994). *Concerns of beginning middle and secondary school teachers.* Paper presented at the Annual Meeting of the Eastern Educational Research Association, Sarasota, FL. (ERIC Document Reproduction Service No. ED 373 033)

# Stories of Beginning Teachers

*First-Year Challenges and Beyond*

# chapter one

# Introduction

Every autumn, many schools across the country welcome beginning teachers. What is virtually certain for most of them is that their job will be very demanding. The teachers may feel overwhelmed. Some will have such a tough year that the first year will be their last year in teaching. In fact, many young teachers do not even make it through the first year. This book is about the challenges faced by young people as they launch careers in education at the beginning of the new millennium.

The authors of this book are affiliated with a graduate teacher education program conducted by the University of Notre Dame. Ours is an alternative certification program. All of the students in the program have already earned a bachelor's degree, typically in a field other than education. The participants did well in their undergraduate programs, and most came from elite universities. They are good candidates for the master's degree they pursue at Notre Dame and good candidates to become fine teachers.

Participants begin their program with a summer session of coursework. This is followed by serving a year as the teacher of record in a school in the southern United States. Then, it is back to campus for a second summer session, followed by a second year of teaching. During both years of teaching, participants stay in contact with campus faculty, using the Internet to be part of seminars in education.

The faculty and staff have noticed that it is much easier to teach students during the second summer session than during the first. After a year of teaching, participants in the program seem acutely aware that there is much that they need to know, that teaching is a very demanding profession. In contrast, during the first summer, program participants are much more nonchalant about coursework, less convinced that teacher education courses have much to offer them. What happened during that first year of teaching that made our students so much more receptive to learning about teaching than they were during their first summer? Every one of them found the first year of teaching to be demanding. We would be less than candid if we did not admit a certain pleasure when first-year teachers call in November and December and admit that they wish they had taken the first summer session more seriously! It takes just a few months of being in charge of a classroom for young people to understand that teaching well requires more than a college education, more than just knowledge of subject matter content.

This is not news to many education professionals, from career teachers to principals to superintendents to educational researchers. Everyone with experience in the education business knows that the first year of teaching can be plenty rough and is always demanding. Many, many formal analyses of the challenges of beginning teaching have been published, from Dewey (1904/1965) to U. S. Department of Education analyses at the end of the 20th century (Lewis et al., 1999).

Researchers interested in the topic were particularly active in the middle part of the twentieth century. Barr and Rudisill's (1930) analysis continues to be cited. The authors found that beginning teachers had difficulties controlling students, dealing with individual differences among students, instructional presentations, pupil motivation, planning and organizing for teaching, poor working conditions, assessing students, encouraging student participation in class, and devising effective assignments for students. Other midcentury analyses—Wey (1951), Lambert (1956), Dropkin and Taylor (1963), Hermanowicz (1966), Broadbent and Cruickshank (1965), Ryan (1974), and Johnston and Ryan (1980)—produced similar lists of challenges. One of the most famous analyses was Lortie's (1975) *Schoolteacher: A Sociological Study.* A frequently cited insight from that work was that teaching is exceptional as a profession in expecting so much so soon from the beginning professional, who is "fully responsible from the first working day . . . and performs the same tasks as a twenty-five year veteran" (p. 72). Virtually everyone who has looked at beginning teaching found young people who were doing much more than teaching their classes: They were also learning to teach and learning to deal with the many challenges that are part of teaching.

A nontrivial proportion of new teachers do not make it through the first year; many others do not return for a second year (Olson, 2000). This attrition is a problem, since the nation will need 2 million new teachers in the first decade of the 21st century; the challenges of beginning teaching are a known contributor to the attrition (Boser, 2000).

The main motivation for our writing this book was to provide information to students who aspire to be teachers—to let them know about the challenges ahead so that they can prepare for them better.

## VEENMAN'S SUMMARY OF THE CHALLENGES OF BEGINNING TEACHING

A good starting point for anyone wanting to know about the challenges of teaching is a summary of the research on the topic published in 1984 by Simon Veenman. Veenman began with a description of the "reality shock" of the first year of teaching. First-year teachers are often very aware that they are having many more problems than they anticipated. Sometimes they feel pressured to behave in ways they never thought they would behave (e.g., be a strict disciplinarian, or assign drill-and-practice despite their philosophical objections to such an approach; see Feiman-Nemser, 1983; Ryan, 1979). First-year teachers often find their attitudes changing, sometimes in ways they regret (e.g., their desire to serve the poor begins to be undermined by the difficulties of teaching children who live in poverty; see Hoy, 1968; Iannaccone, 1965; Jacobs, 1968; Lacey, 1977; Muuss, 1969). New teachers' emotions can get out of control (e.g., being overwhelmed by the demands of the job, with accompanying feelings of depression and helplessness). Their perceptions of themselves can be affected as well, as when the former honors college student in literature begins to perceive her- or himself as a failure because of unsuccessful struggles to get eighth graders to understand even short stories—or get them to read the stories at all. Veenman made a strong case based on research that the shift from being a college student to being a classroom teacher can be a dramatic one.

Veenman summarized the large body of literature that specified just what the challenges of beginning teaching are. At the time of his review, there had been a number of studies conducted, most of them in the quarter of a century preceding his review. Such research was produced all over the world, although the clear majority of it originated in the United States.

Most of the studies Veenman summarized used questionnaire methodology, although a few involved face-to-face interviews with researchers or combined questionnaires and interviews. That is, beginning teachers were asked to rate a number of potential problems that one might encounter as a teacher, indicating whether they had experienced each of the problems. Veenman identified the 24 challenges mentioned most often in the 91 studies that were reviewed. Although there were some slight differences in the relative frequencies of the 24 problems among elementary versus secondary teachers, the problems reported were, in general, similar. Combining elementary and secondary teacher responses, Veenman concluded that the following challenged beginning teachers (listed from most frequent to least frequent):

- Classroom discipline
- Motivating students
- Dealing with individual differences
- Assessing students' work
- Relations with parents
- Organization of class work
- Insufficient materials and supplies
- Dealing with problems of individual students
- Heavy teaching load resulting in insufficient prep time
- Relations with colleagues
- Planning of lessons and school days
- Effective use of different teaching methods
- Awareness of school policies and rules
- Determining learning level of students
- Knowledge of subject matter
- Burden of clerical work
- Relations with principals/administrators
- Inadequate school equipment
- Dealing with slow learners
- Dealing with students of different cultures and deprived backgrounds
- Effective use of textbooks and curriculum guides
- Lack of spare time
- Inadequate guidance and support
- Large class size (Veenman, 1984)

One way of alerting students in teacher education to the problems that they might encounter in the classroom during their first year of teaching could be to present this list to them. Even so, presenting such a list generally has not been the method of alerting young teachers to potential difficulties they will face. Rather, students in teacher education often are introduced to the problems of beginning teaching through the study of case studies of first-year teaching.

## CASE STUDIES OF BEGINNING TEACHING

When we first began discussing our interest in the challenges facing beginning teachers, several colleagues referred us to a book edited by Kevin Ryan (1970), *Don't Smile Until Christmas: Accounts of the First Year of Teaching*. Although now out of print, this book can be found in virtually every university library serving a teacher education program. The book contains six case studies of first-year teachers, all of whom were participating in a master of arts in teaching program at the University of Chicago. It is a really interesting read because of the depth of the cases.

For example, one case about "Gail" begins by introducing the challenging urban school environment she entered as a first-year teacher. The case explores in depth what she was confident about as a young teacher and what she was concerned about, especially illuminating how dramatically and quickly her confidence eroded as she experienced the reality of an inner-city school and classroom, which contrasted with what she had imagined teaching would be like. The nitty-gritty of overwhelming paperwork and not always competent administrators was included in the case. Gail's class gained students over the first month of school, with many demands created by a constantly changing enrollment. Although Gail anticipated the amount of planning she would have to do, she did not anticipate some of the misbehavior she would encounter. Student misconduct really irritated her. When it occurred in her class, it also stimulated attitudes in fellow faculty members that insulted her (e.g., a male colleague insinuating that she would need help keeping high school boys in order). There were some really frightening moments, such as when fights broke out in her class. Then, there was a dramatic upheaval in the school following the death of Martin Luther King (this first-year case was based on school year 1967–68), with a number of changes made in reaction to resentful students who wanted more control of the school. Gail was relieved when the end of the year came; she left the school and chose to make her teaching career elsewhere.

Such a case provided much material for reflection, as did the other five in the Ryan book. Since the appearance of *Don't Smile Until Christmas,* the case-study approach to teacher education has increased in popularity, stimulating the development of many case studies for teacher education students (see Carter & Anders, 1996), including some case volumes dedicated to describing the perils of first-year teachers (Dollase, 1992; Henson, 1994; Kane, 1991; Kowalski, Shapiro, 1993; Weaver, & Ryan et al., 1980). We came to some very interesting insights as we read these volumes of cases.

First, many of the categories in Veenman's (1984) list sprang to life, with the teachers reporting, for example, specific instances of discipline problems. Even so, there were some challenges not well captured by Veenman's categories. If the researchers did not think to ask about an issue, there was no way the issue could be represented in the outcomes of the study (Johnston & Ryan, 1983).

Veenman relied on studies that used researcher-designed questionnaires and interviews. Although some of the questionnaires and interviews (e.g., Adams, Hutchinson, & Martray, 1980; Cruickshank, Kennedy, & Myers, 1974; Kennedy, Cruickshank, & Myers, 1976; Koontz, 1963; Lee, 1974; Moller, 1968; Rapp, 1986) were informed by a broad range of opinion about potential challenges to beginning teachers and were based on reviews of the literature on the topic or on interviews with beginning teachers, this essentially was deductive research, with the researchers' theories of beginning teaching often resulting in studies sensitive to their theoretical preconceptions. There, of course, is another way to do research, which is to use induction.

The recognition of an inexact match between Veenman's categories and the challenges represented in the case studies set in motion an analysis to categorize the many challenges reported by first-year teachers, as represented by the published case studies. We thought this might give us a more complete window on the challenges of first-year teaching than Veenman had established.

In qualitative studies, categories of challenge are inferred from data. Thus, we used the published case studies of first-year teaching as the raw data for our analysis, treating these case-study reports, most of which were written by the beginning teachers themselves, as something like open-ended responses to the question, "What challenged you during your first year of teaching?"

Specifically, we used a method called grounded-theory analysis (Strauss & Corbin, 1998). We read five volumes of case studies of beginning teaching—Dollase (1992), Kane (1991), Kowalski, Weaver, and Henson (1994), Ryan et al. (1980), and Shapiro (1993)—noting any challenges of first-year teaching mentioned in the case study.* As we continued to read cases, we began to categorize the challenges reported by the teachers in the case studies. By the time we had completed all five volumes of cases, no new major categories of challenges were emerging in the data; indeed, very few specific new instances of challenges were emerging. By this point, we had identified more than 500 different specific challenges confronted by beginning teachers, although these could be organized into 22 categories.

In the remainder of this section, we detail the 22 categories of challenges that we detected in the case studies that we read. Many of the categories that emerged in our analyses mapped directly onto categories reported by Veenman (1984). Others were less exact fits. A few were not included in the Veenman list at all. Even in those cases when we perceived our categories to be identical or similar to Veenman's, we emerged from reading the cases feeling that we understood much better just what each category was about than through reading Veenman's analyses. The many specific instances in the case studies of category members permitted insights about the breadth of each of the categories coming out of our analyses. In order to provide readers with a similar experience, without having to read all of the case studies that we read in the preparation of this book, each of the 22 categories identified in our analyses is described and several examples of specific challenges encountered in the case studies are provided. The complete list of challenges in each of the 22 categories can be found in the appendix to this chapter.

---

*Something that we had become aware of in searching for case studies to analyze was the popularity in the current teacher education market of a set of case studies developed by Kowalski, Weaver, and Henson (1994). At first, we were reluctant to admit these case studies because they were invented cases, ones constructed by Kowalski et al. in collaboration with a number of teacher educators to represent the issues faced by first-year teachers. In the end, we did go through these cases, in the fifth and last volume of cases we read. Although a few new specific challenges were reported in these cases that were not reported in the first four volumes we read, no new major categories emerged.

## Category 1: Classroom Discipline

Challenges with discipline are represented extensively in the case studies we reviewed. There are many sub-issues in this category, from concerns about spending too much time on discipline to fears about not disciplining enough. Some of the particular discipline tactics used in schools concern beginning teachers. For instance, whenever paddling is mentioned in the cases, the beginning teacher expressed concern about doing it, although there are teachers in the case studies who decided to administer corporal punishment. When and how to punish students is definitely on the minds of the beginning teachers contributing to the case studies.

## Category 2: Student Misbehavior

We felt that student misbehavior was a category that could be separated out from discipline issues. There are many, many student misbehaviors that are reported as challenging in the case studies. Student misbehavior ranges from cutting class and being inattentive to causing serious disruptions to the rest of the class. Students throw things, heckle other students, and talk back to their teachers. Some violent and criminal behaviors that occur outside of the classroom but still pose problems to beginning teachers are student fighting, student alcohol abuse and smoking, student theft, and weapon violations.

## Category 3: Motivating Students

Beginning teachers highlight many problems involving the motivation of their students. There are plenty of reports of undermotivated students, with Category 3 representing many nuances of undermotivation (e.g., bored with material the teacher is covering, not liking school in general) and its effects on performance (e.g., not doing homework, doing sloppy work). Other concerns included those involving students who are under too much pressure to do well, who do not know how to do well, or who do not believe they can do well. They are also faced with students who are withdrawn or apathetic. Beginning teachers are often not well prepared to motivate the many types of undermotivated students.

## Category 4: Dealing with Individual Differences

The case-study teachers report many concerns about individual differences among students. The variety of differences that cause difficulties span the entire range of ways that humans can differ from one another with respect to personality traits, health status, and consequences of socioeconomic status. Beginning teachers report being challenged by the diverse special needs of students who are immature, angry, depressed, abused, gifted, learning disabled, emotionally disturbed, physically handicapped, or affected by the demands of poverty, or who cannot read or write. Balancing the needs of individuals with the needs of the entire class is also a challenge when teachers are faced with students with vastly different abilities and characteristics.

## Category 5: Assessing Students' Work

The beginning teachers in the case studies face a wide range of challenges with assessment that are rooted in their students' reactions and in the teachers' own lack of time, knowledge, or confidence. Teachers express concerns about how to do assessment. They can lack confidence in their ability to judge student work and struggle with how to grade so as to inform students how they can do better. Beginning teachers can have trouble keeping up with the large amount of assessment required of them and can get behind on grading. They are challenged by the reactions of students to assessments (e.g., students who argue with them about their grades). Teachers also can have difficulty finding the balance between giving students the grades they deserve and having the students like them.

## Category 6: Relations with Parents

There were a number of ways that relations with parents are challenging to the beginning teachers in the case studies. Beginning teachers experience frustrations in working with parents due to parental characteristics (e.g., parents were alcoholic or divorced) or at least the teachers' perceptions of parental characteristics. Many other frustrations are produced by the way the parents respond to the teacher. It is challenging when beginning teachers lack support and backing from parents. Some parents are neglectful of their children, some are unable to give academic help to them, some disagree with the teaching method or with what is being taught, and some disagree with the grades teachers give. Teachers struggle with getting parents to come in for conferences, and if they do come in, the ensuing discussions can be difficult or anxiety producing for new teachers.

## Category 7: Classroom Management

The case-study teachers provide a great deal of information about the challenges they confront in managing their classrooms. There are challenges in managing the physical classroom environment (e.g., some teachers struggle to organize their classrooms, while others do not even have their own classroom and have to move from room to room). There are many challenges in managing the students (e.g., teachers struggle when there is tension in the classroom over who controls the class—the students or the teacher—when they try to establish classroom routines, when they find it difficult to teach and monitor students at the same time). There are also challenges in managing other adults who are in the classroom (e.g., when "specials" teachers, like art and music teachers, do not arrive on time or come unannounced, when the noise from another class disturbs the beginning teacher's class, when the classroom aide is not very helpful, or when visitors to the room or at the door interrupt teaching).

## Category 8: Resource Issues

The case studies are filled with concerns about insufficient materials and supplies, inadequate equipment, and large class sizes. Some teachers lack materials essential for teaching the curriculum, and others have an insufficient number of textbooks, or the textbooks they have are weak, inappropriate, or outdated. Some teachers are challenged when there are not enough computers, while others lack even a comfortable building and have to struggle with rooms that are too small, in disrepair, too hot or too cold, or infested with mice or other vermin. Beginning teachers also report that caring for their students' basic needs is a struggle when there is a lack of social services or security and safety in schools.

## Category 9: Teacher–Student Communications/Interactions

The case-study teachers express many concerns with teacher-student communications and interactions issues. Teachers find learning the names of students and getting to know students to be challenging. Some new teachers are too friendly, to the point that students take advantage of them. It is challenging for the teachers to relate to students who just want to be left alone, who hate the teacher, or who think the teacher hates them. They also report having difficulties dealing with students who have outbursts of rage or intentionally try to make the teacher angry, and some teachers even have difficulties in controlling their own anger.

### Category 10: School-Based Demands on Time

The case-study teachers report many nonteaching school-based demands on their time, making it clear that teachers have much to do during the school day besides teach. They report having too much paperwork for them and their students to fill out. Committee work is also difficult, with administrative responsibilities sometimes producing anxiety. Extracurricular assignments such as coaching are draining for beginning teachers. Teachers are frustrated when they have to spend time on low-level tasks such as overseeing study halls, monitoring the playground, or patrolling the bathroom.

### Category 11: Relations with Colleagues

Relations with colleagues can be challenging to the new teacher, ranging from too little communication or interaction between the new teacher and other teachers to negative interactions with other teachers. Beginning teachers have difficulties when they feel they cannot discuss their problems with other teachers. Other teachers can be cliquish, cold, "burned out," or insulting to students. Being confronted by or having a conflict with another teacher is a challenge, as is another teacher's being tactless, rude, insulting, or critical of the new teacher. Other stressful, negative interactions include disagreements with other teachers about what the fundamental goals of the school should be, and other teachers being suspicious or disapproving of the new teacher or his or her teaching methods.

### Category 12: Planning of Lessons and School Days

There are many ways that beginning teachers find planning difficult. When new teachers do not receive enough information early on about the types of students in their classes, the school policies, the school year schedule, the curriculum that is to be taught, or the textbooks they are to use, they have to play catch-up the rest of the year. They report not having enough time to read the textbooks being used in class and are stressed by staying just one chapter ahead of the students. Meeting all the demands of the job and not having enough time to prepare for class is often reported as a challenge, with time management something new teachers struggle with, especially when extracurricular assignments like coaching take up valuable evenings and weekends. New teachers also worry about covering enough material, deciding what to teach, and designing effective lessons to achieve specific aims.

### Category 13: Classroom Instruction

Beginning teachers can have many different problems with classroom instruction. Finding the balance between the teaching of process and of factual content is troublesome, especially when teachers struggle with getting students to think critically. Teachers also struggle to find the balance between child-centered activities (e.g., student construction of understandings) and teacher structuring of learning (e.g., more direct instruction). It is hard for new teachers to meet the needs and demands of individual students while meeting the needs and demands of the class as a whole, and it is difficult to adapt materials and lessons to provide challenge for students who are having no difficulties understanding the material.

### Category 14: Teacher Knowledge Base and Curriculum

Instructional challenges can be compounded when the new teacher lacks curricular knowledge. Teachers are thrown when they encounter situations that teacher education did not prepare them for. Also, it is a challenge for them to teach at a developmental level for which they were not trained to teach.

### Category 15: Induction, Mentoring, and Inadequate Guidance

The beginning teachers express many concerns about the induction and mentoring they receive. Sometimes they are challenged because they do not receive enough mentoring or feedback about their teaching, especially when they need help with some aspect of teaching but do not get it. And sometimes being observed is trying in and of itself, especially when they are being evaluated or the visits are a surprise. In general, lack of knowledge about folkways, rules, policies, or procedures poses a challenge to new teachers.

### Category 16: Conflicts with School Culture

New teachers can have a number of different conflicts with school culture. Teachers struggle when they disagree with or perceive a problem with school policies or methods, such as the school's approach to tracking. The "goodness of fit" between the teacher and the school can also be an issue, for example, when the new teacher feels that the school is either too rigid or too unstructured.

### Category 17: Relations with Principals/Administrators

Beginning teachers are often challenged by their relations with principals and other administrators. Sometimes the principal or another administrator is too critical of the beginning teacher or does not respect the beginning teacher's authority. The principal's directives can be so general or vague that the beginning teacher does not know how to carry them out. The teacher and the principal can disagree on approaches to grading, teaching, or disciplining. Teachers can struggle as schools attempt to upgrade academic standards, do action research, or win awards. The power that administrators have over hiring decisions makes many interactions with them difficult, especially when teachers worry about being rehired for the next year or being dismissed.

### Category 18: Diversity Issues

Often, beginning teachers teach students different from themselves. Beginning teachers find teaching students who are bilingual or culturally different from themselves to be challenging, and they struggle when they do not know how to refer to members of ethnic minority groups (e.g., Blacks or African Americans). Sometimes the teacher is a victim of racial resentment, and other times students or parents feel they are victims of discrimination by the beginning teacher. It can also be difficult to deal with students who show racial prejudice and to help students cope with racial prejudice directed against them.

### Category 19: Personal Life Issues

There are many personal life issues that affect beginning teachers. Not having any spare time is reported often, with teachers spending vacations trying to get out from under piles of work and their teaching assignment interfering with their continuing education. Physical illnesses and injuries can negatively affect teachers, and sometimes the illness is actually a reaction to the stress of the job. Not being able to get a substitute when the teacher needs to be absent from school is a hassle. And sometimes the demands of the job keep the beginning teachers from being as creative as they want to be. Beginning teachers can also feel isolated and lonely.

### Category 20: Unconstructive Attitudes and Perceptions

Many challenges for beginning teaching are created by the young teachers themselves, challenges in the form of unconstructive attitudes and perceptions they hold. Although these attitudes and perceptions are a diverse group of feelings, all have the potential to undermine the motivation of the young teacher. Teachers are challenged when they feel anxious, overwhelmed, incompetent, or ineffective. Things are also difficult when the teachers feel that the rewards of teaching are not great enough or feel unsupported in or unrecognized for their teaching. And it is particularly hard for teachers to teach material that they do not believe is important, useful, or appropriate.

### Category 21: Gender and Sexual Issues

The case studies include a number of reports of gender- and sex-related matters. These include issues of both sexism and sexuality. Others in the school can have feelings toward the teacher, such as when another faculty member sexually harasses the teacher or a student flirts with the teacher. But sometimes the challenge is generated by the young teacher's own feelings, as when the teacher finds a student attractive.

### Category 22: Concerns about the Greater Community

Beginning teachers often teach in communities that are new to them. The challenges of working and living in a new community are apparent in some of the case studies. Teachers usually struggle when the community is deteriorating, negatively affecting life in the school. Sometimes the community is not a stimulating place for the teachers to live or work, or teachers have trouble establishing themselves in it or finding their way around.

## FURTHER REFLECTIONS ON THE CHALLENGES OF TEACHING

A review of the chapter appendix can create the impression that beginning teaching is filled with an overwhelming number of challenges. What we emphasize, however, is that the table summarizes *potential* challenges of teaching. Each of the many case studies included only a few of the challenges detailed in this chapter.

## Who Is Challenged?

Are some beginning teachers more challenged than others? The answer is a definite yes. That said, however, researchers have not been very successful in identifying just who is most likely to be challenged as a beginning teacher. Thus, there are not reliable differences between the genders with respect to susceptibility to challenges (Grantham, 1961; Koontz, 1963; Rapp, 1986; Sandidge, 1989; Stone, 1963). How well a beginning teacher did in undergraduate school or during practice teaching does not seem to predict how challenged the individual will be during the first year (Brock, 1988; Dropkin & Taylor, 1963; Rapp, 1986). That is not to say that there are no predictive differences, however: When the data across studies are examined, it seems that teachers serving urban schools are more challenged than those in suburban or rural schools (Dropkin & Taylor, 1963; Kennedy, Cruickshank, & Myers, 1976; Rapp, 1986; Sandidge, 1989). Also, if anything, the older the students being taught, the greater the challenges faced by the beginning teacher (Rapp, 1986; Sandidge, 1989; Stegall, 1966; Stone, 1963; Thomas & Kiley, 1994).

## Recent Qualitative Studies

Is the list of challenges contained in the appendix complete or close to complete? That very few new challenges emerged when we read last few volumes of cases suggests that there might not be many more challenges to detect. That is, the challenges reported in them sounded very similar to those in cases we had read previously.

There have been several studies in recent years involving qualitative analyses of the pressures on beginning teachers. For example, Martin (1991) conducted open-ended interviews with ten first-year elementary teachers in California. She conducted a grounded-theory analysis on the challenges mentioned by the teachers in her study. She reported no challenges that are not contained in the appendix. Olson and Osborne (1991) asked four Canadian elementary teachers to write about their experiences during the first year of teaching and followed up with interviews of the teachers. Again, in reading their results, we found no challenges not covered in the table. Thompson (1991) studied six first-year secondary English teachers. She also used qualitative methods to develop categories of challenges they experienced. Again, all of the challenges she detected were represented in the table. Featherstone (1993) studied six first-year teachers in depth, collecting narratives about first-year challenges from her participants. Again, their reports reflected challenges detailed in the table. In short, reading these qualitative analyses confirmed that the analysis of the case studies that we conducted yielded close to an exhaustive inventory of challenges of beginning teaching. Although these recent qualitative analyses included variations on the themes summarized in the table, that is what they were—variations on themes, rather than new categories or new specific instances of challenges.

## The Beginning Teacher's World of Challenges

Is there any way to create greater order from the vast array of challenges represented in the appendix? We think there are five superordinate categories that capture the challenges of beginning teaching.

### Self Challenges

Some challenges are within oneself. For example, the beginning teacher's knowledge (or lack of it) and attitudes can create challenges for him- or herself. As summarized in Category 14, there are many aspects of curriculum and instruction that are foreign to the beginning teacher. Such lack of knowledge can cause many problems and produce many challenges. Similarly, lack of knowledge about the folkways of the school, its rules and procedures, or its organization (see Category 15) can place the beginning teacher in difficult situations. If the teacher's attitudes are different from attitudes favored in the school culture (Category 16), there is the potential for problems. If the teacher does not like teaching or the school, feels incompetent or overwhelmed, or has any of a number of unconstructive feelings, there is the potential for these feelings to interfere with her or his effectiveness in the school (Category 20). If the teacher has inappropriate sexual feelings toward a member of the school community or feels the school community is sexist, that can undermine the teacher's effectiveness (Category 21). Physical illness or injury can impair a young teacher's functioning (Category 19). In short, there is much about the young teacher's self that can lead to challenges in his or her performing well as a teacher.

### Student Challenges

Students can be challenging, from their behaviors and misbehaviors (Categories 2 and 21) to motivations (Category 3) to individual differences (Category 4), including differences reflecting diversity (Category 18). Communicating with students is much of what teaching is about, and thus teacher-student communications and interactions provide many possibilities for challenges (Category 9).

## Professional Responsibility Challenges

All of the young teacher's professional responsibilities provide potential for challenge. The professional teacher has to be curriculum and lesson planner (Category 12), classroom instructor (Category 13), assessor (Category 5), classroom manager (Category 7), and disciplinarian (Category 1). Then, there are the demands the school makes on a teacher that do not involve classroom teaching (e.g., paperwork, coaching; Category 10). Quite often, lack of sufficient material and mentoring resources (Categories 8 and 15) challenges the teacher in the exercise of her or his professional responsibilities.

## Challenging Adults Associated with the School Setting

Although the most important people in the professional teacher's world are the students, there are also adults in the school who can cause difficulties for the beginning teacher. These other adults include parents (Category 6); teaching colleagues (Category 11), including mentors (Category 15); and principals and other administrators (Category 17). Sometimes relationships with other adults are so bad that the beginning teacher believes she or he is not accepted by the larger school community (Category 16), with these feelings sometimes due to a mismatch between the beginning teacher's culture and the cultural identification of other teachers in the school. Sometimes a teaching colleague makes an unwelcome sexual overture or otherwise sexually harasses a young teacher (Category 21).

## Outside-the-School Challenges

A beginning teacher's parents, roommates, and significant other all can impact in ways that are very, very challenging to the young professional (see Category 19). Sometimes the problem is lack of human contact with other people outside of school; many beginning teachers find themselves alone in new communities, places they do not know, and perhaps places they actually find threatening (Categories 19 and 22). Not making much money while trying to deal with the bureaucracies of a new setting (e.g., the professional licensing process) can also challenge beginning teachers (Category 19). Even if the community is inviting, often there is just not much free time for the beginning teacher (Category 19).

## Summary

The beginning teacher is immersed in layers of potential challenges, summarized in Table 1.1. Of course, these various sources interact. For example, the beginning teacher's sense of self can definitely be affected by how students, other adults, and significant others react as she or he struggles to be a professional. Also, the behavior of students often reflects the community, with a deteriorating community sending different types of students to school than would a prosperous community. How students behave in the beginning teacher's class often reflects their previous interactions with their parents, other teachers, and the school's administrators.

Thus, although our analysis of the case studies of beginning teachers produced an inventory of diverse challenges, it often will be more useful in the chapters that follow to think about the various challenges as self challenges, student challenges, professional challenges, challenging adults in school, and outside-the-school challenges.

## What follows

In the next two chapters, the actual challenges confronted by beginning teachers will be covered in several ways. Samples of first- and second-year teachers were asked to review all of the challenges identified in the case studies, indicating which ones they experienced. In addition, beginning teachers were asked to appraise the seriousness of the challenges identified in the case studies. When these two analyses were combined, it was possible to draw some conclusions about the likelihood of a beginning teacher experiencing serious challenges versus not-so-serious ones. The same set of challenges was also provided to more experienced teachers, with the goal of this analysis to determine which are unique to beginning teaching and which apply to teaching in general. At the end of these two chapters, a number of

**TABLE 1-1**

*Five Sources of Beginning Teaching Challenges*

SELF

Lack of knowledge about teaching/curriculum (Category 14)
Induction and mentoring issues (some of Category 15)
Conflicts with school culture (some of Category 16)
Personal life issues (some of Category 19)
Unconstructive attitudes/perceptions (Category 20)
Gender/sexual challenges (some of Category 21)

STUDENTS

Misbehavior (Category 2)
Motivation (Category 3)
Individual differences (Category 4)
Teacher-student communications (Category 9)
Diversity issues (Category 18)
Gender/sexual challenges (some of Category 21)

PROFESSIONAL

Classroom discipline (Category 1)
Assessment (Category 5)
Classroom management (Category 7)
Resource issues (Category 8)
Nonteaching school-based demands (Category 10)
Planning lessons and school days (Category 12)
Classroom instruction (Category 13)
Induction and mentoring issues (some of Category 15)

OTHER ADULTS IN SCHOOL

Relations with parents (Category 6)
Relations with teaching colleagues (Category 11)
Induction and mentoring issues (Category 15)
Conflicts with school culture (Category 16)
Relations with principals/administrators (Category 17)
Gender/sexual challenges (Category 21)

OUTSIDE OF THE SCHOOL

Personal life issues (some of Category 19)
Outside community issues (Category 22)

conclusions about the challenges of beginning teaching will be possible that are not possible from previous analyses.

Readers then will have an opportunity to apply these insights to some case studies of beginning teachers generated by teachers in the teacher education program we oversee. The eight case studies included in this volume represent well what happens when young people try their hand at teaching. As a group, however, they confirm that what happens to each individual can be understood in retrospect by reflecting on the data base about the challenges of teaching. Even so, there is no predicting just which challenges will arise for any given young teacher. The case studies also provide valuable data about how young people cope with the challenges of beginning teaching; our expectation is that readers will sometimes agree with how the young teachers coped and sometimes disagree.

One insight that we have had from working with young teachers is that the challenges just keep coming, day in and day out, week in and week out. Thus, we also conducted a study in which we contacted beginning teachers in our program over a period of a few months and asked them to tell us about the challenges they faced on the day of the call. This analysis, probably more than anything else offered in this book, makes clear that young teachers are always facing challenges and always having to rise to those challenges if they are to get through their days and weeks successfully.

# REFERENCES

Adams, R. D., Hutchinson, S., & Martray, C. (1980). *A developmental study of teacher concerns across time.* Paper presented at the Annual Meeting of the American Educational Research Association, Boston, MA. (ERIC Document Reproduction Service No. ED 189 181)

Barr, A. S., & Rudisill, M. (1930). Inexperienced teachers who fail—and why. *Nations Schools, 5,* 30–34.

Boser, U. (2000). A picture of the teacher pipeline: Baccalaureate and beyond. *Education Week, 19* (18), 16–17.

Broadbent, F., & Cruickshank, D. (1965). *The identification and analysis of problems of first year teachers.* Brockport, NY: State University of New York. (ERIC Document Reproduction Service No. ED 012 786)

Brock, B. L. (1988). *First year teachers in Catholic schools: A study and analysis of perceptions of undergraduate preparation, entry level assistance, and problems, and development of a model of assistance* (Doctoral dissertation, University of Nebraska–Lincoln, 1988). *Dissertation Abstracts International, 50–01A,* 117.

Carter, K., & Anders, D. (1996). Program pedagogy. In F. B. Murray (Ed.), *The teacher educator's handbook.* San Francisco: Jossey-Bass.

Cruickshank, D. R., Kennedy, J. J., & Myers, B. (1974). Perceived problems of secondary school teachers. *Journal of Educational Research, 68,* 154–159.

Dewey, J. (1904/1965). The relation of theory to practice in education. In M. Borrowman (Ed.), *Teacher education in America: A documentary history.* New York: Teachers College Press.

Dollase, R. H. (1992). *Voices of beginning teachers: Visions and realities.* New York: Teachers College Press.

Dropkin, S., & Taylor, M. (1963). Perceived problems of beginning teachers and related factors. *Journal of Teacher Education, 14* (4), 384–390.

Featherstone, H. (1993). Learning from the first years of classroom teaching: The journey in, the journey out. *Teachers College Record, 95,* 93–112.

Feiman-Nemser, S. (1983). Learning to teach. In L. Shulman & G. Sykes (Eds.), *Handbook of teaching and policy.* New York: Longman.

Fuller, F. F. (1969). Concerns of teachers: A developmental conceptualization. *American Educational Research Journal, 6,* 207–226.

Grantham, J. W. (1961). *A study of the problems of beginning teachers in selected secondary schools of Mississippi* (Doctoral dissertation, Indiana University, 1961). *Dissertation Abstracts International, 22A,* 1520.

Hermanowicz, H. J. (1966). *The real world of the beginning teacher: The pluralistic world of beginning teachers.* Washington, DC: National Education Association. (ERIC Document Reproduction Service No. ED 030 616)

Hoy, W. (1968). The influence of experience on the beginning teacher. *School Review, 76,* 312–323.

Iannaccone, L. (1965). On becoming a teacher of readers. In M. Douglass (Ed.), *Claremont Reading Conference: 29th Yearbook.* Claremont, CA: Claremont Graduate School and University Center.

Jacobs, E. (1968). Attitude change in teacher education: An inquiry into the role of attitudes in changing teacher behavior. *Journal of Teacher Education, 14,* 410–415.

Johnston, J. M., & Ryan, K. (1980). *Research on the beginning teacher: Implications for teacher education.* Washington, DC: Department of Education, National Institute of Education. (ERIC Document Reproduction Service No. ED 209 188)

Johnston, J. M., & Ryan, K. (1983). Research on the beginning teacher: Implications for teacher education. In K. Howey & W. Gardner (Eds.), *The education of teachers.* New York: Longman.

Kane, P. R. (1991). *The first year of teaching: Real world stories from America's teachers.* New York: Walker.

Kennedy, J. J., Cruickshank, D. R., & Myers, B. (1976). Problems of beginning secondary teachers in relation to school location. *Journal of Educational Research, 69,* 167–172.

Koontz, J. E. (1963). *Problems of Arkansas secondary school teachers in certain selected schools* (Doctoral dissertation, University of Arkansas, 1963). *Dissertation Abstracts International, 24A,* 1493.

Kowalski, T. J., Weaver, R. A., & Henson, K. T. (1994). *Case studies of beginning teachers.* New York: Longman.

Lacey, C. (1977). *The socialization of teachers.* London: Methuen.

Lambert, S. (1956). Beginning teachers and their education. *Journal of Teacher Education, 7* (4), 347–351.

Lee, C. S. (1974). *An investigation of the frequency, bothersomeness, and seriousness of classroom problems as perceived by first and fifth year secondary teachers* (Doctoral dissertation, University of South Carolina, 1974). *Dissertation Abstracts International, 35–10A,* 6576.

Lewis, L., Parsad, B., Carey, N., Bartfai, N., Farris, E., Smerdon, B., & Greene, B. (1999). *Teacher quality: A report on teacher preparation and qualifications of public school teachers* (NCES Publication No. 1999080). Washington, DC: U.S. Department of Education.

Lortie, D. C. (1975). *Schoolteacher: A sociological study.* Chicago, IL: University of Chicago Press.

Martin, G. J. (1991). *Teachers' perceptions of their first year of teaching* (Doctoral dissertation, Claremont Graduate School, 1991). *Dissertation Abstracts International, 52–03A,* 885.

Moller, G. E. (1968). *A comprehensive study of problems of beginning teachers in selected large senior high schools* (Doctoral dissertation, University of Nebraska Teachers College, 1968). *Dissertation Abstracts International, 29A,* 1722.

Muuss, R. (1969). Differential effects of studying versus teaching on teachers' attitudes. *Journal of Educational Research, 63,* 185–189.

Olson, L. (2000). Finding and keeping competent teachers. *Education Week, 19* (18), 13–18.

Olson, M. R., & Osborne, J. W. (1991). Learning to teach: The first year. *Teaching & Teacher Education, 7,* 331–343.

Rapp, P. R. (1986). *A study of problems confronting first-year teachers with recommendations for their remedies* (Doctoral dissertation, University of North Carolina at Chapel Hill, 1986). *Dissertation Abstracts International, 48-02A,* 367.

Ryan, K. (1970). *Don't smile until Christmas: Accounts of the first year of teaching.* Chicago: University of Chicago Press.

Ryan, K. (1974). *Survival is not good enough: Overcoming the problems of beginning teachers* (Report No. AFT-Pop-15). Washington, DC: American Federation of Teachers. (ERIC Document Reproduction Service No. ED 090 200)

Ryan, K. (1979). Toward understanding the problem: At the threshold of the profession. In K. Howey & V. Bents (Eds.), *Toward meeting the needs of the beginning teacher.* Minneapolis: Midwest Teacher Corps Network. (ERIC Document Reproduction Service No. ED 206 581)

Ryan, K., Newman, K., Mager, G., Applegate, J., Lasley, T., Flora, R., & Johnston, J. (1980). *Biting the apple: Accounts of first year teachers.* New York: Longman.

Sandidge, R. F. (1989). *Perceptions of beginning teacher concerns, problems, and support within the context of the Kentucky beginning teacher internship program* (Doctoral dissertation, University of Kentucky, 1989). *Dissertation Abstracts International, 50-11A,* 3558.

Shapiro, M. (1993). *Who will teach for America?* Washington, DC: Farragut.

Stegall, H. H. (1966). *A study of the induction of new teachers and the problems encountered by the new teachers in the public schools of Jefferson County, Alabama* (Doctoral dissertation, University of Alabama, 1966). *Dissertation Abstracts International, 27A,* 2808.

Stone, E. H. (1963). *Personal and professional problems recognized by beginning junior and senior high school teachers and the relationship of the number of these problems to personal characteristics, professional preparation, teaching assignment and career plans* (Doctoral dissertation, University of Denver, 1963). *Dissertation Abstracts International, 25A,* 1037.

Strauss, A., & Corbin, J. (1998). *Basics of qualitative research: Techniques and procedures for developing grounded theory* (2nd ed.). Thousand Oaks, CA: Sage.

Taylor, J. K., & Dale, I. R. (1971). *A survey of teachers in their first year of service.* Bristol: University of Bristol, Institute of Education.

Thomas, B., & Kiley, M. A. (1994). *Concerns of beginning middle and secondary school teachers.* Paper presented at the Annual Meeting of the Eastern Educational Research Association, Sarasota, FL. (ERIC Document Reproduction Service No. ED 373 033)

Thompson, M. H. (1991). *A classroom of one's own: An ethnographic account of the induction process focusing on problems experienced by first-year, secondary English teachers* (Doctoral dissertation, University of California, Los Angeles, 1991). *Dissertation Abstracts International, 53–01A,* 59.

Veenman, S. (1984). Perceived problems of beginning teachers. *Review of Educational Research, 54,* 143–178.

Wey, H. W. (1951). Difficulties of beginning teachers. *School Review, 59* (1), 32–37.

# APPENDIX

## Category 1: Classroom Discipline Issues Represented in Case Studies of Beginning Teachers

1. Devising/establishing effective classroom rules.
2. Getting students to understand classroom rules.
3. Getting students to obey classroom rules.
4. Finding the *balance* between the teacher being in control and being too autocratic (between having a happy and friendly classroom and a disciplined one).
5. Coping with being an authority figure (because of the beginning teacher's anti-authority feelings).
6. Feeling concerns about not disciplining (punishing) students enough.
7. Feeling concerns about not being strict enough.
8. Sensing that students think she/he is a pushover.
9. Being too patient or tolerant of misbehavior, with misbehavior increasing as a consequence.
10. Having to show the students who is boss.
11. Administering punishment.
12. Experiencing pressure from principal (or some other administrator) or other teachers to be more punitive.
13. Administering corporal punishment.
14. Experiencing pressure from principal (or some other administrator) or other teachers to use corporal punishment.
15. Feeling too much time is spent disciplining students.
16. Being consistent with punishment.
17. Finding discipline methods ineffective.
18. Students not listening to or obeying him/her.
19. Students obeying rules much better when teacher is in room (e.g., students begin to talk or horse around when teacher leaves the room).
20. Disagreeing with another teacher's discipline tactics.
21. Disagreeing with an expulsion or suspension decision made by the school.
22. Not knowing how to cope with students cheating.
23. Feeling students are obeying blindly rather than out of respect.

## Category 2: Student Misbehavior Issues Represented in Case Studies of Beginning Teachers

24. Students being inattentive.
25. Hyperactive students being disruptive.
26. Students severely "acting out."
27. Students sleeping during class.
28. Students chewing gum.
29. Students smoking.
30. Students wearing inappropriate dress.
31. Students passing notes.
32. Students throwing objects at one another.
33. Students freeing animals in the room, causing disruption.
34. Students sitting inappropriately (e.g., sprawled over/sitting on a desk, leaning back on a chair).
35. Students misbehaving when principal or other outside evaluators visit.
36. Students coming to school unclean.
37. Students being absent/truant.
38. Students being tardy.
39. Students cutting classes.
40. Students cutting exams.
41. Students refusing to take a test.
42. Students talking too much.
43. Students yelling too much.
44. Students using profanity.
45. Students fighting.
46. Students lying.
47. Students abusing alcohol.
48. Students abusing drugs (e.g., teacher catching students with/using drugs).
49. Students interrupting class with pranks (e.g., pulling fire alarm, setting off firecrackers in restroom).
50. Students harassing teacher.
51. Students taking advantage of or hassling substitute teacher.
52. Students physically attacking/hitting teacher.
53. Students verbally abusing teacher (e.g., "talking back").
54. Students insulting teacher.
55. Students being cruel to other students (e.g., heckling them).
56. Students being rude/disrespectful.
57. Students plagiarizing (e.g., students in class plagiarize; students plagiarize because they do not know what plagiarism is).

58. Students cheating.
59. Students being suspected of involvement in illegal activity (e.g., selling drugs).
60. Having evidence that a student committed a crime
61. Students stealing.
62. Students extorting money or other goods/services from other students.
63. Students carrying guns or other weapons (e.g., someone enters teacher's class/school with a gun).
64. Students vandalizing (e.g., teacher is a victim of student vandalism).
65. Students belonging to gangs.
66. Students dropping out of school.
67. Students committing or threatening to commit suicide.

### Category 3: Issues about Motivating Students Represented in Case Studies of Beginning Teachers

68. Students not caring about school.
69. Students not liking school.
70. Students not showing energy or enthusiasm in class.
71. Students not sharing the teacher's "hard work" ethic.
72. Students working only if they are threatened.
73. Students not having a good time in class.
74. Students not liking the material being covered.
75. Students being disinterested.
76. Students being bored.
77. Students hating the class.
78. Students turning in sloppy work.
79. Students complaining about homework or assignments.
80. Students doing homework/assignments haphazardly.
81. Students doing homework/assignments late.
82. Students not doing homework/assignments.
83. Not knowing how to motivate students.
84. Trying to get students to work hard and have fun while doing it.
85. Students being indifferent to the teacher/what the teacher is teaching.
86. Students thinking that what is taught is irrelevant to them (e.g., they do not care about the material).
87. Students seeming not to care about anything teacher cares about.

88. Students passively resisting what the teacher is trying to teach.
89. Other teachers turning the teacher's students off to school.
90. Wanting students to have a voice in the classroom, but having trouble convincing them that they do because of their experiences in other classes.
91. Students feeling too much academic pressure (e.g., to get into college).
92. Students feeling defeated, believing there is no way they can succeed.
93. Students not accepting responsibility for their own failures.
94. Students believing there is no way they can do well on an upcoming standardized exam.
95. Students having negative self-images and/or low expectations about themselves.
96. Students acting withdrawn/passive.
97. Students acting apathetic.
98. Students not answering the teacher's questions.
99. Students not knowing how to do better in school.
100. Students lacking confidence that they can learn on their own.
101. Getting students to take academic risks.
102. Getting students to trust each other.
103. Having know-it-all students (e.g., students who believe there is nothing beginning teacher can teach them).
104. Having students with special talents who want to focus on their talents rather than on the school curriculum.
105. School making the students feel badly about themselves.

## Category 4: Individual Differences Issues Represented in Case Studies of Beginning Teachers

106. Students being immature.
107. Students being transient (e.g., students who frequently move in and out).
108. Students being angry.
109. Students being overly tired.
110. Students being depressed.
111. Students being very shy.
112. Students being social misfits (e.g., loners).
113. Students being mean.
114. Students being hard to reach.
115. Students being infected with the AIDS virus.

116. Students being abused.
117. Students being angry about/hurt by life.
118. Students being low in ability.
119. Students being gifted (e.g., more able) students.
120. Students being emotionally disturbed.
121. Students living in disorganized, dysfunctional families (e.g., divorcing parents, father coming and going, child abandoned by parents to grandmother).
122. Students being parents of children, with their parenting responsibilities interfering with schoolwork.
123. Students being affected by the demands of poverty (e.g., students coming to school hungry, students who must hold employment outside of school, students who do not have the resources to wear appropriate dress).
124. Students having short attention spans.
125. Students having high test anxiety.
126. Students having bad tempers.
127. Students having vastly different abilities (e.g., from well below grade level to well above grade level).
128. Students having special education needs (e.g., they are learning disabled, retarded, etc.).
129. Students having problems in understanding the material.
130. Students having been wrongly classified as in need of special education.
131. Students having eating disorders (e.g., anorexia, bulimia).
132. Students having physical handicaps.
133. Students having asthma.
134. Students having mental handicaps due to head injury.
135. Students having not had required inoculations.
136. Students having parents who feel worthless.
137. Students having a parent who dies.
138. Students being unable to read.
139. Students being unwilling to read.
140. Students watching too much television.
141. Students being unable to write (e.g., compose).
142. Students being unwilling to write (e.g., compose)
143. Students varying greatly in their physical size/physical abilities.
144. Students needing glasses but not having them.
145. Students despising their parents/families.
146. A student dying.
147. A student being murdered.

## Category 5: Assessment Issues Represented in
## Case Studies of Beginning Teachers

148. Feeling unsure about how to grade.
149. Not knowing how to assess students.
150. Lacking confidence in her/his ability to judge student work (e.g., deciding who gets high marks, who gets average, and who gets below average).
151. Not know how to grade (mark) so as to inform students about how they can do better.
152. Having to give Fs to students.
153. Feeling she/he must lower her/his grading standards to pass a sufficient number of students.
154. Asking students to evaluate other students' work, and finding they are very harsh.
155. Finding the *balance* between giving students the grades they deserve and having them like the beginning teacher.
156. Getting behind on grading.
157. Having a large amount of grading/correction of papers that must be done.
158. Failing to grade enough items in a grading period to give students grades.
159. Students thinking teacher's standards are too high.
160. Students believing teacher is unfair (e.g., her/his tests are unfair).
161. Students reacting emotionally to or being discouraged by bad grades.
162. Students arguing about their grades.
163. Students disagreeing with the "correct" answers on a test.
164. Students disagreeing with how teacher grades.
165. Students seeing one of the teacher's exams before it is administered.

## Category 6: Relations with Parents Issues
## Represented in Case Studies of Beginning Teachers

166. Parents being immigrants.
167. Parents being divorced.
168. Parents being alcoholics.
169. Students having no parents.
170. Parents being angry.
171. Parents neglecting their children.

172. Parents having to work so much that they do not have time to help their children.
173. Parents seeming afraid of school or of teacher.
174. Parents being unable to give academic help to their children.
175. Parents not being interested in (or being indifferent about) their child.
176. Students getting angry/objecting when teacher calls their parents.
177. Parents objecting to assignments teacher makes (e.g., reading of controversial books).
178. Parents objecting to teacher's approach to teaching a subject (e.g., teacher favors a progressive approach and parent favors a traditional approach).
179. Parents disagreeing with teaching methods or what is being taught
180. Parents not backing teacher on important issues (e.g., discipline).
181. Parents being unsupportive (e.g., parents are not concerned about child's education).
182. Parents not agreeing on the grades teacher gave or the teacher's approach to grading.
183. Parent requesting that his/her child be moved to another class.
184. Parent threatening to ask that teacher be dismissed.
185. Parents blaming teacher for their child's difficulties.
186. Parents not respecting teacher's authority.
187. Parent questioning teacher's fairness.
188. Parents feeling that teacher is attempting to interfere with how they handle their children.
189. Parents having a wide range of expectations about what should be going on in the class.
190. Parents refusing to give academic help to their students.
191. Parents being overly punitive to their child when teacher calls them about their child.
192. Parent conferences/discussions being difficult or producing anxiety.
193. Persuading parents to come in for a conference.
194. Parents challenging a grade teacher gave to their child.
195. Having to make a moral compromise to keep the peace with parents.

## Category 7: Classroom Management Issues
## Represented in Case Studies of Beginning Teachers

196. Establishing classroom routines.
197. Organizing the classroom.
198. Not having own classroom (e.g., teacher has to move from classroom to classroom).
199. Individual students being disruptive or uncontrollable.
200. Students not liking one another.
201. Discussions getting out of control (off the topic of the lesson).
202. Students refusing to work constructively in groups.
203. Students experiencing difficulty with cooperative learning (e.g., one student dominates interactions in her/his group).
204. Monitoring what is going on when students are working together (e.g., during cooperative learning).
205. Students working together when they are supposed to be working alone.
206. Getting students to work autonomously (e.g., in a self-regulated fashion).
207. Working with "hard-to-know" students
208. Students disappearing from classroom (e.g., teacher cannot find a student who is supposed to be with her/him).
209. Students leaving the school/class and not returning—ever.
210. Having to make a moral compromise to keep the peace with students.
211. Students questioning the legitimacy of the system (e.g., the authority of teachers).
212. Tension existing in the school over who controls the school—the students or the teachers.
213. Tension existing in the classroom over who controls the class—the students or the teacher.
214. Students seeming to control the classroom (e.g., students are unresponsive to teacher directions and do what they want to do).
215. Students not remaining on task and orderly when teacher working intensely with one or two students.
216. Teaching and monitoring students at the same time.
217. Wasting time handing back papers, with students not productively engaged.
218. Students leaving the room messy.

219. "Specials" teachers not arriving on time or arriving unannounced.
220. Disagreeing with students being released from teacher's class for another activity.
221. Students arriving late for class because another teacher does not dismiss them promptly.
222. Students arriving late for class because of a late school bus.
223. Noise from another class disturbing teacher's class.
224. Bringing in an outside speaker and finding that things do not go well (e.g., the speaker says something to class that the teacher did not expect).
225. Person entering classroom without authorization and refusing to leave.
226. Classroom aide not being very helpful.
227. Classroom aide having other responsibilities that interfere with her/his helping the teacher.
228. Public address announcements interrupting teaching
229. Visitors to room or at door interrupting teaching.
230. Wanting to schedule special activities.
231. Being asked to substitute in an unruly class.
232. Having a civil or other disruption (e.g., hurricane) in the school's neighborhood that interferes with school.
233. Unscheduled school closures (e.g., due to weather, labor disputes) disrupting teaching.

## Category 8: Resource Issues
## Represented in Case Studies of Beginning Teachers

234. Lacking materials essential for teaching the curriculum.
235. Lacking materials that would be helpful (but are not essential) in teaching the curriculum (including, paper, pens, etc.).
236. Suspecting that the school has materials teacher needs or could use but teacher does not know where to find them or how to access them.
237. Students not bringing necessary supplies to class/school.
238. Classes being too large.
239. Classrooms being are too small.
240. School being too small, so that it seems overcrowded.
241. Having too few desks in the classroom.
242. Having outdated texts.
243. Having weak or inappropriate/unattractive textbooks.

244. Having an insufficient number of textbooks.
245. Lacking a curriculum guide or an effective curriculum guide.
246. Having methods or materials in use at the school are inconsistent with methods or philosophies that teacher prefers.
247. Having too few computers.
248. Not knowing how to use a classroom computer or computer program.
249. Having unfamiliar audio-visual equipment.
250. Audio-visual materials not being accepted by students (e.g., inattentive to a dated filmstrip or a black-and-white movie).
251. Classroom/building being too hot or too cold for comfort.
252. Mice or other vermin being in the classroom/school.
253. School building having been constructed for another purpose, not well suited as a school.
254. School building being in disrepair in ways that interfere with teaching.
255. Construction/cleaning/work crews interrupting class to do their work.
256. Lacking social services help needed for a student.
257. Having security/safety concerns in the school.

## Category 9: Teacher–Student Communications/Interactions Issues Represented in Case Studies of Beginning Teachers

258. Giving directions to students that prove to be unclear.
259. Students challenging what teacher says.
260. Students not accepting the teacher's teachings.
261. Students who "crawl into their shell" and stop participating as a result of teacher's reaction to them.
262. Learning the names of students.
263. Trying to get to know students.
264. Trying to get to know students without getting too friendly/close to them.
265. Being unsure about whether to attend a social function organized by students, for fear of getting too close to students.
266. Getting friendly with students to the point that the students take advantage of the teacher.
267. Disliking students.
268. Students remaining anxious even though teacher tries to help them.

269. Students asking for privileges other students do not receive.
270. Students not being able to answer questions.
271. Students asking questions so stupid or naive that they are not worth addressing.
272. Having academic discussions in class that die too quickly.
273. Students forgetting important information teacher gave them (e.g., day of an important exam).
274. Students comparing teacher's teaching practices negatively with those of another teacher (e.g., Ms. X lets us . . .).
275. Students wanting only *not* to make waves.
276. Students wanting just to be left alone.
277. Students being scared of school.
278. Students apple-polishing or trying to be the teacher's pet (e.g., playing up to the teacher).
279. Students leaving class without authorization.
280. Students requesting to transfer out of teacher's class.
281. Students hating teacher.
282. Students not trusting teacher.
283. Students thinking teacher hates them.
284. Students having outbursts of rage.
285. Students with bad tempers who are physically big enough to be threatening to the teacher.
286. Students intentionally trying to make teacher angry.
287. Being afraid of students.
288. Reaching students who are "at risk."
289. Students not understanding what teacher is trying to say.
290. Having personality conflicts with student(s).
291. Having to break very bad news to a student.
292. Controlling own anger.
293. Worrying about falsely accusing a student of something.
294. Accusing a student of something and later finding out that the accusation was false.
295. Looking so young that students do not take the teacher seriously.

## Category 10: Non-Teaching, School-Based Demands on Time Represented in Case Studies of Beginning Teachers

296. Having too much paperwork to fill out.
297. Having too much paperwork that students must fill out.
298. Having too many money collections to oversee.

299. Doing committee work that is difficult (e.g., too much of it, committee members do not agree).
300. Having administrative responsibilities which are anxiety-producing.
301. Spending time on low-level tasks (overseeing study hall, hall/ playground/bus monitoring, bathroom patrol).
302. Having extracurricular assignments (e.g., coaching) that are draining.
303. Having to perform the pastoral duties that are expected of a teacher (e.g., having to counsel a student who is pregnant/might be pregnant).
304. Substituting for another teacher during what was supposed to be a free period.
305. Having more detailed written plans required than the teacher believes are necessary.

### Category 11: Relations with Teaching Colleagues Issues Represented in Case Studies of Beginning Teachers

306. Engaging in "teachers'-room talk."
307. Other teachers being insulting about students.
308. Other teachers being pessimistic about the students in the school.
309. Other teachers seeming stupid, undereducated, incompetent, etc.
310. Other teachers being rumor-mongers.
311. Other teachers seeming cliquish.
312. Other teachers not respecting the teacher's authority.
313. Having too little communication/interaction with other teachers.
314. Having a conflict with another teacher.
315. Not knowing how to address other teachers (e.g., Mrs. Smith or Susan, Mr. Jones or Ralph).
316. Feeling pressures from the teacher's union or similar association.
317. Other teachers telling the teacher what he/she "can't do."
318. Other teachers resenting the teacher (e.g., perceiving him/her as too competent, enthusiastic, or energetic).
319. Other teachers not acting in a professional manner toward the teacher.
320. Co-teaching with someone who does not treat the teacher as an equal.

321. Co-teaching with someone who does not do her/his share of the work.
322. Other teachers seeing the faculty as a team, and the teacher not perceiving herm- or himself as a member of the team.
323. Other teachers being critical of the teacher; being tactless, rude, or insulting to her/him.
324. Disagreeing with other teachers about what the fundamental goals of the school should be.
325. Other teachers being suspicious of the teacher and/or her/his teaching methods (e.g., they do not think the teacher's classes are quiet or orderly enough).
326. Other teachers disapproving of the teacher and/or her/his teaching methods.
327. Other teachers seeming to watch for the teacher's mistakes.
328. Receiving a sharp note from the office or another teacher.
329. Other teachers opposing innovations the teacher wants to make.
330. Other teachers being "burned out."
331. Other teachers being cold.
332. Teachers generally not cooperating with one another.
333. Another teacher not cooperating with the teacher on an important issue.
334. Another teacher not discussing with the teacher an issue that she/he believes needs to be discussed.
335. Other teachers disapproving of what the teacher is teaching.
336. Being concerned that other teachers will find out what is going on in the teacher's class.
337. Other teachers feeling the teacher's teaching should be more structured.
338. Being concerned that other teachers do not agree with the teacher's approach to teaching.
339. Having a confrontation with another teacher.
340. Feeling unable to discuss problems with other teachers.
341. Other teachers expecting the teacher's class to be quieter than he/she can keep it.
342. Other teachers evaluating the teacher too much on the basis of how quiet her/his classroom is.
343. Other teachers comparing the teacher negatively to previous teachers (e.g., "You aren't like so-and-so").
344. Having to make a moral compromise to keep the peace with other teachers.

### Category 12: Issues about Planning of Lessons and School Days Represented in the Case Studies

345. Not receiving enough information about the (types of) students in a class.
346. Not receiving enough information in advance about the school's policies.
347. Not receiving information about the school year schedule.
348. Not receiving enough information in advance about the curriculum that is to be taught.
349. Not receiving the textbooks sufficiently in advance of the school year so that they could be used in planning the term.
350. Extracurricular assignments (e.g., coaching) taking valuable time away from teaching and preparing for teaching.
351. Not having enough time to do the professional reading that needs to be done.
352. Not having time to read the textbooks being used in a class.
353. Being stressed by staying just one chapter ahead of the students (e.g., the teacher must learn for him- or herself the content to be taught).
354. School emphasizing adherence to publisher guidelines in using textbooks and curriculum materials.
355. Some students having already read something teacher wants to assign.
356. Feeling she/he is using the textbook too much.
357. Feeling she/he is relying too much on the teacher's guide that accompanies the text.
358. Having to juggle more than one goal at a time.
359. Having trouble being decisive.
360. Not having enough energy to meet all the demands of the job (e.g., exhausted from working so hard).
361. Not having enough time to meet all the demands of the job.
362. Not having enough time to prepare for class.
363. Spending too much time preparing for class.
364. Working much too late at night to be ready for the next day.
365. Not reflecting on teaching as much as she/he should.
366. Being overprepared for a class (e.g., reading from a script and/or not being flexible enough to make sure that students actually "get it").
367. Feeling that she/he does not know how or what to plan.
368. Facing deadlines that are too demanding.
369. Having too many course preps.

370. Having more course preps than other teachers.
371. Not being prepared for a lesson.
372. Not completing a lesson in the allotted time.
373. Planning a lesson that fails to fills up its allotted time.
374. Feeling that she/he is not covering enough materials.
375. Having too much material to cover in the school year.
376. Not being sure about whether to assign homework.
377. Not being sure about how much homework to assign.
378. Not having enough time to help each student as much as needed.
379. Deciding what to teach.
380. Not knowing what information (e.g., test scores, past grades, etc.) to use to organize students for instruction.
381. Identifying the specific aims of lessons or major concepts in lessons she/he is teaching.
382. Creating lessons intended to achieve specific aims.
383. Teaching a mixed-grades classroom.
384. Needing to give a little more structure to class.
385. School expecting students to do a lot of memory work.
386. Lessons being driven too much by what is on a standardized test (e.g., a state test).
387. Students having to take school/state/standardized exams that include material teacher has not covered.

### Category 13: Problems of Classroom Instruction Represented in the Case Studies

388. Doing demonstrations (e.g., science experiments).
389. Using the board (e.g., finding it hard to know what to put on the board).
390. Not liking to write on the board.
391. Making the class interesting.
392. Feeling he/she is lecturing too much.
393. Balancing teaching of process (e.g., teaching "how to" read, write, think, problem solve) and teaching of factual content.
394. Making the material relevant to the students.
395. Adapting materials/lessons to provide more challenge for students who are having no difficulties understanding the material.
396. *Balancing* child-centered activities (e.g., student construction of understandings) and teacher-structured learning (e.g., more direct instruction).

397. Getting students to understand a lesson.
398. Getting students to think critically.
399. Getting students to think about material.
400. Matching lessons/work to students' level of understanding.
401. Knowing why students are studying what they are studying.
402. Students not following teacher's directions in doing an assignment.
403. Students not responding to teacher's teaching.
404. Students being unable to handle the amount of homework teacher wants to assign.
405. Students having difficulty answering higher-order questions, that is, questions requiring more than factual recall.
406. Meeting the needs/demands of individual students while meeting the needs/demands of the class as a whole.
407. Students having misconceptions that interfere with their learning new content (e.g., in mathematics).
408. Students learning material for a test but not seeming to understand it (e.g., they can't apply it in new situations, do not recognize its relevance in a new situation).
409. Students not self-correcting.

## Category 14: Lack of Knowledge about Teaching and the Curriculum Represented in the Case Studies

410. Encountering a situation that teacher education did not prepare the teacher for.
411. Not teaching as well as possible because unable to see links between theory and practice.
412. Not knowing how to teach writing (e.g., composing) to students.
413. Not knowing how to teach reading to students.
414. Being asked to substitute in a class the teacher is not qualified to teach.
415. Not understanding the purpose and value of the material/curriculum teacher is teaching.
416. Not understanding the philosophy for the curriculum teacher is teaching.
417. Having to teach material teacher does not understand or know.
418. Not understanding the history of the curriculum teacher is teaching.

419. Finding curriculum materials hard to understand (e.g., teacher does not know or is not sufficiently familiar with the content he/she is expected to cover in class).
420. Student/Practice teaching at a different level/in a different content area than present position.
421. Encountering content that should be taught but not knowing it well enough to teach (i.e., teacher lacks content knowledge).
422. Not knowing how to teach something that needs to be taught.
423. Teaching subjects/a developmental level that she/he was not trained to teach.
424. Not knowing answers to student questions.
425. Not knowing how to question students about content (or experiencing difficulties in doing so).

### Category 15: Induction and Mentoring Issues Represented in the Case Studies

426. Being ignorant of some folkways of the school and its staff.
427. Not knowing what material should be censored out of a class as inappropriate.
428. Having surprise evaluation visits by principal or others (e.g., school board members).
429. Needing help with some aspect of teaching and not getting it.
430. Not knowing a law that a teacher needs to know (e.g., what to do if a child is suffering abuse at home).
431. Receiving little or no feedback about teaching.
432. Not understanding how the school is governed.
433. Not understanding how the school is financed.
434. Not understanding the community served by the schools.
435. Not understanding the philosophy of the school.
436. Not understanding the history of the school.
437. Not knowing how far to go with students on moral or political issues or controversial subjects.
438. Having teaching evaluated (e.g., observations by mentor teacher or principal or some other administrator).
439. Having another teacher who is supposed to be mentoring the teacher not doing so.
440. Not knowing how to fill out paperwork/forms.
441. Not knowing all of the school rules, procedures, or policies.

442. Not knowing how to dress for school or school events.
443. Not knowing how to implement the curriculum guide.
444. Not knowing the school's curriculum.
445. Not knowing the organization of the school.
446. Having to determine whether a student is athletically eligible and not knowing how to do it.
447. Not knowing how to deal with substance abuse.
448. Not knowing how to teach to assessments students are going to face.

### Category 16: Conflicts with School Culture Represented in the Case Studies

449. School's approach to Catholicism (i.e., in a Catholic school) being more traditional or more liberal than the teacher's own approach
450. School being generally more traditional than what the teacher is accustomed to.
451. Perceiving a problem with the school's approach to "tracking."
452. Disagreeing with school policies/methods for assigning students to special education.
453. Disagreeing with the school's approach for handling special-needs students.
454. Perceiving the curriculum as too rigid.
455. The school being too unstructured for the teacher.
456. Students not being accustomed to the teacher's methods of teaching because they differ from the methods typically employed in the school.
457. Disagreeing with some aspects of the religious observances at the school (i.e., in a Catholic school).
458. Students seeming to have different values than the teacher has (e.g., they are more traditional or more liberal).
459. Other teachers seeming to hold different values (e.g., more traditional) than the teacher does.
460. Administrators seeming to have different values than the teacher has (e.g., they are more traditional or more liberal).
461. School being generally more nontraditional than what the teacher is accustomed to.
462. Not knowing whether she/he is accepted by the school community.

463. School not seeming to accept the teacher.
464. Very powerful individuals harboring beliefs about teaching that are inconsistent with what the teacher learned in teacher education and/or believes.
465. School rule/procedure/policy preventing the teacher from doing something she/he wanted to do with students.
466. Disapproving of a school censorship policy/decision (e.g., a certain book or story cannot be read by the students).
467. Perceiving the school as too high pressure and achievement oriented.
468. Perceiving the school as not achievement oriented enough.
469. School's expectations being too low.

### Category 17: Issues Involving Relations with Principals/Administrators Represented in the Case Studies

470. Principal or another administrator expecting teacher's class to be quieter than she/he can keep them.
471. Principal or another administrator evaluating teacher too much on the basis of how quiet her/his classroom is.
472. Principal/assistant principal criticizing teacher (e.g., believes she/he is too soft on students, does not plan enough, does not give enough tests, does not give enough homework, etc.).
473. Member of the administration (e.g., principal) vetoing an activity teacher wants to do.
474. Administrators not respecting teacher's authority.
475. Principal's (or some other administrator's) directives being so general or vague that teacher does not know how to carry them out.
476. Feeling concerned that the principal (or some other administrator) will find out what is going on in her/his class.
477. Feeling concerned that the principal (or some other administrator) does not agree with her/his approach to teaching.
478. Principal (or some other administrator) and beginning teacher not agreeing on how to discipline students.
479. Principal (or some other administrator) being ineffective in disciplining students.
480. Being criticized for not following a school policy.

481. Not knowing how to respond to pressure to do "action research" on her/his teaching.
482. Being under high pressure in the school to win awards, for teachers/programs to be prominent in the state, for the school to be recognized, etc.
483. Principal (or some other administrator) and teacher not agreeing on approach to grading.
484. Principal (or some other administrator) not supporting a decision teacher made or the teacher's approach to an issue.
485. Principal/supervisor feeling teacher's teaching should be more structured.
486. Principal, other administrators, or other teachers being able to listen in on what goes on in teacher's classroom.
487. Worrying about whether she/he can meet the high expectations of the principal or others.
488. Feeling that she/he cannot discuss problems with principal (or some other administrator), perhaps because the administrator will use the information against her/him.
489. Principal visiting teacher's class too often.
490. Principal not visiting teacher's class enough.
491. Having a confrontation with the principal or another administrator.
492. Having a run-in with a member of the school's support staff (e.g., secretary, cafeteria worker).
493. Other staff members being cold.
494. Principal or other administrators or other teachers opposing beginning teacher's use of cooperative learning or active learning because students are not enough under control (e.g., not quiet enough).
495. Being threatened with dismissal by principal or other administrator.
496. Feeling uncertain whether she/he will be rehired next year.
497. Administrators comparing teacher negatively to previous teacher (e.g., "You aren't like so-and-so").
498. Too much emphasis being placed on accountability (e.g., standardized tests).
499. Being under pressure to upgrade the academic standards of the school.
500. Becoming immersed in a controversial issue (e.g., taking a politically unpopular stand).

## Category 18: Diversity Issues
## Represented in the Case Studies

501. Students or their parents accusing teacher of racial prejudice.
502. Minority students (or their parents) feeling they are victims of discrimination by teacher.
503. Not knowing how to refer to members of ethnic minority groups (e.g., Blacks or African Americans).
504. Teaching students who are culturally different than the teacher.
505. Interacting with students from a number of different language/cultural groups.
506. Having bilingual students.
507. Individual students showing racial prejudice.
508. Class/school exhibiting general racial prejudice.
509. Helping students cope with racial prejudice directed against them.
510. Having students face the demands of being *illegal* immigrants.
511. Being a victim of racial resentment.
512. Other teachers being suspicious of teacher because she/he comes from a different cultural background.

## Category 19: Personal Life Issues
## Represented in the Case Studies

513. Not having any spare time.
514. Spending much of vacations getting out from under a pile of work.
515. Having headaches caused by teaching.
516. Having physical illness as a reaction to stress on the job.
517. Teaching assignment interfering with continuing teacher's education (e.g., going to/doing the work for graduate school courses).
518. Being physically injured in a classroom/school accident.
519. Having physical illness that negatively affects teaching.
520. Living with others who feel they are not getting enough attention because of the heavy job demands on teacher's time.
521. Suffering a setback in self-esteem/confidence.
522. Teacher's parents having unfavorable opinions about decision to teach.

523. Finding the first year of teaching so demanding that teacher cannot be as creative as she/he would like.
524. Having to deal with the bureaucratic red tape associated with the licensing process.
525. Finding no substitute available when teacher needed to be absent from school.
526. Getting to and from school.
527. Living on beginning teacher's salary.
528. Boyfriend/girlfriend/fiancée living somewhere else.
529. Meeting members of the opposite sex.
530. Finding the time to make living arrangement seem like home.
531. Experiencing interpersonal difficulties with those the teacher lives with.
532. Feeling isolated/lonely.

### Category 20: Unconstructive Attitudes and Perceptions Represented in the Case Studies

533. Not liking teaching.
534. Feeling very dissatisfied with her/his teaching job.
535. Not liking the courses she/he is teaching.
536. Feeling ineffective.
537. Feeling incompetent in the classroom.
538. Having doubts about her/his ability as a teacher.
539. Feeling overwhelmed by what she/he has to do.
540. Encountering content that teacher knows she/he should teach but does not like.
541. Having to teach material that she/he does not believe is important or useful.
542. Feeling material on an upcoming standardized test is inappropriate content for her/his students to be covering.
543. Feeling that her/his students are not growing intellectually
544. Feeling that her/his students are not growing morally.
545. Feeling too critical, criticizing more than teaching.
546. Feeling she/he entertains more than teaches.
547. Feeling she/he has nothing to say to students.
548. Lacking confidence in/feeling anxious about teaching.
549. Being challenged to appear confident while teaching, but appearing/feeling tentative or lacking in direction.
550. Fearing to take risks in teaching.

551. Perceiving that students feel her/his teaching is too structured or rigid—or feel the teacher is too structured or rigid.
552. Feeling unsure of the soundness or appropriateness of her/his decisions.
553. Feeling that she/he needs to be more understanding of students (e.g., there have been occasions when she/he has been a bit hard on them).
554. Feeling powerless.
555. Feeling unsupported in/unrecognized for her/his teaching.
556. Feeling the students are driving her/him crazy.
557. Experiencing depression because of her/his teaching.
558. Feeling depressed by the circumstances of students (e.g., she/he believes there is no hope for them).
559. Feeling that her/his authority as a teacher is illegitimate.
560. Feeling the rewards of teaching are not great enough (e.g., teaching seems thankless to her/him).

### Category 21: Gender/Sexual Challenges
### Represented in the Case Studies

561. Perceiving the school as sexist.
562. Experiencing an unwanted romantic overture from another faculty member.
563. Being sexually harassed by another faculty member or subjected to sexual innuendo by another faculty member.
564. Learning of a seduction attempt of a student by another teacher.
565. Experiencing flirtation from a student.
566. Experiencing a homosexual overture from a student.
567. Finding a student attractive.
568. Students engaging in sexual misconduct.

### Category 22: Outside Community Issues
### Represented in the Case Studies

569. Community deteriorating, negatively affecting life in the school.
570. Community being an unstimulating place for the teacher to live or work.
571. Having difficulties getting established in the community (e.g., finding where services are—shoe repairmen, auto mechanic, dentist, dry cleaner, etc.).

**I**

# An Overview of the Challenges of Beginning Teaching and Beyond

# chapter two

# The Challenges Reported by Beginning Teachers in the Notre Dame Teacher Education Program

In this chapter we take up a study designed to illuminate just how likely it is that young teachers will experience the challenges detailed in Chapter 1. The method used was simple and consistent with the method used in many previous studies of teacher challenges: We had young teachers complete a questionnaire. There was one question for every one of the 571 issues identified in Chapter 1 (i.e., there was one question for every challenge listed in the Appendix to Chapter 1). Specifically, first- and second-year teachers rated how often they encountered each of these challenges, from never (0) to every day or almost every day (5).

The respondents were all participating in the teacher education program sponsored by the Alliance for Catholic Education of the University of Notre Dame. The first-year teachers had completed one summer of coursework and were at the midpoint of their first year of teaching when they were given the questionnaire. The second-year teachers had one summer of education coursework followed by a year of teaching followed by a second summer session of coursework before returning for the second year of teaching. Most of the second-year teachers were in the same school they had served in during their first year in the program. The second-year teachers were also given the questionnaire at midyear. Even though the questionnaire was distributed in the middle of the year, participants could complete the questionnaire immediately or wait until later in the school year. In fact, the majority of the teachers chose to wait until quite late in the school year or until the school year was over before they completed the questionnaire.

The teachers served in Catholic elementary, middle, and high schools across states in the South, including Alabama, Florida, Georgia, Louisiana, Mississippi, North Carolina, Oklahoma, South Carolina, and Texas. Most of the elementary teachers taught the entire curriculum, although there were a few elementary teachers with more specialized assignments that required them to coach, teach French, teach reading to several classes, or teach one of the elementary content areas to several classes. There were middle and high school teachers in all of the content areas typical at these levels. In short, the sample of teachers spanned the full range of teaching responsibilities possible in Catholic K–12 education.

With 571 questions, the questionnaire was perceived as very long by the participants, requiring about two hours on average to complete. Because participation in the study was unambiguously voluntary, consistent with University of Notre Dame and professional psychological research standards, we did not expect 100% participation in the study. Of the 73 first-year teachers in the group, 50 replied with usable data (68% participation). Of the 57 second-year teachers, 27 provided usable data (47%). The sample was culturally diverse (African American, European American, Asian American, and Hispanic), with approximately equal numbers of males and females in the group.

## ARE CHALLENGES FREQUENT?

A very important first question was whether challenges in teaching were frequent for the sample of beginning teachers. Determination of this was easy: We counted the number of nonzero responses for each participant. The minimum number of challenges reported by a participant was 49; the maximum number reported was 440. The mean number of challenges reported was 207.48 (SD = 90.90). In short, the participants reported plenty of challenges, although, on average, they reported experiencing only 35% of the total pool of challenges identified in Chapter 1.

The next question was how many of the challenges reported occurred infrequently and how many occurred very frequently. The relevant data are displayed in Table 2-1. Challenges are a daily thing, with the teachers reporting on average 23 challenges on a daily or almost daily basis. Another 31 challenges on average were reported as occurring several times this week, with 53 challenges on average being reported as experienced monthly. Based on these responses, we conclude that beginning teachers are immersed in challenge. If there is good news in this analysis, it is that almost half of the challenges cited by the teachers were reported as relatively infrequent (i.e., happening once or only a few times during the year).

One expectation that we had was that there might be fewer challenges reported by second-year compared to first-year teachers. In fact, there were slight trends in that direction in every nonzero category of response, although none of the trends was statistically significant. The differences in the number of challenges reported by women and men were miniscule. In general, the number of challenges reported by elementary, middle school, and high school teachers were comparable.

## WHAT CHALLENGES ARE MOST FREQUENT?

Although beginning teachers experience many challenges, that does not necessarily mean they experience many different types. We explored that issue by calculating the mean frequency ratings for each of the 571 challenges tapped in the survey. One finding was that every one of the 571 had happened to at least one of the beginning teach-

**TABLE 2-1**
*Mean of Challenges Receiving Each Rating*

| RATING | MEAN | SD |
| --- | --- | --- |
| 0 = Never this year | 363.42 | 90.90 |
| 1 = One time this year | 20.03 | 18.25 |
| 2 = A few times this year | 79.12 | 44.61 |
| 3 = A few times this month | 53.52 | 26.69 |
| 4 = A few times this week | 31.78 | 21.92 |
| 5 = Every day or almost every day | 23.14 | 21.21 |

ers in our sample. That is, all of the challenges in the list do, in fact, happen in school.

Even so, only 16 challenges emerged in this analysis as occurring frequently for the sample as a whole (i.e., either 3 = several times a month, 4 = several times a week, or 5 = daily or almost daily); Table 2-2 summarizes this set of challenges. Another 44 challenges were cited as frequent for identifiable subsets of teachers (i.e., first or second year; male or female; elementary, middle, or high school). What is most striking about Table 2-2 is that the clear majority of frequently encountered challenges are about students. Student misbehavior, motivation (or lack of it), and individual differences are the daily challenges confronting teachers. The inexperienced teachers are confronted often by inattentive and hyperactive students plus students who come to class late and talk too much in class. Getting students to do homework on time also challenges many beginning teachers. What was absolutely salient to our sample of beginning teachers, however, was that the students they were serving were diverse, including some students with characteristics that make teaching them difficult (i.e., they are immature, angry, overly tired, etc.).

Yes, there were some frequently encountered challenges in categories other than the "student" category. Nonetheless, many of the "professional" challenges cited also involved students. Summing up the high-frequency challenges recorded in Table 2-2 in a nutshell, we conclude that it is the students who are challenging for beginning teachers.

In this analysis, there was evidence that first-year teachers experienced a greater variety of frequent challenges than did second-year teachers. For example, Table 2-2 includes 16 items that were rated as frequently occurring only by the first-year teachers. In contrast, there were only 3 items in Table 2-2 that were frequent for second-year teachers but not for first-year teachers.

The number of frequent challenges was slightly greater for men than for women beginning teachers. The only striking general conclusion was that men reported more difficulties in motivating students.

The grade level where there were the most specific challenges perceived as frequent was high school. It was very striking that 9 of the items that were judged as frequent at high school but not at the lower grade levels pertained to student motivation. If the students are the challenge in general, which is what our sample of teachers told us, students seem even more challenging in high school than in elementary or middle school.

**TABLE 2-2**

*Challenges Rated as Occurring Frequently, by Category*

SELF

**Lack Knowledge of Teaching**

Encountering a situation teacher education did not prepare you for[1,f,E,H]

**Personal Life Issues**

Not having any spare time[1]

First year of teaching so demanding teacher cannot be as creative as would like to be[1,f,E]

**Conflicts with School Culture**

Expectancies of school seeming too low[H]

**Unconstructive Attitudes and Perceptions**

Feeling overwhelmed by what there is to do[1,m,H]

Having doubts about ability as a teacher[1]

PROFESSIONAL

**Classroom Discipline**

Finding balance between being in control and being too autocratic[1,m,E,H]

Getting students to obey classroom rules[M]

Being consistent with punishment[1,m,H]

Feeling she/he is not being strict enough[H]

**Classroom Instruction**

Trying to meet needs/demands of individual students while meeting needs/demands of class as whole[1,f,E]

Getting students to think critically[2,m,H]

Getting students to answer higher-order questions—that is, questions requiring more than factual recall[m,H]

**Classroom Management**

Students leaving the room messy[1,E,M]

Individual students being disruptive or uncontrollable

**Planning Lessons and School Days**

Not having enough time to teach each student as much as needed[f,E,M]

Not completing lesson in allotted time[E]

Not reflecting on teaching as much as she/he should[H]

**Assessment**

Having large amount of grading/correction of papers that must be done[1,E]

Getting behind on grading,[H]

*(Table 2-2 continued)*

**TABLE 2-2 *(cont'd.)***

**Resource Issues**
  Students not bringing necessary supplies to class/school [1,M]

**Planning Lessons and School Days**
  Not having enough time to do professional reading[1]

**STUDENTS**
  Misbehavior
  Students being inattentive
  Hyperactive students being disruptive
  Students sitting inappropriately (e.g., sprawled over or sitting on desk)[1,E]
  Students being tardy[1]
  Students talking too much
  Students severely "acting out"[1,E,M]
  Students being cruel to one another[f]

**Motivation**
  Students not doing assignments/homework
  Students doing assignments/homework late[f]
  Students doing homework/assignments haphazardly[M,H]
  Students turning in sloppy work
  Students not accepting responsibility for their own failures[m,H]
  Students not showing energy or enthusiasm in teacher's class[H]
  Students thinking what teacher is teaching is irrelevant to them[m,H]
  Students feeling bored[m,H]
  Students feeling apathetic[H]
  Students feeling disinterested[m,H]
  Students complaining about homework/assignments[m,M,H]
  Many students not sharing teacher's "hard work" ethic[H]

**Individual Differences**
  Students who are immature
  Students who are angry[f,2,E,M]
  Students who are overly tired
  Students who are social misfits[1,m,M]
  Students who are mean
  Students who are hard to reach
  Students with low ability
  Students who are gifted
  Students living in disorganized/dysfunctional families
  Students with short attention spans
  Students with vastly different abilities
  Students with special education needs[f,2,H]
  Students with problems understanding material
  Students who watch too much TV[1,m,M,H]
  Students who are rude/disrespectful[M,H]

Students who are emotionally disturbed[E]
Students with bad tempers[E,M]
Students who are very shy[H]

---

Items with superscript numbers and letters were frequent only for the groups indicated.
[1]First-year teachers
[2]Second-year teachers
[f]Female teachers
[m]Male teachers
[E]Elementary school teachers
[M]Middle school teachers
[H]High school teachers

In summary, only a small portion of the total number of challenges in the survey was rated as occurring frequently. That is, there are some challenges that do occur for many beginning teachers quite often. The many other challenges that beginning teachers face—and recall, in the analyses reported in the last section, that beginning teachers are reporting that they have many challenges on a regular basis—seem to be unique to particular teachers. For example, 173 of the 571 challenges had a mean frequency rating of less than 0.50 on the 0-to-5 scale and a mode of 0 (i.e., fully one-third of the items were encountered rarely by the beginning teachers). When the commonly experienced challenges are examined, it is very clear, however, that at the heart of the frequent challenges experienced by teachers lie challenges with students. Students misbehave, are undermotivated, and have diverse talents and needs.

## TEACHING ABILITY AND CHALLENGES

It is always the case in a cohort of beginning teachers that some will be better teachers than others. That was true in this sample as well, as reflected in student teaching grades, which were assigned by a university-based field supervisor who visited the school sites where teachers in the Alliance for Catholic Education program taught. The supervised teaching grades ranged from A to C in the program.

With respect to the number of challenges reported, there were no statistically significant differences as a function of teaching ability.

**TABLE 2-3**

*Challenges More Frequent for Beginning Teachers with Higher Supervised Teaching Grades*

---

SELF

**Personal Life Issues**

Finding teaching so demanding teacher cannot be as creative as she/he would like

Not having any spare time

Having trouble finding the time to make living arrangements seem like home

**Unconstructive Perceptions and Attitudes**

Feeling overwhelmed by what she/he has to do

Having doubts about his/her ability as a teacher

PROFESSIONAL

**Planning of Lessons and School Days**

Having to juggle more than one goal at a time

Having trouble being decisive

Spending too much time preparing for class

Feeling she/he not covering enough material

Having too much material to cover in the school year

Not having enough time to help each student as much as needed

**Classroom Instruction**

Students not following directions in doing an assignment

Meeting the needs/demands of individual students while meeting the needs/demands of the class as a whole

Students having misconceptions that interfere with their learning new content

Students not self-correcting

**Lack of Knowledge about Teaching and Curriculum**

Student/Practice teaching at a different level/in a different content area than present position

**Induction and Mentoring Issues**

Not knowing all the school rules, procedures, or policies

**Diversity Issues**

Not knowing how to refer to members of ethnic minority groups

STUDENTS

**Motivation**

Getting students to work hard and have fun while doing it

---

Pearson correlations between supervised teaching grade and rated frequency of challenge were statistically significant at $p < .05$ for each challenge in this table.

**TABLE 2-4**

*Challenges That Were More Frequent for Beginning Teachers Defined as Less Able by Supervised Teaching Grade*

SELF

**Personal Life Issues**

Being physically injured in a classroom/school accident

Finding no substitutes available when teacher needs to be absent from school

**Unconstructive Perceptions and Attitudes**

Feeling she/he entertains more than teaches

PROFESSIONAL

**Assessment**

Students disagreeing with how teacher grades

**Classroom Management**

Feeling tension in the school over who controls the school—teachers or students

Classroom aide not being very helpful

**Relations with Teaching Colleagues**

Receiving a sharp note from the office or another teacher

Feeling concerned that other teachers will find out what is going on in her/his class

Having a confrontation with another teacher

STUDENTS

**Misbehavior**

Cutting exams

Insulting teacher

Yelling too much

**Individual Differences**

Students being angry

Students being very depressed

Students being very shy

Students being angry/hurt about life

Students having low ability

**Teacher–Student Communications/Interactions**

Students just wanting to be left alone

Note: Pearson correlations between supervised teaching grade and rated frequency of challenge were statistically significant at $p < .05$ for each challenge in this table.

Some specific challenges, however, were statistically more frequent for more able (Table 2-3) and less able (Table 2-4) beginning teachers. There were several aspects of these results that were striking. The less able teachers reported having more problems with students than did the better beginning teachers. The less able teachers also reported less favorable relations with other teachers in the school. In contrast, despite the fact that the more able teachers provided better instruction, they worried more about teaching, having, for example, more planning concerns than less able teachers. The better teachers also reported more challenges in their personal lives, perhaps because they were so consumed with their teaching job that they did not have spare time or time to make home as comfortable as possible. The more able teachers also seemed to be more reflective, reporting self-doubts and more feelings of being overwhelmed than did the less able teachers. In short, the experience of challenge did seem to be qualitatively different for more and less able beginning teachers.

## WHAT ABOUT THE MOST SERIOUS CHALLENGES?

One reaction to the list of 571 challenges is that many of them really do not seem that serious. In response to that perception, we carried out several analyses that included evaluation of the seriousness of the challenges. Specifically, 20 members of the original sample of 77 teachers were paid to go through the list of 571 challenges twice. The 20 teachers doing the rating included an equal number of first- and second-year teachers and an equal number of male and female teachers; 6 of the raters were elementary, 6 middle school, and 8 high school teachers.

On one pass through the items, the 20 raters evaluated which of the challenges would be serious if they occurred frequently (i.e., posed a challenge daily or weekly), using a 1-to-3 scale ($1 =$ not serious, $2 =$ somewhat serious, and $3 =$ extremely serious). The mean ratings in this analysis ranged from 1.05 to 2.95, and most items (64.45%) received at least a rating in the "somewhat serious" range (scoring greater than 1.50), when the rater rated their impact when they occurred frequently. On the second pass, the 20 raters evaluated which challenges would be serious (again on a 1-to-3 scale) even if they occurred infrequently (i.e., posed a challenge only monthly or yearly).

The mean ratings in this analysis ranged from 1.45 to 3.00, with all but two of the items (99.65%) perceived at least in the "somewhat serious" range even if they occurred infrequently.

There was not a single item of the 571 that did not receive a "somewhat serious" or greater rating from at least one rater. We infer that every challenge detailed in Chapter 1 has the potential to be problematic for a beginning teacher.

Even so, we felt that certain items deserved more attention in this analysis than others. Thus, we analyze in the subsections that follow (a) challenges rated as serious if they occurred frequently that did, in fact, occur frequently and (b) challenges that are serious even if they occur infrequently.

## Challenges Serious Only If They Occur Frequently

There were, in fact, challenges that were rated as extremely serious (mean serious rating > 2.50, mode = 3) only if they occurred frequently that were also reported as occurring frequently (mean greater than 2.50 on the 0-to-5 frequency scale). These are reported in Table 2-5. Notably, six of the eight challenges were associated with difficult students. In a nutshell, the message in Table 2-5 is that students who cause serious problems are frequently encountered by the beginning teacher. A secondary message is that the beginning teacher has time neither for all the students who need help nor for her- or himself, with both of these time pressures posing serious problems.

## Challenges Serious If They Occur Even Infrequently

Some challenges do not have to occur frequently to be extremely serious (mean seriousness rating > 2.50, mode = 3). In fact, there are quite a few challenges in this category; these are summarized in Table 2-6 (challenges that occur rarely, with the average rating less than 0.5 on the 0-to-5 frequency scale and a mode of 0) and Table 2-7 (challenges that occur more frequently, with the average rating between 0.5 and 2.50 on the 0-to-5 frequency scale). More positively, there were no challenges in the "serious if they occur even infrequently" category that occurred very frequently (mean greater than 2.5 on the 0-to-5 frequency scale). Although there were a number of serious student-related challenges in Tables 2-6 and 2-7, there were also quite a few serious challenges involving relations with other adults associated with the school, especially in Table 2-6.

**TABLE 2-5**

*Challenges That Would Be Serious If They Occurred Frequently That Occurred Frequently*

**SELF**

**Personal Life Issues**
  Not having any spare time

**PROFESSIONAL**

**Classroom Management**
  Individual students being disruptive or uncontrollable

**Planning of Lessons and School Days**
  Not having enough time to help each student as much as needed

**STUDENTS**

**Misbehavior**
  Students being rude/disrespectful

**Motivation**
  Students not doing assignments/homework

**Individual Differences**
  Students being mean
  Students living in disorganized/dysfunctional families
  Students having special education needs

**TABLE 2-6**

*Challenges That Would Be Serious If They Occurred Even Infrequently That Occurred Infrequently*

**PROFESSIONAL**

**Classroom Management**
  Person entering room without authorization and refusing to leave
  Having to make moral compromise to keep peace with students
  Student disappearing from teacher's classroom (i.e., teacher cannot find
    a student who is supposed to be with her or him)

**STUDENTS**

**Discipline**
  Having to administer corporal punishment
  Being pressured by principal (or some other administrator or teacher) to
    use corporal punishment

## Misbehavior

Being physically attacked/hit by student(s)

Having evidence that a student committed a crime

Being the victim of student vandalism

Student committing or threatening to commit suicide

Students dropping out of school

Students being gang members

Students extorting money or other goods from other students

Students carrying guns or other weapons in the school

Students abusing drugs

## Individual Differences

Students having eating disorders

A student dying

A student being murdered

## Diversity Issues

Minority students (or their parents) feeling they are victims of discrimination by beginning teacher.

Students or their parents accusing teacher of racial prejudice

## Gender/Sexual Issues

Student engaging in sexual misconduct

## OTHER ADULTS IN SCHOOL

## Relations with Parents

Parent threatening to ask that beginning teacher be dismissed

## Relations with Teaching Colleagues

Other teachers being critical of the teacher; being tactless, rude, or insulting to the teacher

Having to make a moral compromise to keep the peace with other teachers

## Relations with Principals/Administrators

Being threatened with dismissal by principal or other administrator

Being uncertain about being rehired next year

## Gender/Sexual Issues

Being sexually harassed by another faculty member or subjected to sexual innuendo by another faculty member

Learning of a seduction attempt of a student by another teacher

**TABLE 2-7**

*Challenges That Would Be Serious If They Occurred Even Infrequently That Occurred Moderately Frequently*

---

**STUDENTS**

**Misbehavior**
Students harassing beginning teacher
Suspecting that a student is involved in illegal activity (e.g., selling drugs)
Students stealing
Students fighting
Students abusing alcohol

**Individual Differences**
Student being abused
Student having a parent who dies
Students being unable to read

**Diversity Issues**
Individual students showing racial prejudice

---

The second-year teachers reported many more items as not serious (mean = 289, SD = 106.56) than did first-year teachers (mean = 197, SD = 63.21), $|t|$ (18) = 2.03, $p < .03$. Consistent with their reduced concern, the second-year teachers also rated fewer items as very serious (mean = 68, SD = 34.98) than did first-year teachers (mean = 119, SD = 41.60), $|t|$ (18) = 2.98, $p < .008$. What is obvious from reviewing these data (see Table 2-8) is that there is a broad array of concerns that are more troubling to first-year than to second-year teachers.

Middle school teachers reported more challenges as extremely serious than did high school teachers. The middle school mean of 129 (SD = 42.27) challenges rated as extremely serious was greater than the high school mean of 70 (SD = 33.93), $t$ (12) = 2.91, $p < .02$.

The particular items rated more serious by middle school than by high school teachers are in Table 2-9. There is a wide range of issues that are perceived as more serious by beginning middle school compared to beginning high school teachers.

**TABLE 2-8**

*Challenges Rated as More Serious by First- Than by Second-Year Teachers*

SELF

**Conflicts with School Culture**

Disagreeing with school's approach for handling special needs students

Disagreeing with school policies/methods for assigning students to special education

Perceiving the school as too high pressure and achievement oriented

**Personal Life Issues**

Having a physical illness as a reaction to stress on the job

Suffering a setback in self-esteem/confidence

Having a physical illness that negatively affects teaching

**Unconstructive Attitudes and Perceptions**

Being challenged to appear confident while teaching, but appearing/feeling tentative or lacking in direction

Feeling powerless

Experiencing depression because of her/his teaching

Feeling that students are driving her/him crazy

**Gender/Sexual Challenges**

Perceiving the school as sexist

PROFESSIONAL

**Assessment**

Students disagreeing with how teacher grades

**Classroom Management**

Students working together when they are supposed to be working alone

Student disappearing from the classroom

**Resource Issues**

Classes being too large

Having weak or inappropriate/unattractive textbooks

Having no textbooks or an insufficient number of textbooks available

Classroom/building being too hot or too cold for comfort

Lacking social services help needed for a student

School building being in disrepair in ways that interfere with teaching

Mice or other vermin being in the classroom/school

School building having been constructed for another purpose, not well suited to being a school

Audio-visual materials not being accepted by students

*(Table 2-8 continued)*

**TABLE 2-8** *(cont'd.)*

**Teacher–Student Communications/Interactions**

Students asking questions so stupid or naive that they are not worth addressing

Disliking students

Students intentionally trying to make teacher angry

Worrying that she/he might be falsely accusing a student of something

Students not understanding what teacher is saying

Giving directions that are unclear

Being unsure about whether to attend a social function organized by students, for fear of getting too close to students

Students hating the teacher

Students not trusting the teacher

Students hating class

**Planning of Lessons and School Days**

Students having to take school/state/standardized exams that include material that teacher has not covered

School emphasizing adherence to publisher guidelines in using textbooks and curriculum materials

**Classroom Instruction**

Getting students to understand a lesson

Students not following teacher's directions in doing an assignment

**Knowledge of Teaching and Curriculum**

Finding curriculum materials hard to understand

**STUDENTS**

**Discipline**

Being consistent with punishment

Coping with being an authority figure because of having anti-authority feelings

Having to administer corporal punishment

**Misbehavior**

Hyperactive students being disruptive

Students lying

Students having bad tempers

Students plagiarizing

Students cheating

Students taking advantage of or hassling substitute teacher

Students verbally abusing or "talking back" to teacher

Students throwing objects at one another

Students yelling too much

Students fighting
Students freeing animals in room causing disruption

**Motivation**
Students feeling defeated, believing there is no way they can succeed
Getting students to trust each other
Students passively resisting what the teacher is trying to teach
Students not answering teacher's questions
School making the students feel badly about themselves
Students not caring about school

**Individual Differences**
Students being inattentive

**Diversity Issues**
Individual students showing racial prejudice
Class/school exhibiting general racial prejudice

**OTHER ADULTS IN SCHOOL**

**Relations with Parents**
Parents being angry
Parents not respecting teacher authority
Parents having a wide range of expectations about what should be going
on in the classroom
Parent conferences/discussions being difficult or producing anxiety

**Relations with Teaching Colleagues**
Other teachers insulting about/to students
Other teachers being pessimistic about the students in the school
Other teachers seeming stupid, undereducated, incompetent, etc.
Having too little communication/interaction with other teachers
Having to make a moral compromise to keep the peace with other
teachers

**Relations with Principals/Administrators**
Principal or other administrator expecting students to be quieter than
teacher can keep them
Being pressured by the principal (or other administrator) to use corporal
punishment

---

For all items, Mann-Whitney U $<$ 30, $p <$ .03, for first- versus second-year comparison.

**TABLE 2-9**

*Challenges Rated as More Serious by Middle School Than by High School Teachers*

SELF

**Personal Life Issues**
Meeting members of the opposite sex

**Unconstructive Attitudes and Perceptions**
Having to teach material that the teacher does not believe is useful or important
Being afraid to take risks in teaching
Being depressed by the circumstances of students (e.g., teacher believes there is no hope for her/his students)
Feeling material on an upcoming standardized test is inappropriate content for his/her students to be covering

PROFESSIONAL

**Assessment**
Too much emphasis being placed on accountability (e.g., standardized tests)

**Classroom Management**
Students not remaining on task and orderly when teacher is working intensely with one or two students
Wasting time handing back papers, with students not productively engaged

**Teacher–Student Communications/Interactions Issues**
Students requesting to transfer out of the teacher's class

**Planning of Lessons and School Days**
Planning a lesson that fails to fill up its allotted time

**Induction and Mentoring Issues**
Not knowing how to implement the curriculum guide
Not understanding how the school is governed
Not understanding the community served by the school

**Diversity Issues**
Students or their parents accusing teacher of racial prejudice

**Outside Community Issues**
Community deteriorating, negatively affecting life in school

## STUDENTS

### Individual Differences

Students being gifted

Students having vastly different abilities

Students watching too much TV

Students being inattentive

Students being parents of children, with their parenting responsibilities interfering with schoolwork

Students being affected by the demands of poverty

Students being wrongly classified as in need of special education

Students having eating disorders

Students having parents who feel worthless

Students having bad tempers who are physically big enough to threaten teacher

Student having no parents

### Misbehavior

Students harassing teacher

Students stealing

## OTHER ADULTS IN SCHOOL

### Relations with Parents

Communicating with divorced parents

Communicating with alcoholic parents

Parents being unable to give academic help to their children

Parents being unwilling to give academic help to their children

Persuading parents to come in for a conference

### Relations with Principals/Administrators

Having a run-in with a member of the school's support staff

---

For all items in the table, Mann-Whitney $U < 30$, $p < .03$, for middle school versus high school teachers.

# Summary

There are many challenges involving students that can be very serious, with some of these occurring frequently (and hence likely in the beginning teacher's world) and others occurring less frequently. Looking across the tables in this chapter, there can be little doubt that students are the source of many of the most serious challenges to the beginning teacher. That said, our young teachers often reported a lack of time for themselves and a lack of time for their most needy students. Then, there are the politics of the job, which can become extremely serious if parents, other teachers, or principals think ill of the new teacher. Conflicts with the young teacher's morals can also be a source of serious problems, either if the young teacher feels she/he has to morally compromise to keep peace with students or teachers or if members of the faculty are engaging in inappropriate sexual behaviors (e.g., harassment, seduction). Compared to the entire list of 571 potential challenges, however, it is encouraging that less than 8% of the total pool of challenges proved to be extremely serious.

One finding that deserves emphasis is that second-year teachers perceived fewer challenges as serious than did first-year teachers. Life in school gets better for young teachers as they acquire experience, even the little bit of experience that distinguishes first- from second-year teachers.

# chapter three

# What Lies Ahead?
# The Challenges of
# Experienced Teachers

What lies ahead for these young teachers? If they are like young people in previous generations who began teaching, many will leave the profession. But what about those who stay? Will the job remain challenging? Based on research focusing on the problems faced by experienced teachers, the most likely answer is that current beginning teachers will be challenged throughout their careers as teachers.

There were a number of studies in the second half of the 20th century that tapped the challenges faced by experienced teachers. We studied 10 of the more prominent of these studies in order to understand the types of challenges that have been documented with experienced teachers. Our sample of studies included Adams, Hutchinson, and Martray (1980); Dunn (1972); Echternacht (1981); Koontz (1963); Leiter (1995); Litt and Turk (1985); Olander and Farrell (1970); Pharr (1974); Rudd and Wiseman (1962); and Thomas and Kiley (1994). In all these investigations, experienced teachers responded to questionnaires about the challenges of teaching.

As was the case with beginning teachers, we found evidence of "self" concerns, including unconstructive attitudes and perceptions by the teacher (3 of the 10 studies), personal life issues (3 of 10 studies), conflicts with school culture (2 studies), and teacher knowledge concerns (2 studies). There also were professional practice issues, including discipline (1 study), classroom instruction (4 studies), assessment (1 study), planning (3 studies), nonteaching responsibilities (5 studies), and limited resources (2 studies). Students were cited as a source of challenge, including dealing with individual differences among students (4 studies) and motivating students (6 studies). These studies also cited challenges in dealing with other adults associated with the school, including other teachers (2 studies), parents (5 studies), and administrators (3 studies). Outside-the-school challenges, which were very apparent in the studies of beginning teachers, were not reported in the questionnaire studies of experienced teachers. In short, however, many of the challenges reported by beginning teachers, including those in the questionnaire study reported in detail in this book, have also been reported by more experienced teachers.

In reviewing the research, it was salient to us that nobody had ever tapped the challenges of experienced teachers as completely as we tapped the challenges of beginning teachers in the questionnaire we employed in our investigation. The purpose of the investigation covered in this chapter was to determine how experienced teachers would respond to the instrument employed in our study of beginning teachers. In doing so, we expected to be able to come to insights about challenges of teaching that endure beyond the initial years of teaching. Thus, we sought a sample of experienced teachers who were as similar as possible to the sample of beginning teachers we had studied. Specifically, we identified a sample of experienced teachers (with teaching experience ranging from 3 to 55 years) who taught in the same schools as the beginning teachers who were surveyed in the study reported in Chapter 2 of this book. In fact, the experienced teachers had served as mentors for the first-year class reported on earlier, so that their teaching assignments often were very similar to the teaching assignments of the beginning teachers who were surveyed by us. That is, there were elementary, middle school, and high school teachers. At the middle and high school levels, the full range of subject-area teaching was represented in the sample. As mentors to the beginning teachers, these experienced teachers were making their careers in southern Catholic schools, as far east as Charleston and as far west as Texas and Oklahoma.

We were very successful in recruiting the mentors to complete the questionnaire. There were 66 mentor teachers for the first-year teacher education class, and 55 of them completed the questionnaire (83% participation rate). Twelve of these experienced respondents were elementary teachers; 24 were middle school teachers; and the remaining 19 taught at the high school level.

The questionnaires were sent to these teachers in the mail, and they returned their responses in the mail. Participation was unambiguously voluntary, although each mentor who completed a questionnaire received a $24.00 gift certificate redeemable at one of the national chain bookstores. The questionnaires were mailed in May 1999, with follow-up phone calls three weeks after mailing to solicit the cooperation of those teachers who did not respond immediately. Responses continued to come in until October 1999.

## ARE EXPERIENCED TEACHERS CHALLENGED FREQUENTLY?

We established in Chapter 2 that beginning teachers are challenged a great deal, with multiple confirmations that beginning teaching is challenging every day (see Chapter 13, where many days of beginning teachers are taken up in some detail). We assessed whether challenges were frequent for the experienced teachers exactly as we did with the beginning teachers: We counted the number of nonzero responses to the 571 questionnaire items. The minimum number of challenges reported by a teacher was 9; the maximum was 553. This contrasted with a considerably smaller range for the beginning teachers, whose minimum was 49 and maximum was 440. The mean number of challenges for the experienced teachers was 153.64 (SD = 95.65), which was fewer than the mean number of challenges for the beginning teachers (207.48, SD = 90.90), $t$ (130) = 3.29, $p < .001$.

Table 3-1 reports the number of challenges as a function of the frequency of occurrence for the experienced teachers. The table also contains the corresponding information for the beginning teachers reported in Chapter 2, for the purpose of comparison. As was the case with the beginning teachers, the experienced teachers reported many challenges, and they were a daily occurrence. Most striking, however, was that the experienced teachers reported fewer frequent challenges, significantly so with respect to those reported as happening several times a month and several times a week.

Experienced high school teachers reported 154.42 challenges on average (SD = 103.70); middle school teachers cited a mean of 165.46 challenges (SD = 106.94); and elementary teachers reported a mean of 128.75 challenges (SD = 49.18). None of the pairwise

**TABLE 3-1**

*Mean Number of Challenges Receiving Each Rating*

|  | EXPERIENCED | | BEGINNING | |
| --- | --- | --- | --- | --- |
| RATING | MEAN | SD | MEAN | SD |
| 0 = Never this year | 417.36 | 95.65 | 363.42 | 90.90* |
| 1 = One time this year | 23.71 | 28.72 | 20.03 | 18.25 |
| 2 = A few times this year | 70.95 | 39.67 | 79.12 | 44.61 |
| 3 = A few times this month | 27.33 | 20.23 | 53.52 | 26.69* |
| 4 = A few times this week | 14.33 | 13.87 | 31.78 | 21.92* |
| 5 = Every day or almost every day | 17.33 | 30.83 | 23.14 | 21.21 |

:Total at each experience level = 571 questionnaire items.

*Significantly different, $p < .05$.

differences was statistically significant; all pairwise $ts < 1.00$. In short, regardless of teaching assignment in the K–12 range, experienced teachers are challenged in their work.

## WHAT CHALLENGES ARE MOST FREQUENT FOR EXPERIENCED TEACHERS?

A fairly small set of challenges was rated as occurring frequently by the beginning teachers. Just as we did with the beginning teachers, we calculated the mean frequency ratings for all 571 challenges tapped in the survey of experienced teachers. Whereas the beginning teachers rated 30 challenges as occurring frequently (having a mean rating of 2.50 or higher on the 0-to-5 scale—rated as occurring several times a month or more on average), the experienced teachers rated only 17 challenges as occurring several times a month or more frequently (see Table 3-2). For the beginning teachers the clear majority of the frequently encountered challenges involved students, and all 17 of the challenges frequently encountered by the experienced teachers were also with students. Student misbehavior, motivation, and individual differences are what frequently challenged the experienced teachers.

In the beginning teacher data, there were indications that challenges decreased with a little bit of experience. Specifically, there were

**TABLE 3-2**

*Challenges Rated as Occurring Frequently by Experienced Teachers*

| CHALLENGES | MEAN FREQUENCY | SD | MODAL FREQUENCY |
|---|---|---|---|
| **MISBEHAVIOR** | | | |
| Students being inattentive | 3.24 | 1.47 | 2 |
| Hyperactive students being disruptive | 2.75 | 1.82 | 5 |
| Students being tardy | 3.07 | 1.64 | 4 |
| Students talking too much | 3.33 | 1.49 | 3 |
| **MOTIVATION** | | | |
| Students not doing assignments | 2.71 | 1.44 | 3 |
| Students turning in sloppy work | 2.62 | 1.38 | 3 |
| **INDIVIDUAL DIFFERENCES** | | | |
| Students being immature | 3.67 | 1.23 | 5 |
| Students being angry | 2.67 | 1.38 | 2 |
| Students being overly tired | 2.93 | 1.45 | 2 |
| Students being hard to reach | 2.60 | 1.44 | 2 |
| Students having low ability | 3.40 | 1.84 | 5 |
| Students being gifted (more able) | 3.33 | 1.87 | 5 |
| Students living in disorganized, dysfunctional families | 3.18 | 1.61 | 5 |
| Students having short attention spans | 4.18 | 1.16 | 5 |
| Students having vastly different abilities | 3.36 | 1.86 | 5 |
| Students having problems understanding the material | 3.40 | 1.23 | 2 |
| Students watching too much television | 3.22 | 2.02 | 5 |

Rated on 0-to-5 scale: 0 = never, 1 = one time this year, 2 = a few times this year, 3 = a few times a month, 4 = a few times a week, 5 = every day or almost every day.

descriptively fewer challenges—albeit not at a statistically significant level—reported by second- compared to first-year teachers. In the experienced teacher sample, it was possible to calculate the correlation between number of years of experience and the number of challenges reported, with $r = -.288$, $p < .05$ (i.e., there was a tendency for reported challenges to decrease with increasing experience). That is,

473 of the 571 challenges declined descriptively in frequency with increasing experience. (Similar conclusions about experience emerged when the responses of the experienced teachers were compared with the responses of the beginning teachers. For 460 of the 571 items, experienced teachers had a descriptively lower mean frequency than beginning teachers.) Within the sample of experienced teachers, for 35 of the items, there was a significant decline ($p < .05$) in reported frequency with increasing experience (see Table 3-3).

Life at school definitely is less challenging for more versus less experienced teachers. Their personal lives are better, with fewer

**TABLE 3-3**

*Challenges That Were Significantly Less Likely with Increasing Experience among Experienced Teachers*

SELF

**Conflicts with School Culture**
  School being generally more traditional than what the teacher is accustomed to

**Personal Life**
  Having headaches caused by teaching
  Not having any spare time
  Meeting members of the opposite sex
  Feeling isolated/lonely

**Unconstructive Attitudes and Perceptions**
  Feeling students are driving her/him crazy

PROFESSIONAL

**Classroom Discipline**
  Finding balance between being in control and being too autocratic

**Assessments**
  Lacking confidence in ability to judge student work

**Classroom Management**
  Discussions getting out of control (i.e., getting off topic of the lesson)
  Students questioning the legitimacy of the system (e.g., authority of teachers)
  Tension existing in school over who controls school, teachers or students
  Unscheduled school closures disrupting teaching

### Resources Issues
Lacking a curriculum guide or an effective curriculum guide
Lacking resources essential for teaching the curriculum
Lacking social services help needed for a student
Classroom building being too hot/cold for comfort

### Teacher–Student Communications and Interactions
Having an outburst of rage with a student

### Nonteaching Responsibilities
Having extracurricular assignments that are draining (e.g., coaching)

### Relations with Colleagues
Other teachers telling teacher what she/he "can't do"

### Planning Lessons and School Days
Not having enough time to plan for class

### Classroom Instruction
Feeling she/he is lecturing too much

### Lack Knowledge of Curriculum
Teaching subjects/a developmental level not trained to teach
Not knowing answers to students' questions

### Relations with Principals/Administrators
Principal's directives being so general or vague that teacher doesn't
know how to carry them out

### STUDENTS

### Misbehavior
Students not wearing appropriate dress
Student lying

### Motivation
Other teachers turning teacher's students off to school
Students thinking what teacher is teaching is irrelevant to them
Students having negative self-image and/or low expectations about
themselves
School making students feel badly about themselves
Students not knowing how to do better in school
Students being bored
Having know-it-all students (i.e., students believing there is nothing
teacher can teach them)

### Individual Differences
Students being mean
Students having problems understanding the material

**TABLE 3-4**

*Challenges Considered Extremely Serious If They Occurred Even Rarely*

STUDENT-CENTERED ITEMS

**Student Behavior**
  Students stealing
  Students fighting
  Discipline Issues
  Students not listening/obeying teacher at all

INTERACTIONS/COMMUNICATIONS WITH OTHER ADULTS

**Relations with Parents**
  Parents neglecting their children
  Parents not being interested in (or being indifferent to) their child

**Relations with Other Teachers**
  Teachers insulting about/to students

headaches, less loneliness, and more spare time. With experience, the teacher is more likely to feel in synchrony with the school culture and at peace with the students. The greatest improvements, however, are with respect to professional challenges. With experience, classroom discipline, management, and communications are less difficult. Relations with other teachers and administrators are better. Instructing is easier, as is assessing students, as well as managing available resources and being less hassled by nonteaching responsibilities. Lessons go smoother, from planning them to dealing with the questions students ask. The students are also less challenging as years of experience increase, with issues of student motivation being less salient in the reports of experienced compared to less experienced teachers. (Similar conclusions emerged when the challenges of the experienced teachers were compared with those of the beginning teachers. For example, 230 challenges were reported as significantly less frequent [$p < .05$] by the experienced compared to the beginning teachers, with only 7 challenges reported as significantly less frequent [$p < .05$] by the beginning compared to the experienced teachers.)

As was true for the beginning teachers, there were very few items that were perceived as seriously challenging that were also reported as occurring frequently by experienced teachers (see Tables 3-4 and 3-5).

**TABLE 3-5**

*Challenges Considered Extremely Serious If They Occurred Frequently*

STUDENT-CENTERED ITEMS

**Individual Differences in Students**
Students living in disorganized, dysfunctional families
Students being angry
Students being hard to reach

**STUDENT BEHAVIOR**
Students being tardy
Hyperactive students being disruptive

**Student Motivation and Affective Issues**
Students not doing assignments or homework
Students turning in sloppy work

# SUMMARY

Based on the responses of the experienced teachers, today's beginning teacher can expect that teaching will remain demanding, although the challenges decline substantially with increasing experience. Most of the challenges that occur are small irritations rather than major crises.

Perhaps most striking in these data is that dealing with individual differences among students and challenges posed by students were the most salient problems in the lives of the experienced teachers, just as in the lives of the beginning teachers. We think this finding has major implications for teacher training: Much more time and effort in teacher education should be directed at learning how to deal with challenging students. On the positive side, much is now known about how to manage misbehaving students and how to increase academic motivation. Also, much has been learned about how to increase learning and performance in students who experience difficulties with schoolwork. What is needed now is significant effort to increase teacher knowledge about techniques that work with various types of problem students. That even experienced teachers report frequent difficulties in dealing with the types of students who are commonly encountered in school makes clear the need for such work. An important direction in the Notre Dame teacher education effort is increasing the knowledge of young teachers in our program about how to deal with challenging students. We think this is an important key to developing better teachers.

## REFERENCES

Adams, R., Hutchinson, S., & Martray, C. (1980, April). *A developmental study of teacher challenges across time.* Paper presented at the annual meeting of the American Educational Research Association, Boston.

Dunn, L. E. (1972). Problems encountered by the Northwest State University secondary education graduates: A comparative study of problems of beginning and experienced teachers (Doctoral dissertation, Northwestern State University of Louisiana, 1972). *Dissertation Abstracts International, 33*, 156.

Echternacht, L. (1982). Instructional problems of business teachers perceived by first-year teachers and experienced teachers. *College Student Journal, 15*, 352–358.

Koontz, J. E. (1963). A study of the relationship between the problems of Arkansas secondary school teachers in certain selected schools and the factors of professional preparation, teaching experience, the sex of the teacher, and the size of the school system (Doctoral dissertation, University of Arkansas, 1963). *Dissertation Abstracts International, 24*, 146.

Leiter, M. P. (1995, June). *Burnout in the 1990s: Research agenda and theory.* Invited symposium, Canadian Society for Industrial/Organization Psychology, annual convention of the Canadian Psychological Association, Charlestown, PEI.

Litt, M. D., & Turk, D. C. (1985). Sources of stress and dissatisfaction in experienced high school teachers. *Journal of Educational Research, 78* (3), 178–185.

Olander, H. T., & Farrell, M. E. (1970). Professional problems of elementary teachers. *Journal of Teacher Education, 21*, 276–280.

Pharr, H. J. (1974). *A study of skills and competencies identified as problem areas for beginning and experienced teachers* (Doctoral dissertation, University of Northern Colorado, University Microfilms International 74-24503).

Rudd, W. G. A., & Wiseman, S. (1962). Sources of dissatisfaction among a group of teachers. *British Journal of Educational Psychology, 32*, 275–291.

Taylor, B. L. (1961). The in-service education needs of new teachers. *California Journal of Educational Research, 12*, 221–223.

Thomas, B., & Kiley, M. A. (1994, February). *Concerns of beginning, middle, and secondary school teachers.* Paper presented at the annual meeting of the Eastern Educational Research Association, Sarasota, FL.

# II

# *B*eginning Teachers
# *Tell Their Stories*

*The second part of this book is all about the bringing to life of the challenges of beginning teaching outlined in the first part. Current and former students of the Notre Dame teacher education program were invited to write about the challenges of their first year of teaching. They chose what to write about and what style to write it in. Their efforts resulted in eight stories about their most memorable challenges. These compelling stories (chapters 4 to 11), some of which include descriptions of quite serious problems, are complemented by a series of 16 mini-cases on the daily hassles first- and second-year teachers face (chapter 12). We hope, by providing stories of beginning teachers who are able to work through their challenges, as well by demonstrating that most of the challenges that beginning teachers face are more hassles than serious problems, that this perspective will help to quell the fears of new or aspiring teachers, as well as to guide the topical focus of instruction in teacher education programs.*

*The challenges described in chapters 4 through 12 come from all five sources described in chapter 1 (Table 1-1): self, students, professional responsibilities, other adults in school, and outside of school. But, just as in the results of the questionnaire studies described in chapters 2 and 3, the bulk of the teachers' challenges come from dealing with their students and issues of misbehavior, motivation, and individual difference. As beginning teachers, their professional challenges also frequently include issues of classroom discipline (which is also highly student centered) and issues of planning and instruction. Their stories are diverse and together provide rich descriptions of all 22 categories of challenge outlined in the Appendix to chapter 1.*

THE 22 CATEGORIES OF CHALLENGES

1. *Classroom Discipline*
2. *Student Misbehavior*
3. *Motivating Students*
4. *Dealing with Individual Differences*
5. *Assessing Students' Work*
6. *Relations with Parents*
7. *Classroom Management*
8. *Resource Issues*
9. *Teacher–Student Communications or Interactions*
10. *Nonteaching, School-Based Demands on Time*
11. *Relations with Colleagues*
12. *Planning of Lessons and School Days*
13. *Classroom Instruction*
14. *Lack of Knowledge about Teaching or Curriculum*
15. *Induction, Mentoring, and Inadequate Guidance*
16. *Conflicts with School Culture*
17. *Relations with Principals or Administrators*
18. *Diversity Issues*
19. *Personal Life Issues*
20. *Unconstructive Attitudes or Perceptions*
21. *Gender or Sexual Issues*
22. *Concerns about the Greater Community*

*The stories in chapters 4 through 11 are presented in order of grade level taught, beginning with the stories of the elementary teachers and concluding with those of the high school teachers. The mini-cases in chapter 12 are presented in the same order. At the beginning of each of the teacher's autobiographical chapters as well as the mini–case studies, we provide an overview of the issues that the teacher dealt with to help guide your reading. In addition, preceding each of the autobiographical stories, we list questions that highlight which of the 22 categories of challenge the teacher touches upon. These will help to get you reflecting on the teacher's options and effectiveness, as well as your own experiences.*

*To protect the privacy of the students, staff, and parents described in the stories, pseudonyms were used for all schools, students, staff, and parents mentioned throughout this section of the book. Furthermore, because the descriptions of the situations in the mini-cases were elicited in the context of a study, the names of the teachers in chapter 12 are also pseudonyms.*

# chapter four

# Discovering Love, Laughter, and Learning in an Inner-City First Grade

## Amy's Story

*Amy entered a school world very different from anything she had experienced previously. She taught first grade in a high-needs school, experiencing firsthand the many challenges in a school serving at-risk children. As sometimes occurs, this first-year teacher was assigned the most challenging group of children in the school. Amy did not give up, however, and she describes in this essay how she dealt with the scant resources in the impoverished school where she taught as well as the emotional upheavals that occur in such a school. Amy did a lot of exploring of options during her first year of teaching and, in doing so, discovered how to make much progress with her class.*

## QUESTIONS FOR REFLECTION WHILE READING AMY'S STORY

1. How would you have handled the misbehavior in Amy's class?
2. What student motivation challenges did Amy face?
3. What types of individual differences increased teaching challenges in Amy's class?
4. What were the assessment challenges that Amy faced?

5. Evaluate Amy's approach for obtaining resources for her class. What else might she have done?
6. What were the challenges facing Amy with respect to classroom interaction?
7. What were the challenges facing Amy in planning?
8. What knowledge of teaching and the curriculum did Amy lack?
9. How well did mentoring serve Amy?
10. Were there diversity issues in Amy's class? If so, did she handle them well?
11. What unconstructive attitudes and perceptions did Amy have?

# THE STORY

The first thing I noticed when I stepped through the doors of the school was the smell. Sickeningly sweet, the odor was a cross between rotting orange peels and damp leaves. I pushed the double glass doors back open, gulped the outside air, then sat on the outside steps, willing my stomach to settle.

After several minutes, I took a deep breath and reentered the building. As my eyes adjusted to the dim light, I peered down a wide hallway with doors lining both sides and a filthy, ancient, circular water fountain in the middle. Splintered wooden benches leaned wearily against the walls and cracks made the floor tiles an eerie mosaic.

A shiver spiraled down my back. This wasn't what I had pictured.

I had arrived that morning, and I was eager to explore my new school. The superintendent had described it as a small private school, in a downtown area that houses 130 children in grades preschool–8. I later learned that most children in the school come from neighborhoods where gangs, drugs, and violence are the norm. The majority of students receive scholarships from private donors, enabling them to avoid the overcrowding and gang-related problems in the neighborhood public schools.

I had come to the large southwestern city from a small town on the New England coast, eager to experience the newness of working with at-risk students in an unfamiliar part of the country. I had been assigned to teach first grade, and I was looking forward to setting up my classroom and preparing for the first day of school. I did not come with clearly defined expectations of my role at my new school. I felt lucky to have been placed in a school that really needed me, and I wanted to do whatever I could to make the most of my time there. By the end of my first day, however, I had learned several things that made me very nervous about beginning the school year.

The smell that had sent me reeling when I first arrived that morning was mold. The basement, which housed Grades 5–8 and the cafeteria, was covered with mold. It bubbled under the peeling paint, streaked the windows, and created damp spots underneath the carpet. Students and teachers had experienced respiratory problems for years, but it was only when the beams supporting floors and ceilings began to rot that the district administration brought in inspectors to assess the building's condition.

The inspectors condemned the basement and the two top floors of the four-story building. The main floor was deemed habitable because it was built on a concrete base that had not been affected by the mold. I often wondered, however, how the main floor could be safe if the floors above it were unstable. I couldn't understand how a concrete base would help me if the two floors above came crashing down.

Because of the building's condition, the students were divided between two locations. Preschool through fourth grade would stay on the main floor of the condemned building, while the middle school would be housed in rooms donated by a church five blocks away.

The first day of school was thus extremely disorganized. The main hallway was filled with people—young students trying to find their classrooms, middle school children who had been dropped at the wrong location, and news crews who were eager to survey the building's condition. I watched this activity from my classroom doorway, waiting nervously for my class to arrive and hoping that my long skirt made me look older than my 22 years. I was surprised by how few parents came to meet me; most children were simply dropped off by their parents in the parking lot.

As I look back, the first day of school was probably the best day we had between August and November. The children were quiet and nervous, but they completed each activity carefully and seriously. I laugh now when I think of my "lesson plans" for those first few days: I wrote out everything I planned to do, minute by minute, on a yellow legal pad and referred to it constantly throughout the day.

My lesson plans were based solely on my own research, since the school did not have a formal curriculum. The older grades had 20-year-old textbooks that the teachers used to plan lessons, but first grade had merely a math workbook for each child. I didn't find this out until three weeks before I arrived, so I spent those weeks frantically searching for information on first-grade curriculum. Desperation breeds creativity, I guess, and I came up with many sources of information in a very short time. I obtained copies of the state curriculum. I borrowed textbooks from other schools and photocopied the tables of contents. I used reference books on early reading and writing to determine how best to structure these subjects. By the time school began, I had a vague yearlong plan for each subject and a month's worth of specific lessons.

By the end of the first week of school, however, these lessons became impossible. My classroom was in chaos, and it was then that other teachers revealed their "secret": The former first-grade teacher had left because she didn't want to deal with this group of children. They had been through four kindergarten teachers, each of whom had left after several months.

There were 13 boys and 5 girls in the class. They were typical of the students in my new school in many ways: Most were from single-parent families or homes where grandparents or other relatives served as their caregivers. Most of their parents worked at least two jobs, and the children, for the most part, took care of themselves. What was unusual about this group were the additional burdens that they faced in their young lives. The emotional needs of the class overwhelmed me, and the stories of these children's lives filled me with despair.

Anton had spent the first six years of his life in an orphanage in Eastern Europe. He was adopted by a middle-class family and he had attended the school for the last two months of kindergarten. Anton trusted no one; he hoarded food from home in his backpack and hid money in his socks. When we ate, he hunched over his lunchbox and gulped down his food, afraid that the other children would take it. Anton had been abused for most of his young life, and he was extremely aggressive.

William was the youngest of three children, all of whom had different fathers. William lived in an apartment with his mother and her current boyfriend, who would lock the children in the bedroom so he could have "peace" when he came home from his job running drugs.

Zach's father had died of dementia several months before. Zach and his siblings had literally watched their father wither away on the couch, and Zach was grieving in the only way he knew. He spent hours in the coatroom banging his head against the wall and sobbing.

As these and other stories unfolded, the class spun out of control. If Zach wasn't screaming, Anton was hitting someone. If William was awake, he was absolutely listless. The children were constantly crying and fighting, and I found myself losing sight of my goals for the class. I yelled constantly, and I cried every morning before the children arrived. The school schedule did not help my situation. I spent 7 1/2 hours each day with the children without a break or even a change of scenery. There were no art or gym classes. There was no cafeteria or playground. We ate lunch at our desks and played in the parking lot each afternoon.

Academics were not a priority for me during the first few months of school. The children were not ready to learn reading, math, and writing; they first needed to learn about hope, trust, and inner peace. I couldn't establish order without giving these children a classroom community where they felt safe, loved, and important. I realized this after several weeks, and it was difficult for me to accept that I was failing to provide the class with any of this.

This crisis required a lot more work than photocopying resources and networking with other schools. I turned to the school principal for help, but she wanted no part of this group of children. As far as she was concerned, if I could keep the class inside the classroom, everything was fine. There was no school counselor or special services team. All the support services I had learned about during my education classes were nonexistent.

> The only outside resource I found was Angel Ford, a fourth-grade teacher at the school. Angela had been teaching there for fifteen years, and her classroom was a sanctuary for her students. Soft music played while children worked in small groups, and the students radiated joy and self-confidence.

I first approached Angela late one September afternoon after everyone else had gone home. Angela stayed late to hang stars with her students' names and accomplishments from the ceiling, and I was trying to type a disciplinary report. Anton had kicked me in the face at recess, and my lip was still swollen and sore. Angela looked at me as I stood in her doorway, and without saying a word, she put her arms around me and smoothed my hair as I sobbed for what felt like hours. It wasn't anything she said that afternoon that changed my outlook on teaching; it was what she did. She held me without asking questions, she listened without offering judgment, and she made me believe that I had the talent and power to turn my class around. She showed me by example what I wanted to be for my students—comforting arms, unconditional ears, and unending confidence.

I returned to school the next day feeling recommitted to my students, and I noticed small changes right away. Instead of shouting, I used silence to get the children's attention, and the whole demeanor of the class calmed as a result. Instead of asking sarcastic questions and barking orders, I let the children suggest ways that they could do things better, and I could see them slowly becoming more self-directed. I learned to love each child, even the difficult ones, and I found that when I let this love show, the children responded by trying to be members of our classroom community. By inviting each child to become a part of something special in our classroom, I found that they all blossomed socially and spiritually.

Things were far from perfect, of course, but soon Zach cried only about once a week, Anton occasionally offered to share his lunch with a friend, and William confided that if he could read, the time he spent locked in the bedroom might pass faster. The other children cried less, talked to me more, and became more focused too. Finally, by mid-November, we were ready to begin our schoolwork.

This presented its own unique set of challenges, and again, I was faced with obstacles that I never imagined were possible. Besides lacking textbooks, the school lacked other basic materials, such as pencils, paper, glue, and story books. At first, I bought these things for the students, but I soon realized that I could not keep spending my own money on such basic supplies. I asked the principal for suggestions on obtaining resources, and she pointed me toward several social service organizations. I obtained crayons, pencils, and paints from the Salvation Army and some story books from a local homeless shelter that had surplus donations. I also called several businesses and asked them to donate paper. Some companies sent us new reams of paper, while others sent used computer paper. Both types of donations were helpful, for we used the scrap paper for art projects and rough drafts in writing. Later in the year, I summoned the courage to call some of the wealthier schools in the area (without my principal knowing), and I asked their first-grade teachers for old books and materials.

In a strange way, this experience of trying to find resources for our classroom helped me to better understand my students' lives.

They were often forced by their socioeconomic status to wait in line for free meals or to wear secondhand clothes, and I gained a sense of appreciation for the dignity with which they accepted help from other people. I learned to hold my head high as I carried used books from wealthy schools, and I no longer hesitated when asking others for assistance.

Despite my success in obtaining supplies for the classroom, our academic program did not take off the way I had hoped it would. I tried everything I could think of—hands-on activities, small-group work, whole-class projects—but the children struggled with even the most basic concepts. They seemed so unmotivated and defeated, as if, at this tender age, they had already been told that they would never be successful and they had accepted this without question.

Learning to read was especially difficult for the students. I checked out as many Dr. Seuss books at a time as I could from the public library, and I used these as reading textbooks. The children loved these books at story time, but whenever I took one out for reading instruction, fear clouded their eyes. This lack of confidence affected the class in every subject. They were too afraid to try anything on their own, and for weeks, we did every assignment together. My grand plans of writing workshops fizzled into dictation sessions. I wrote a story on the board, and the children copied and illustrated it.

Once again, I found none of the support services to which all schools are "entitled." I knew that most of my students were eligible for Title I instruction, but the school had never been assessed for this program. I suspected that one of the children had a language-processing problem, but there was no way to have him tested. At times, I felt like I was in another time, or at least in another country. It seemed to me that no child should be deprived of the basic educational resources that these already at-risk students were lacking.

A breakthrough finally came, quite by accident, in January. I needed a break from Dr. Seuss, and I decided to teach a unit about fairy tales. Most of the children hadn't heard these familiar stories, and I knew they would enjoy them. I had learned that reading stories about "real" people was ineffective with these students. They couldn't relate to stories about going to the park or playing with a pet. Castles and princesses were easier for them to imagine.

We read and studied fairy tales for several weeks and then began to rehearse for a play that I had written called "First-Grade Fairy Tales." I typed scripts for each skit, and I read them to the class until each child had memorized his part. We acted out "The Three Little Pigs,"

"The Little Red Hen," and "Goldilocks and the Three Bears," and the children loved it. We made costumes and scenery, wrote playbills, and performed our show for the rest of the school. The children glowed for days after the performance. For many of them, it was the first time that they had ever been successful in school.

After the play, I was determined to sustain and nurture the children's newfound enthusiasm and confidence. I realized that the students had turned to me to find their "identity," and they hung onto every word I said. This was thrilling in one sense, but terrifying in another. I held these fragile hearts and wounded souls, and I feared that one hasty action or word said in anger could shatter them.

After much thought, I cautiously devised a plan to build self-esteem and camaraderie within the class. I praised the children whenever I could, and I urged them to support each other. I wanted to empower them to be successful wherever they were; I did not want them to depend on me for self-assurance and confidence. I encouraged the children to support each other, and we practiced finding the good in others. We made "Friendship Books" listing what was special about each member of the class. Whenever we successfully completed an assignment, the children turned to each other and shouted, "You're a genius!"

Little by little, I noticed the children becoming bolder in their academic work. Several children began to write their own stories, and the class began to ask for more independent assignments. We took standardized tests late in the winter, and I worried that the children would become disheartened and frustrated. Fortunately, my fears were allayed during the second test. I read the directions, reminded the children that they should do their best work without any help from me, and circulated quietly around the room. As I passed William's desk, I heard him whisper to himself, "You're a genius! You're a genius, William!" To me, his score on that test was unimportant as long as he continued to believe this.

As happy as I was with the students' progress, there were still issues with which I continued to struggle. I knew that school was a refuge for most of the children, and I longed to help them find peace at home as well. I had met most of the children's parents, but our relationships did not develop beyond a polite hello as I released the children at dismissal each afternoon. I sent newsletters home to parents to let them know what we were studying in school, but they usually came back the next day, still untouched in the children's folders.

Although I knew how much progress the children could make if their parents worked with them at home, I could not find a respectful way to reach these parents. One father warned me before we had a required conference that he "didn't need some white, East Coast college girl telling him how to raise his daughter." Another parent asked me how I could possibly know the first thing about relating to a black child.

I was also disturbed by the prevalence of corporal punishment in the children's homes. These children were not just spanked; they were "whupped," as the children called it, with everything from belts to sticks to fists. Some days, I would touch a child's back as he entered the classroom, and he would flinch in pain. After the first month of school, I stopped calling parents or sending home "sad notes" for serious discipline problems. I couldn't bear to be the impetus for a child's being beaten. I asked the principal if she had ever addressed corporal punishment with parents, and she warned me that it was "part of the culture."

Another source of frustration for me was the children's schoolwork. Although the class made a lot of progress academically, they were still months behind the "typical" first grade. I struggled all year to help the children catch up to their grade level, but I know that they didn't come nearly as far as they needed to. Even today, I think about ways that I could have helped those children do better academically.

By the end of the year, though, we had all come a long way. There were no more tantrums and fights, and the children had grown to respect and care for each other. I, too, was a different person. The nervous young woman in the long skirt had been replaced by a seasoned, confident teacher. Working with that first class taught me that teaching is about much more than academics. It's about respect and love and involvement in children's lives.

After that year, I accepted a job at a school as different from my first school as I could ever imagine. Eight hundred children in Grades K–2 come to school with every possible privilege. We have more supplies than I know what to do with, computers in every classroom, and every imaginable support team.

Although I am learning a lot at my new school, a big piece of my heart is still with my first students. I think about those children constantly and pray for their safety and well-being. My early teaching experiences opened my eyes to the plight of our nation's poorest families, and I developed a strong sense of commitment to children in poverty.

When I recently returned for a visit, I was amazed by the changes. The building has been renovated, and a new principal has begun to try to change the image of the school. The student body has become more diverse economically and culturally, and resources are slowly being updated. At first, I worried that "my kids" would be lost in all of the changes, but the ones who were still there seemed to be thriving academically and emotionally.

In retrospect, my first year of teaching was the most difficult I have ever faced. But in spite of the tears and the frustration and lack of support, I found something wonderful there. The trust and the love that my students developed were precious gifts, and their small successes still amaze me. Despite the "ugliness" of their lives, my students found beauty within themselves.

During that year I was faced with weaknesses within myself, and I found strength that I never knew I had. I lived, through my students, a life completely different from the one to which I was accustomed, and I will never forget my first class. Those little children taught me lessons about hope and self-reliance that I will carry with me forever.

My first year of teaching was frustrating, difficult, and, at times, overwhelming, but I wouldn't trade it for anything. No, it was not at all what I had pictured. But sometimes the greatest blessings are those that we do not at first recognize.

### Author Biography

*I received my master's in teaching from Notre Dame, and I have been teaching first grade for five years. I will receive an MEd in educational administration in June 2001. I hope to become a school administrator, and I am especially interested in working in early childhood education.*

# chapter five

# Tips and Tales from the Third Grade

## Sarah's Story

*Sarah taught third grade her first year. During that year she faced a number of realizations about what works and what does not, particularly in respect to classroom management procedures. She struggled with many of the less serious but frequent hassles enumerated in the first part of this book, and she wound up learning a lot.*

## QUESTIONS FOR REFLECTION WHILE READING SARAH'S STORY

1. What about classroom discipline was challenging for Sarah?
2. How would you have handled the misbehavior in Sarah's class?
3. What student motivation challenges did Sarah face?
4. What types of individual differences increased teaching challenges in Sarah's class?
5. What were the assessment challenges that Sarah faced, and do you think she made the right choices?
6. What about relations with parents was challenging for Sarah?

7. Why do you think some of the classroom management strategies Sarah tried worked and some did not?
8. Did resources pose a challenge for Sarah?
9. What were the challenges facing Sarah with respect to classroom interaction?
10. What were the challenges facing Sarah in planning?
11. In what ways was classroom instruction a challenge to Sarah?
12. What knowledge of teaching and the curriculum did Sarah lack?
13. How important was the support of Sarah's colleagues and principal?
14. Did Sarah have any unconstructive attitudes or perceptions that posed challenges for her?

# THE STORY

Now in my second year of teaching, I reflect back on all of the trials and tribulations, the successes and the failures, of the first year. I reflect upon how I have grown as a person as well as a teacher. Those nine months went by rather quickly, but at times I felt as though I would never get through them. I quickly learned that teaching was not an eight o'clock in the morning to three o'clock in the afternoon job, as I would stay every day first semester after school until six o'clock preparing for the next day, organizing my classroom, and conversing with other teachers or with the principal about the occurrences of the day. Now, here I am reflecting on my first year as a new third-grade teacher and on all of my challenges as a beginning teacher and how I overcame them. I will say that my second semester showed much improvement over my first semester. Experienced teachers always say that the first year of teaching is the hardest, and that there is a huge difference between one's first year of teaching and one's second year of teaching, which gives me hope as a person who would like to continue teaching.

I remember when I first drove up to the school. After picturing what it would be like, I was finally seeing it face-to-face. The school itself was actually broken up into four buildings. When I first glanced at these small buildings, I felt as though I had just reached camp for the summer. They looked like the cabins I used to stay in at summer camp with wooden steps leading up to the door. The prekindergarten class occupied one building, while the kindergarten, the first grade, the second grade, and the science lab shared another building. The library and the newly added computer lab shared their own building. My classroom was in the slightly larger main building.

As I made my way to the main building, I walked under the awning just recently built to welcome visitors. In the main office, I met my principal, whom I had spoken on the phone with several times. From her accent, I knew that I would stick out like a sore thumb every time I opened my mouth. She gave me a tour of the school and showed me my room. The principal's office and the main office had just undergone reconstruction. Since my room was right next to the office, most of the office items were stashed in my room. Right then and there, I knew that I had my work cut out for me this year. Upon entering the main building for the first time, I was also surprised to see that the school building did not have the typical school hallways. Instead, there was one large room with the classrooms surrounding it. The large room served many purposes but mostly served as our school cafeteria. Grades 3 through 8 were located in this building, and each classroom had a door leading to the outside of the building as well. I guess I had just expected to see a more traditional-looking school, or one with halls leading to the classrooms. I had never seen a school quite like this one.

My school serves the suburbs of a southern city. It is a nonaccredited school with 180 students and only one class per grade. The majority of the students live outside the city limits in rural areas and are Caucasian and Catholic. Most of the students in the school have siblings who also attend here. I learned that the families of the school are blue-collar families. Most of the fathers are tradesmen, such as farmers, shrimpers, and fishermen. The majority of the families make under $50,000 a year. These demographics were very different from the areas I knew back in my hometown. I was entering a whole new environment.

Looking back, I can say that teaching second semester seemed so much easier than starting school in August. I could really see a difference in my teaching, my planning, and my organization. First semester, I was just concentrating on keeping my head above water, and second semester, I felt as though I could breathe a little easier when teaching. I am still nowhere near where I want to be in my teaching career, but I can honestly say that I can see improvement. I did not feel as bogged down in my planning second semester, and I could focus more of my time on other aspects of teaching and other projects that I wanted to get started. I had a bright group of children, and I wanted to be able to give them more opportunities to be creative and not just follow the book all of the time.

I must also point out that the first year was extremely challenging in many respects. The biggest issues that I faced during the year were classroom management, discipline, student and parent interaction, organization, and just teaching as a whole. I have tried to face these problems head-on because with teaching one must deal with the problems. If they are not dealt with, they are just going to get worse; they do not disappear. The teacher who can sight the problem and fix it or attempt to do so becomes the better teacher in the long run. I am slowly learning the ropes, and I hope to continue to learn and grow as my teaching career blooms. I truly feel as though teaching has been a roller coaster ride, but I do like it and am sure I will like it even more as I become more experienced over time.

A couple of things that helped me through this semester were the other teachers in my school, including my mentor teacher and my principal, because they have been very supportive and extremely helpful; observing an experienced third-grade teacher; and reading different case studies for beginning teachers. There were several case studies that really hit home with me, and these made me feel as though I was not alone in the teaching world. I could relate to some of the problems these new teachers were facing, and I realized that every teacher started out as a new teacher.

## CLASSROOM MANAGEMENT

Classroom management is an issue that every teacher must deal with, and the challenge is finding what works best for the teacher as well as the students. There are so many little things, for example, rules for handing in papers, rules for going to the bathroom, rules for sharpening pencils, rules for lining up, and every possible movement in the classroom that one does not think of until faced with it. In one of my MEd classes, I had to give a group presentation on classroom management. My group did very well, and I was under the false impression that I had everything I possibly needed for classroom management and that I had it all under control. I found out, however, that I was blindly mistaken when I arrived in my classroom one week before the first day of school and realized that I did not know how to set up my classroom or how to handle anything else in getting ready for school over the days that were soon to come. The following several paragraphs list some of my initial ideas for classroom management that I have had to change due to difficulty.

For my bathroom procedure, I planned that I would know at a glance which student was taking a restroom break by providing a Bathroom Bear for my students. I would decorate a small, laminated, brown-paper bear that had a string attached to it to be worn around one's neck, and it would be labeled the "Bathroom Bear." When a child left to visit the restroom, he or she would quietly place the Bathroom Bear on his or her desk so as to not disturb class, then replace the bear when he or she returned. There would be one boys' Bathroom Bear and one girls' Bathroom Bear.

The rules for sharpening pencils would be as follows: At the beginning of the day, students would be allowed to sharpen three pencils. If at any time during the day all three of the pencils were dull or broken, the student would not be able to resharpen his or her pencils. Instead, the student would have to write all of the assignments in crayon, then recopy them during recess.

As for lining up procedures, I would have the students line up differently by weeks or however I felt necessary. One way I would dismiss them would be to ask them questions; the first person to get the question right would line up first. Then, I would ask another question, and I would keep asking questions until everyone was lined up at the door in a single-file line. Another way to line up the students would be to compliment a student who was sitting nice and quiet at his or her desk and let him or her get in line first. Then, I would let the other students sitting quietly at their desk line up at the door. I would also let the first row sitting "like third-grade students" line up at the door.

In order to control the noise level, I would remind my students to be quiet by using a traffic signal. I would make a large stoplight cutout. I would cut out three circles to fit the traffic light—one green, one yellow, and one red. I would tape a black arrow next to the red circle to indicate "silence," the yellow circle for "whisper," and the green circle for "talk freely." I might also create a student job titled "traffic controller." He or she would change the color of the light at my signal.

These were my classroom procedures when I first started school, but I made many changes to them because many things did not work with my class or with my style of teaching. I changed the Bathroom

Bear idea because my students were taking advantage of it. For example, I would be in the middle of a lesson and a student would get out of his or her chair to get the Bathroom Bear, disrupting other students as well as my lesson. Another example of misuse was the fact that some students would use the Bathroom Bear four or five times during the day, mostly just to leave class for a while. It was hard for me to keep track of who went to the bathroom how many times a day. Finally, I decided to give each student one bathroom pass that he or she could use at his or her discretion throughout the day.

I also started taking my students to the bathroom as a class because I had several reports from other teachers of misbehavior in the bathroom. We would line up in a boys' line and a girls' line outside the bathroom, and I would send three girls and four boys in the bathroom at a time, with only one boy and girl at the drinking fountain at a time. I would take them right after morning break and right after lunch recess, but I found that this procedure took too much time away from my teaching. I also got frustrated that the students would not stand in line the way I wanted them to stand. Finally, I just started letting them go row by row first thing in the morning when we were doing seatwork and right after lunch recess. This routine seemed to be working fine, but my principal decided that she did not want any of the teachers letting students go to the bathroom first thing in the morning or just after a break. She saw the same people going to the bathroom every morning and after certain breaks. She was concerned that it had become too much of a routine for these students, whether they actually had to go to the bathroom or not. She said that they have just developed a habit, and they should go to the bathroom during their breaks because she does not want them to take away from our teaching. So, a couple of months after the start of school, I began dismissing my students to go to break a couple of minutes early so that those students who needed to go to the bathroom could go. I also began telling them to go to the bathroom during lunch, first asking my permission. They still had their bathroom passes, and sometimes I took class bathroom breaks in the afternoon around two o'clock.

Another procedure I changed several times is the procedure to sharpen pencils. I changed from originally letting students sharpen pencils in the morning because it took too much time, they made too much noise, and it was hard for me to talk over them to take lunch count. I started to let the students have their own pencil sharpeners at their desks, but they would be sharpening their pencils at their desks during a lesson, which meant they were not paying attention.

They would also leave lots of pencil shavings all over the floor, making a mess. The students loved to sharpen pencils and would go through a pencil a day because they would sharpen it too much. A pencil a day can be an expensive habit, and we, as a class, were constantly at a loss for pencils. Therefore, I changed the procedure again to the rule I used for the rest of the year. I collected all of the pencils, and I had two cups—one cup had sharpened pencils and the other cup had unsharpened pencils. I was the only one who sharpened pencils, and if a student's pencil broke, he or she just put it in the cup with broken pencils and took a pencil from the cup of already sharpened pencils. I had a helper who would sharpen the pencils for me before lunch and at the end of the day. I found this procedure to be rather successful.

My stoplight system did not work very well at all, and I think that was mainly because I did not practice it enough with the students for it to become a habit. I learned that in order for something to become a habit, it must be practiced between seven and ten days. Halfway through the first semester I started giving the students key words that, when I said them in my "teacher voice," meant for them to sit in their "listening positions." I would say, "Pencils down, eyes up." They were very responsive to this phrase, especially when I said it in my teacher voice. I would also say, "Salami," which stands for "Stop and look at me." If a student was talking and I wanted the other students to pay attention to him or her, I would say, "Salami, Jenny," or "Salami, Eddy." Then, all of the students knew to look at that student immediately. It is important that the students learn to look at the student who is speaking because they will not hear what the student says otherwise. I could also use this phrase to direct their attention to their books.

My students had a hard time with their listening skills, and I noticed that at times I was the only person listening to the student who was speaking. As a teacher, I have to make sure that I know what every person is doing in the classroom and that each is on task. I also began using my bell to get their attention when the noise level had gotten too high. If I did not see an immediate reaction after the first bell, then I would discipline them. I have found the bell to be a good attention getter. One ding of the bell meant "Stop and sit in listening positions." Two dings meant "Get on task."

My procedures for getting the students to line up worked really well, but after a couple of months, I also started to make the children stand in line with one finger over their mouth and their other hand behind their back. If their finger is over their mouth, they are less likely to talk, and if their other hand is behind their back, then they do not have another hand to touch the person next to them in line. It seemed to work well with my students, although they still need a reminder every now and then about how to stand in line appropriately. As long as I practiced a procedure with my students, I found that it eventually became a habit.

# Discipline

My biggest challenge the first year was discipline. I truly think that I started out too soft with my students. I think the fact that it was my first year teaching and I looked rather young were factors that did not help me much either. School seemed to start too fast for me, so I did not truly understand how important it was to start off extremely firm. I guess I did not know how to be tough the first couple of months. I messed up and smiled the first week, and I tried to be the students' friend, which is not the best thing to strive for as a teacher. I think it is possible to smile when appropriate yet be a firm disciplinarian, because I have observed good, experienced teachers who can do that. I tried several different approaches, but I think that some of the students already had me figured out. I will say that by the middle of the first semester, my discipline had improved, but it took time. For a while, I just wished for next year because then I could start over altogether and be much firmer. I know the first year is definitely a learning year. I learned what I needed to do differently, and I desperately wanted to try it. What worried me the most was that if my class was out of control in November, how was I going to last rest of the year?

I had a couple of students who were very trying, and they would get the other students going. I met with my principal and my mentor teacher a couple of times first semester about discipline, and they felt there was a lack of it in my classroom. Their suggestions were helpful, and over the course of the year they told me that they were able to see improvement. My class had known no limitations, so it was a challenge to enforce limitations and rules. Many days I went home very frustrated because I just felt as if I was not receiving the respect that I deserved. I will admit that when I started teaching, I was surprised to realize that just because I was the teacher that did not mean that all my students would respect me. I experienced a rude awakening when I witnessed the lack of discipline in the students' homes. I realized that teachers are left to discipline, making up what is being left out at home. I was thankful, however, that I had a group of students who, on the whole, were respectful of my authority and wanted to do anything to please me, their teacher.

Before Christmas and springtime were the hardest times to teach because the children were excited about the holidays and summer-time and did not want to learn. I had to adjust my teaching approach and have the students do more hands-on learning activities and do the more important lessons in the morning when they could focus better. The students also benefited from bribery in the form of positive reinforcement.

One of my ways to positively reinforce the students the first half of the year was to put an "X" on a chart every time the whole class did something well. When they received 100 X's, we had an ice cream party at the beginning of the second semester. I decided to change this technique somewhat for second semester because I wanted to start rewarding the students on a smaller level, especially those students who behaved all the time. I still, however, wanted to keep the idea of teamwork. Therefore, I decided to award tally points to those rows that got their books out quietly, did their work quietly, were sitting like third-grade students, finished their homework assignments, got their homework journals signed, and so on. Then, the row that had the most tallies at the end of the day got to pick out of the treasure box. I found it to work rather well, and the students really helped each other out. I later decided to keep the tallies for the whole week, and the row with the most tallies at the end of the week got to pick out of the treasure box. I wanted to extend the reward to a week to make sure that the students worked hard every day, because their tallies would not start over the next day as they had so far.

The discipline system I implemented at the beginning of the year was based on the following classroom rules that I made up but discussed thoroughly with the students:

1. Treat others the way we want them to treat to us.
2. Follow the directions the first time.
3. Raise your hand and wait to be called on before speaking.
4. Do not interrupt.
5. No teasing or name-calling or talking back to the teacher.
6. Keep hands, feet, and objects to yourself.
7. Walk in the classroom and in the hallways.

During the first semester I also had a system for keeping track of student misbehavior:

1. Individual student bees posted at the front of the room.
2. All students' bees start the day in the hive.
3. Bee flies to each color as misbehavior occurs:
   Yellow = warning
   Blue = lose 5 minutes of recess
   Green = lose all of recess
   Orange = note home
   Red = visit the principal

*Home/school Connection:* If bee is still in hive, student receives a sticker on a daily calendar. If not, color is noted.

Halfway through the first semester, I decided to primarily reinforce the following three rules: (1) Raise hand to walk; (2) raise hand to talk; (3) avoid disrupting others. These rules were the ones I tended to focus on every day, and they seemed the most important. Since there were only three of them, it made it easier for my students to remember and follow them. I posted them on the chalkboard for them to see every day.

Second semester, I changed the students from bees to cars that start out each day in the street. When they misbehaved, they moved to the same consequences, but the consequences had new theme names: The green light was warning, the yellow light was lose five minutes of recess, and the red light was lose all of recess; the next move was to a traffic jam, which was a note home; and the police officer was a visit to the principal. The students made their own cars. I like that I changed the system a little instead of staying with the same one. The students, too, liked the change, and they were used to the consequences by then so it was not confusing for them in any way. I tried to be more strict with my system with the cars, but I still had behavior problems

Even though I changed some things about my discipline procedures, I was still not happy with my discipline in the classroom. So, I continued my search for better discipline, and I attended a workshop about how to deal with oppositionally defiant students. This workshop proved to be very helpful in how to detect certain student characteristics and how to deal with the resulting misbehavior. We learned that there is a difference between discipline problems and behavior problems. The speaker said that no one should have discipline problems in his or her classroom past October, because they should be solved at the beginning of the school year. We are to set straight our rules, regulations, and procedures right away; that was defined as discipline. The problems we deal with throughout the whole year are behavior problems, and these are associated with students' temperaments. There are different kinds of temperaments a person may have, and we are to realize that we cannot change someone's temperament. What we can do is be aware of the kind of temperament the person has and how we can change the environment to create a better fit for that person. It is possible to control behavioral outcomes better when there is a good fit between people's characteristics and their environment. For example, we each have a certain threshold for the amount of anxiety we can tolerate, and for a normal student just getting called back to talk to the teacher could hit that student's threshold anxiety level and serve as a punishment. However, for a student who is oppositionally defiant, just talking to that student will not hit his or her threshold anxiety level and thus will not serve as a deterrent. Students who are oppositionally defiant have much higher thresholds, so they need more severe consequences. On a more positive note in dealing with these oppositionally defiant students, the workshop directed me to do small activities or games with the oppositionally defiant student to get him or her to behave in the class. I was to focus on one aspect of misbehavior to improve on at a time, but the game had to be made so that the student would be successful at it so that he or she would continue to keep up with it.

The area schools use the discipline system called Discipline With Purpose (DWP), designed by Barbara Vasiloff and Paula Lenz. It has proven to be very successful when the whole school implements it and the teachers really enforce it. Halfway through the first semester the new teachers including myself attended a DWP workshop, which proved to be extremely helpful. The hard thing to accept is that DWP takes a couple of years to be fully implemented, before the whole school is really familiar with it and the students can do a good job of following it. The aims of education and classroom discipline are the same in DWP—to help children and youth become self-directing people.

The key to developing Discipline With Purpose is that there is a hierarchy of skills that can be identified and coordinated with a person's growth and development to provide an objective standard to define self-disciplined behavior. Therefore, DWP has fifteen skills, not rules, for the students to learn. These skills are ones that students will need later on in life. They make the students proactive in their decision-making process.

DWP works to prevent misbehavior by reminding the students of skills rather than punishing them.

The first five skills are the basic skills taught in Grades pre-K through 3 and include listening; following instructions; questioning; sharing time, space, people, and things; and basic social skills. The next five skills, called the constructive skills, are taught in Grades 3 through 7. These skills are cooperating with others, understanding rules, figuring out how to accomplish tasks on your own, exhibiting leadership, and communicating effectively. The last five skills, the generative skills, are taught in Grades 7 through 12. These five generative skills are organizing time, space, people, and things; resolving mutual problems; taking the initiative in problem solving; distinguishing fact from feeling; and sacrificing/serving others.

At the workshop, we were given a binder with a set of lesson plans to help us implement the skills properly in the classroom. I tried to implement these skills in my own classroom. We worked on the first skill—listening—extensively, since my students had such a problem with it. I also worked on the second skill—following instructions—because my students had been too dependent on others to tell them what to do in an assignment, when all they needed to do was read the directions. I tried to get my students to learn responsibility, and having them learn how to follow the directions appropriately was one good way. Questioning was another skill that we focused on, because for a while my students would just say, "I don't get it," or "I don't understand." I would tell them that they would have to tell me specifically what they did not understand so that I could help them. I was not going to just spoon-feed them. I also told them that those statements did not sound like questions but more like complaints.

## STUDENT AND PARENT INTERACTION

I had two extremely challenging students, Andrew and Tyler. I had several talks with both students' parents, and they both had issues at home that played a big part in their misbehavior at school and their refusal to do work in class. Tyler lived with his mother and his new stepfather, who was very supportive. However, Tyler used to live with some extended family members right after his mother and his biological father got divorced. They were not a very good influence on him, and Tyler unfortunately learned many inappropriate things as a young child. He had a lot of anger inside because he had not seen his father in almost two years and was still feeling the effects of the divorce. He had grown up with no real limitations and had learned to be very manipulative.

Tyler saw the school counselor every other Friday. He got tested first semester for attention deficit disorder (ADD), and a meeting was held with the counselor, the principal, his parents, and myself. He was diagnosed as having ADD as well as an oppositionally defiant behavior problem. His mother did not want to put him on any kind of medication, which made controlling his behavior at school much harder. I had a talk with the principal and the counselor on how to handle him. They did not have many more suggestions for me, since I had already been trying every kind of approach with him in the classroom. He also walked a thin line with some of my other students' parents, who (for reasons I did not agree with at all) wanted him out of the school. The parents were unhappy with his constant disruption of class. All Tyler really wanted was to be accepted by the other students, but because he had always been somewhat of a troublemaker, the students jumped at the chance to tell on him. Tyler tried the mentor program at school. A seventh grader that is a very good kid and a good student had been partnered with Tyler to help influence him and lead him in the right direction, but the program never really got off the ground. I would be frustrated every morning when I went in to school, wondering how he was going to behave and whether he would do his work or disrupt the class as usual. I could not usually get through a lesson without having to discipline him several times.

The whole year had been a struggle with Tyler because I felt there really was not much more that I could do for him in the classroom to make him behave. The times that I tried to talk to him, I could tell that he did not really care about what I was saying. It was only when I would react and discipline him right away that there would be some reaction from him. Tyler needed to work on many things, such as staying in his desk, not talking out, and getting his work done, but we decided together to start by focusing on not talking out in class. I made a chart for every day, and every time he did not talk out over the course of five minutes he got a tally on his sheet. Then, if he had so many tallies at the end of the day, he could pick out of the treasure box. We were advised to start out at five minutes and gradually move our way up to ten minutes, fifteen minutes, and so on as the student could handle it. Then, the student would be able to see his or her improvement. However, Tyler also had a temper and did not like it when I disciplined him, even though I gave him more chances than any of the other students. Once I moved his car, he would throw his things off his desk and pout for the next fifteen minutes, and I had lost him. He was doing well with our tallies, but during one of his tempers when I had moved his car, he had ripped the sheet off his desk, and we were not able to really get back into it again. Tyler had been my biggest behavior problem the whole year, and toward the end of the year his behavior took a turn for the worse when he refused to do his work or listen to me altogether. Then, some miracle happened, and he was a changed person for the last two weeks of school. (I think his mother promised all of his toys back if he behaved.) I felt that Tyler could behave when he really wanted to behave, and those last two weeks proved it. He had a lot of baggage from his home life that he was dealing with, and though sometimes he would open up to me, I really thought that he needed to get additional professional help from a psychologist. Seeing the school counselor only once every other week was not enough for him.

Andrew, on the other hand, had grown up in a stable environment with two very loving parents. However, his mother was partially deaf and had just found out that she had a degenerative disease in her eyes and was slowly going blind. Andrew was an only child until a year ago, when his mother's best friend and her husband were killed in a car accident, leaving behind their only child—a girl one year younger than Andrew. Andrew's mother, being the closest person to the daughter, decided to adopt her. Andrew had jealous tendencies toward Stephanie because he was no longer the only child and had to share his mother's attention. He still had not really accepted the fact that Stephanie was his sister. I wanted Andrew to start seeing the counselor, but it never happened.

Andrew chose when he wanted to behave appropriately and when he wanted to misbehave, and he defied me when any chance presented itself. He would be on his best behavior when his mother came to class, but when she would leave he was back to his usual self. I had several meetings with my mentor teacher and my principal as well as several phone conversations with his mother about his behavior in the classroom and how to improve it. His mother was very supportive and was concerned about his behavior because it had started to affect his grades. Because he did not like to pay attention in class or do his work, his grades had fallen, and his reading had not improved at all. Instead, his skills had weakened. His mother was not happy with his lack of progress. In particular, he needed help with his math skills; he was still using his fingers for addition and subtraction. I had a sixth grader volunteer to help Andrew and another student with their math skills about three times a week at the end of the day for about twenty minutes. This extra practice proved helpful. By the end of the year, I also noticed a tremendous amount of improvement with his reading skills, because his mother finally decided to give him extra help at home.

I also sent home a daily conduct sheet for Andrew, which helped at times. I think that he might have some kind of an attention disorder. Because he was getting less attention than he was used to at home, he tried to make up for it at school. He constantly acted out in class and talked when he was not supposed to be talking. He also pretended not to understand something when he really did, just to have me next to him while he worked. Tyler also liked me to be next to him while he did his work. I usually had to point to each problem to get these two boys to complete their work. I needed to have a lot of patience to deal with them both, but it was hard to have patience when I was on my last string. However, yelling did not phase them, because they were used to getting yelled at when at home. Throughout the year, I had to work on my patience and on praising them when they did well.

Every day, I wondered how these two were going to act and if I would be able just once to get through a lesson without having to discipline them. At times, I felt as though it was not fair to the students who did behave and really wanted to learn. Even though Tyler was a bright child, he eventually would fall behind because he did not understand how to do something. He was already telling me that he was bored with school and hated it, but I think that was partly because he did not have many friends at school. He really yearned for attention and really wanted the other children to like him, so he constantly acted out. What he did not understand was that the other children were sick of his acting out in class and misbehaving.

My rapport with the parents of my students did improve over the year, or I think that maybe my attitude toward them changed. I finally realized that I could not please all of the parents all of the time. I had a group of parents who never seemed to be pleased and were very reactionary. They had issues with the way some things were run at the school, and sometimes they took it out on me since I seemed to be the easy target. It was as though they looked for things that were wrong, especially since they knew that I was a first-year teacher.

The nice thing was that I had the support of my principal and my mentor behind me. I did not let these parents bother me. I knew that I did have some very supportive parents, and I appreciated these parents very much. I turned to these parents when I needed chaperones for a field trip or other help, and they responded very well. I tried to make sure that I was always kind and confident when dealing with parents. Because it is impossible to please everyone all of the time, I was satisfied knowing that I was doing my best. The people that I concerned myself with the most were the students, even though pleasing them was not easy either. Doing what was best for them, however, was more important than pleasing them.

In fact, at the end of the year, I had to make a very important decision for one of my students. She was not anywhere near where she needed to be as a third grader. Her skills were low across the board. She came into third grade with very poor reading skills. She would get discouraged very easily when she could not read at the pace of the other students. She would not do well in social studies or science because she could not read the material. Her math skills were also very low. Once she got discouraged, she would put her head on her desk and give up for the rest of lesson. There were days when she would really try hard, but I felt as though she should not have passed second grade. However, she had already been held back in kindergarten, so holding her back again would mean that she would be two years older than the other students in her class, and I did not want to hurt her confidence any more. I tutored her after school; she had a reading tutor once a week; I had a sixth grader help her with her math about three times a week for the last twenty minutes of the day; and I had her in my lower-skilled reading group. I saw drastic improvement with her, but I was not sure if it was enough to pass her on to fourth grade.

I did not want to pass her on without trying to get her ready, so I gave her many opportunities at school. She lived in a household of five children with her grandparents, so she did not get as much attention as she needed. There was not much intervention at home with her schoolwork. I sat down and had a talk with our school counselor, and she tested Lisa for learning disabilities, but either way, I thought she needed to practice her math and reading skills over the summer. In the end, I decided to pass Lisa on to the fourth grade for several reasons. One was that she had already been held back a year. Another was that she showed much improvement toward the end of the year, and I felt I could continue to work with her the next year. Finally, many statistics are not favorable for retained students, and it would have definitely killed her self-esteem to be held back again. Maria would just have to work very hard in her studies to keep up.

## ORGANIZATION

Organization was another really challenging part of teaching for me. My first year of teaching, on the whole, was incredibly difficult because from the first day of school, I really had no idea what it all entailed. It was hard for me to get my room settled because I had only one week in my classroom before the first day of school. I had to clean the room and organize it, but I really had no idea how I wanted my own classroom to be. Organization was difficult for me at first, but I found that as I spent more time in my classroom and with my students, I was able to figure out the way I wanted it.

Every Wednesday, I sent home folders with the students' work, an update sheet with the activities in the classroom for that week, and a weekly behavior sheet for each student. The parents signed the behavior sheets as well as the graded papers, so that I would know they saw them. When the folders came back, I needed to have a place to put the students' work so that it did not just pile up on my desk. Therefore, I organized a hanging folder system in my desk drawer for the returned signed graded papers and the behavior sheets of every student. I also made folders for notes that I sent home to parents as well as the notes that I received from parents. I had to be sure to keep all forms of communication as a way to cover my back if a parent were to dispute a grade or disciplinary action with me. I had a parent who came in every Tuesday and Wednesday afternoon to help me put the papers in the folders. I had been staying at school too late trying to file all of the papers away, and asking a very reliable and trustworthy parent to help me made all the difference.

Along with these Wednesday folders, I would send a conduct sheet explaining the student's behavior for the previous week. The note had a star on it, and every time the student stayed in the beehive, he or she received a "Great!" stamp on each arm of the star. Otherwise, I wrote the rule the student broke. Some parents thought it was too hard to discipline their children a week after the fact, so I decided to start sending the conduct reports out on Fridays. For the second semester, I also changed the star sheet to a regular calendar format and used abbreviations instead of writing everything out. The abbreviations were TO for talking out, NFD for not following directions, BO for bothering others, OS for out of seat, NOT for not on task, and a star if the student's car did not get moved. The parents initialed the sheet at the end of the week and returned it with the folder the following week. This system worked much better, and the parents liked it, as well. I learned this calendar system from the second-grade teacher at my school. I also learned that teaching is a profession of sharing and borrowing because teachers are constantly getting ideas from one another.

Organization for me also included getting familiar with the teacher's books, learning how to follow the lessons planned in the books, and then filling up my lesson plan book. It was helpful in the beginning to make sure that there was order to my day, such as starting every morning with spelling, followed by reading, then math, lunch, and in the afternoons doing religion, social studies, and science. Once I felt comfortable with how the day ran as far as teaching the subjects and allowing for enough time, I began to feel more confident about my teaching and myself as a teacher.

I started the school year with my 16 students sitting in groups of 4 because I had learned in my teacher education program that cooperative learning was one of the best ways to help students reach their optimum learning potential. However, I quickly learned that my students could not handle sitting that close to each other. They first needed to be taught how to work cooperatively. Therefore, I rearranged their desks back into basic rows, and they worked well the rest of the year. I tried doing cooperative learning groups with these students, but they had a difficult time working together cooperatively. I did note that whenever I had them work in groups, I had to give specific instructions, preassign groups, and preassign roles for each group.

I also did a running record for each student the first week of school so that I could determine the reading skill level of each student. I was able to decipher that about five of my students were still at the second-grade reading level. My two top students moved up to fourth grade every day during reading, and I divided the rest of my students into two reading groups. My lower readers used the books from second semester, second grade. I put book covers on them so the students did not really know that they were using second-grade books. These students felt much more comfortable reading at their level, rather than being frustrated with the third-grade readers. I found that the reading groups worked rather well, and I saw improvement with the lower-skilled readers. Toward the last few months of school, when we started reading chapter books, I was even able to have one large reading group again.

I had a lot of trouble at first with my reading groups. My confidence was not very high, and I doubted whether the students were really learning. So I went to observe another third-grade teacher who had been teaching for fifteen years and was just an incredible teacher. Her classroom was the perfect classroom, and her students behaved immaculately. She reminded me that she had also once been a first-year teacher and experienced many of the problems that I was facing my first year. She gave me many great ideas on every aspect of teaching. I was also able to see her authoritative interaction style and her students' responsiveness. I sat in on her reading groups, so I was able to see how they can be run effectively. This was the first time I had actually been in a third-grade classroom other than my own. My MEd practicum was in a first-grade classroom, and there is a big difference between the two grade levels. I was blessed to have found such another incredible mentor, and I highly recommend observing another teacher if at all possible.

My first year, I was constantly learning new ways to teach an idea or concept and finding out if these new teaching strategies worked well for my students and for me. What might have worked well with one teacher did not always work well for me. At the end of the first semester, I made a list of some goals for second semester. I wanted to know in advance what each week and each chapter would bring and not just go from day to day. I was spending too much time planning each night for the next day, but it began to take less time as I became more familiar with the concepts being taught in the books.

Some more goals that I had set for myself included the following:

- Set up and organize learning centers.
- Have the students do more writing projects.
- Have the students do book reports and home projects.
- Do some thematic units with the students, especially with science, since the book does not do a great job of following the curriculum.
- Improve the rapport with the parents of my students.
- Have folders with extra and enriched work ready for those students who are brighter than the normal third grader and who complete their work quickly.
- Have the students try to work in cooperative learning groups again.

Second semester allowed me more time to do learning centers. I had wanted to do centers for quite some time, and I finally had the time to organize them. I had a big weekly calendar from Monday to Friday, and I had the students split up into groups according to their row. Each row was assigned a color, and on the daily calendar I color coded and alternated the center activities written under each day. When a student finished his or her work early, he or she looked at the chart and found what center was assigned to his or her group that day. The centers that I offered were the following: math games/manipulatives, silent reading and questions, language arts games and writing, Goodie Box (a folder full of fun worksheets), or the Geo Safari game. The students liked the centers, and they worked rather well. Eventually, I no longer had to tell those students who finished their work early what to do, and some of those students who did not always like to do their work started getting it done so that they could do a center. I started out with some great centers, but they needed to be revamped more often than I was able to. I fell into the rut of not changing my centers often enough because it took a lot of time to put new centers together. The students eventually got bored with some of the centers, and it bothered me that they did not always follow along with the lessons and topics we were covering. However, my students definitely had their favorites, and I think that as I become a more experienced teacher and continue to become more on top of everything, I will be able to make my own collection of centers to choose from at different times of the year. Centers take a lot of work to make and to organize, but I found one of the key factors to having successful centers was the amount of time I spent on teaching the procedure for the centers and how each game works. I found that by spending more time at the beginning when introducing a new learning center, I could save time later.

First semester, I was not pleased with how much I had my students write and practice their writing skills, so I started having my students write in their journals every day after lunch recess for about 15 to 20 minutes. Sometimes I let them share out loud in front of the class, which is good practice for their oral language skills. After reading his or her journal entry, each student got to pick a cheer for the rest of the class to do to recognize the student's good work. First semester, I usually read to them after lunch recess, and we did not do as much journal writing. Second semester, I knew that they really had to start writing more, so I had them write every day. The students liked it because they also got to draw a picture of their story when they were done.

The second semester, I was able to focus more on special projects for my students because I did not have to worry so much about keeping my head above water. In the first two months of the semester, my students completed two home projects. The first project was a book report about an animal, and the students had to present the books in the form of an advertisement. The students were to cut out pictures from magazines, draw pictures, or get them off the Internet to paste onto poster board in order to try to sell their books to their classmates. They were to write the title, the author, and some descriptions of the book on the poster board as well. Then, I had them present their projects to the rest of the class. The students enjoyed seeing their fellow classmates' work. I hung their posters outside the classroom for the other students in the school to see.

For our second home project, I had the students make solar systems. We were studying the planets and the solar system. My students did an excellent job. I was very proud of them. I know that they had a great deal of help from their parents, but I really think that it is important for the parents and the children to bond and for the parents to know what the child is studying in the classroom. Many students used Styrofoam balls, wire, and paint, but each one was unique. The students presented their projects to the class, and the pre-K teacher liked them so much that she had three of my students come over each afternoon to present their projects to her students. I also displayed their projects on tables outside our classroom.

The second book report project I had the students do involved more writing. The students were assigned to read a book about a famous person. They could choose whomever they wanted. I gave them a form to fill out with some questions about the person and the book. Then, when the book report was due, the students had to stand up and tell the class three things about their person. I was going to have them write a paragraph about their famous person, but I had found an easy report form for researching famous people and the students made their own little books. Of course, just trying this approach the first time, it did not go as smoothly as I would have liked. I know for next time to give these research forms out ahead of time and allow the students to have more time for filling them out.

Another book report project idea I had was for the students to put objects in a bag that relate to their book and have them pull out an object and describe its relationship to the story, setting, and characters. We did not get to this project, but it is one that I am trying this year. Another idea I had was for the students to put clothespins on a hanger and then have them hang different parts of the story in order from the clothespins, so they can work on sequencing. The students actually did this project after we finished reading the book *Charlotte's Web*.

Finally, toward the end of the school year, my class and the class of one of my best friends, who is in the Peace Corps in Africa, started corresponding back and forth with each other. My class started by writing letters to my friend and sending her pictures of the school, the playground, the parking lot, and students. She wrote us back and sent pictures of a typical fifth-grade boy in his uniform, a typical fifth-grade girl in her uniform, and their classroom. Her students were very excited to see things common to the American lifestyle, so she also sent us postcards of the country, and a form of money that is almost equivalent to our U.S. dollar. She did a very good job in addressing the students' questions, and my students were very excited about writing to her again. Mail took awhile, however, so it might have been even better had I started the correspondence earlier in the year.

## CONCLUSION

All in all, through the first year, I basically found that classroom management, discipline, student and parent interaction, and organization were some of the most difficult aspects of teaching for me. I am happy to say that the longer I have been teaching and the longer I have been in my classroom, the more organized I have become. I had to change my classroom management systems a couple of times, but I finally found some systems that I feel comfortable with and that work. Classroom management, however, is something that I can always improve upon. It is a continuing learning process. I have to see what works best with the students as well as for myself. Discipline has been and still is at times a problem for me. I have made adjustments, and they have worked. I also tried to start off firm at the beginning of my second school year. I have had success as well as some tension with parents. For the most part, parents are very supportive and very kind, and this seems to outweigh the burden of those hard-to-please parents. I do not let these difficult parents bother me too much, because I know that I have the continuing support of my principal and mentor teacher.

On the whole, I am finally feeling comfortable with my rules and procedures, my classroom, and my organization in the classroom. I think slowly but surely I am getting there. I am now more confident about my approach to teaching and to handling the students. I also feel more confident when approached by some challenging parents. I truly enjoy teaching, although I know that every day has its new challenges and learning experiences. I have just decided to take teaching one day at a time and each trial one at a time and to keep reminding myself that many experienced teachers were once in my position and made it through just fine.

My first year of teaching was extremely challenging. I can honestly say that it was a humbling year. But it was also extremely rewarding. There were many days that I wondered if this was my true calling and if I was really teaching the students and doing them any good. However, every time I doubted, I would see a smiling face or receive a hug from one of my little ones or a compliment from a fellow teacher, and I would know that teaching is where my heart is. I think that as long as I keep an open mind to change and improvement, I can make it. I take this Marian Wright Edelman quote to heart: "Education is for improving the lives of others and leaving your community and world better than you found it." Each day, I try to remind myself that by using my gifts and talents to serve children, I am serving the community as well as providing for a better and brighter future.

### Author Biography

*I am halfway through my second year of teaching third grade. By the end of the year, I will have completed my master's in elementary education through the University of Notre Dame. I intend to continue teaching at the elementary level in Catholic schools, but I plan to leave the South and move back home in order to be closer to my family.*

# chapter six

# Restlessness

## Kimberly's Story

*Kimberly, who taught fourth grade her first year, had many students with striking individual differences that proved to be very serious challenges, not the least of which included the effects one student suffered following a near-fatal car accident. She struggled with self-doubt about her abilities as a teacher throughout the year, and her personal life suffered as she consequently focused all of her energy on teaching.*

## QUESTIONS FOR REFLECTION WHILE READING KIMBERLY'S STORY

1. What student motivation challenges did Kimberly face, and how did she try to increase motivation in her class?
2. What types of individual differences increased teaching challenges in Kimberly's class, and did she handle them well?
3. What about relations with parents was challenging for Kimberly?
4. What were the challenges facing Kimberly in planning?
5. What knowledge of teaching and the curriculum did Kimberly lack?

6. How important was the support of Kimberly's colleagues and principal?
7. How was Kimberly's personal life affected by her job?
8. What unconstructive attitudes and perceptions did Kimberly have?

# THE STORY

"For if I should," said he,
"Bestow this jewel also on my creature,
he would adore my gifts instead of me,
And rest in Nature, not the God of Nature,
so both should losers be."

"Yet let him keep the rest,
But keep him with repining restlessness;
Let him be rich and weary, that at least,
If goodness lead him not, yet weariness
May toss him to my breast."

—*George Herbert, "The Pulley"*

"This can't be right," I muttered, as I stared at the standardized scores floating on the paper before me. I was sitting between two strangers during an afternoon of in-service in what appeared to be and sounded like, to me, a foreign country. Two days earlier, I had arrived in this moderate-sized southern city, during a prophetic sunset with rays streaming from the sky, almost welcoming my arrival. I had been completing the long drive with my new roommate, who shivered with excitement as I did. The next two days whizzed and whirled as I moved into a house with four roommates, met my shy principal and outgoing superintendent, toured the echoing hallway of my new school, and entered a group of people deeply familiar with one another, my faculty. As I wrestled with the thoughts that spring naturally from purposeful displacement for the sake of teaching, I also fought to smother my introverted tendencies. I was determined to change and instantaneously become who I wanted to be in this place where I had no history, only a future. It was a chance to shed my shyness and free my liveliness.

As I stared at the numbers and graphs on the report before me, however, I felt my limbs tighten and my face frown. What kind of teacher was I going to be? What kind of teacher were my circumstances going to make of me when the figures for my rising fourth graders seemed to reveal dismal abilities? The voices and the activity in the room faded as my eyes locked on the pages and my ears thundered with the hollow thumping of my heartbeat. The two-dimensional stories of my future students were almost unbearable: 18 of 20 students from broken or blended homes; more than half of the students below grade level; 10 children with learning differences, five of which were extreme; two sets of parents who were physically abusive; another parent who was a substance abuser. In those moments, I unfairly assumed every responsibility, challenge, and strain for these children I had never met. They became mine, and with that possession came the moral and emotional need to "fix" them. I prayed a prayer of humility:

> It is just hours before I walk into a tremendous new adventure, and I'm exhausted. I profess a tired and weary numbness at the moment for my body craves rest, but I have grown in both nervousness and excitement throughout the day. I find my thoughts revolving around my former teachers, my community, and my students. My dearest God, you watch over me with perfect guidance. I only ask for a drink of your refreshing water tomorrow so that I can grow in confidence from an awareness of your gentle presence. Make me your outlet and be patient with me until I do your will.

And then I met them. Nothing compares to the electricity of the first day of school. With nervous faces, shiny with the kisses of the sunshine, my students slowly entered the classroom, searched for desks and friends, sized up the new teacher, and arranged and re-arranged newly bought school supplies, destined to an early death in the hands of nine-year-olds. Students pulled at their clothes and shoes, much stiffer than the freedom of their summer attire, bathing suits and bare feet. Children hesitantly released parents' arms and gazes. Parents walked with heavy hearts to take the last few steps into the hall. The classroom swelled with life and energy and potential, pausing only to hold its breath at the sound of the bell. And as I was pleasantly robbed of the time to worry about what to do next, school began. The perfectionist in me had spent days drafting and revising the activities of the first half-day down to the precise minute, and I watched in disbelief as the students unintentionally mocked my structure by working at the unique pace of youth, which disregards time in the shadow of fancy.

There was nothing academic to "fix" in those first few days when we established our community, created our guidelines, and assessed our knowledge. We were redefining ourselves in this group, establishing relationships, and adjusting to the feel of school routines. As I reflected in my journal following the first few days, I was enamored with their strength and purity.

> What has stopped me in my tracks, however, is not just their rational minds in action, but the questions and ideas they have. One child chose the word "holy" to describe herself. Another wants to know how God has always existed. . . . It is beautiful and yet sad to hear these children pray—for their siblings who have died, their parents who are ill—but who prays for them? I see such loneliness and need in their eyes. I have already grown cautious of how talkative this group is, but I don't know which messages most overwhelm me, the ones revealed by their lips or those by everything but their lips.

A frenzied panic quickly built a home in my gut, however, when I examined their initial work during the first weekend. I had always been a strong student, a self-motivated overachiever. Faith and academics had been the core of my family, and I struggled at very little until the latter years of high school with advanced classes. As a college student in liberal arts at a prestigious university, I worked with intent purpose to excel in all areas, analytical and creative. I loved school because I was a natural learner, full of the curiosity and awe necessary to be a philosopher, a lover of wisdom. But, for the first time in my life, I was faced with a challenge that was not going to produce beautiful results parallel to the amount of concentrated work I invested. These students were neither influenced by the passions nor exposed to the liberty of my childhood. I identified so many curricular and noncurricular errors to repair, but without experience, I did not know how much to demand from students so far behind and with such a small view of the world. My fourth graders personified the earlier dismal statistics I had been shown, and my romantic mind darkened with thoughts that I could not improve what I saw; I could fail, and thus fail the 20 lives entrusted to me, their families, the school, and the teaching program that had placed me in the school. I highlighted as many of my own shortcomings as I did of the poor basic skills of my students.

I remained in that cocoon of overwhelming self-doubt through most of my first year of teaching, though I hid it from the people whose respect I so wanted to maintain. With ideas of professors, advice of colleagues, and repeated prayers mingling to guide me, I faced each day as a singular opportunity to experiment and to improve. I assumed what one colleague dubbed the "MacGyver" approach, to build something elaborate from random, disconnected items. I placed immense pressure on myself to reach every child and bring every student to a fourth-grade level, an unfair and weighty expectation. I wanted to produce an entire class whose idea of school was a respectful safe haven. I aimed both to ensure that these children learned precise pieces of knowledge and to facilitate the love of learning, so that they could desire and create their own opportunity from what was available around them. I planned creative lessons until I could no longer keep my eyes open. As the nocturnal person in our house, I would cringe when the alarm clock would go off in the morning, and my roommate, who had gotten twice the amount of sleep I had, would suggest that I shower first, enabling her to savor the precious extra moments in bed.

Although the students had broken free of my initial flat impressions of them, their domestic straits shaped how I taught and interacted with them. Poverty now had names and faces and spirits. I lost myself in order to give more to them. After just two weeks of teaching, I set the pace for the year. "I've discovered that I live in a bubble. I teach. I come home to teachers and talk about teaching. I prepare to teach. I reflect on teaching. I don't have a personal side right now. I can't afford to." Even writing in my journal grew sporadic and died after only one month in the classroom, because professional demands always ranked higher on my list of priorities than personal ones. I refused to spend time thinking when that time could be spent doing. After all, I owed it to these children whose lives lacked many of the blessings of my childhood.

My motivation at the start of each day was simply the students. I truly had no favorites and loved them all. I often remarked to my friends, "I have no idea if I'm actually teaching them anything, but we sure do have fun together." Our safe haven was a success, but the academic laurels I had hoped each student would earn were far from our reach. It was then that I began to understand more about the obstacles my students faced in their pursuit of learning, particularly dyslexia, a learning difference with which two students battled.

There was Brandon, who had stolen my heart within hours of the second day of class, when the students were presenting images or physical symbols of the five most important things in their lives. In addition to presenting a painting by his idol, his grandmother, Brandon shared a story of losing his brother.

My heart wept again today since my eyes could not. Brandon shared, in his Paper Bag Stuffer, pictures of his Siamese twin who died as an infant. He is so respectful of him, this creature who shared his organs and very life. The class fearlessly asked him questions about the operation, and the more they asked, the gentler Brandon held the picture in his hands. It was so powerful to see a little boy understand deep love, deep loss.

Brandon had known more strife than I could possibly have imagined. He lived with his grandmother, because his mother was a drug addict who rarely surfaced from her room. He had never known his father. He had an older brother who was part of a gang, and a younger brother who also attended our school. Brandon's mother would not, or could not, afford to give him the eye surgery necessary to correct his physical impairment. Until that impediment was tended to, the state would not offer Brandon special services to address his dyslexia. He was stretched between two parties who did not seem to care.

It hurts me to see him struggle since I know his body restricts his mind. After 10 minutes of reading, he complained about his eyes. How can his mother let him suffer? His grandmother elegantly attempts to hide the atrocity by suggesting that Brandon will grow out of it. Hardly a medical likelihood. Even if he grows out of it, which I doubt, he will have lost years of formation and stimulation. He is too precious to be treated so cruelly and insignificantly.

But his grandmother offered love, unconditional and unyielding. Brandon had his wild side, but that was reserved for after school. He respected the idea of school and worked as much as he could. Like his grandmother, he was a brilliant artist, and when he could do no more schoolwork, out of exhaustion, he would draw with sincere concentration and focus.

And there was Kevin, who I described as follows in the first few weeks: "Makes up for his academic insecurities with his dramatic abilities. He is a true thespian with energy and style. Our Readers' Theatre will be great with his desire to shine and his skill to adopt the traits of other people, even me, all in the name of entertainment." Without a book in his hands, Kevin was bold, silly, romantic, playful, and generous with compliments for other people, however manipulative the motive sometimes was. He had "dated" a classmate for almost two years and had fully given his fourth-grade heart to her. But as whimsical as he was, he sat me down just weeks into the school year to explain why he needed to break up with this girlfriend. "We've just drifted apart as we've gotten older." But capricious and incorrigible Kevin returned to my side many more times to seek advice on how to "get her back. She [was] the best thing that [had] happened to [him]," and he tried with all his charm to win her affection again.

I watched as he flirted with his parents in a similar manner. His parents were separated and filing for divorce, so Kevin had learned to use his dramatic tendencies to gain from each parent what he wanted, although he truly desired nothing more than for his parents to be together. And when he observed that I needed a dose of spirit and energy, he was sure to smother me with sugary words. One day when we were elbow deep in dioramas, the students' voices were unusually piercing. Kevin piped, "Isn't it ironic that we're talking when our teacher is the best teacher in the world?" My mental response: "Grain of salt."

Kevin's composure and confidence vanished when he faced an academic demand, however, so that reading and math became a point of misery for him. I created tools to help him; I referred him to the resource program; I talked with his tutor; and mostly I talked with Kevin, himself, to adapt and adjust our routines and assignments so that he was comfortable. But Kevin became too comfortable. His dyslexia created complications; his laziness created failure. If working meant facing his frustrations, he preferred to make excuses. I was trying, but Kevin was not. I blamed myself for not being an expert who could magically give him individualized attention for the duration of the class while the other students worked independently. I blamed myself for not instilling self-motivation in Kevin so that he really wanted to learn more, even if it was harder than I could comprehend. I already felt that I was robbing other students of their due because I spent such energy and time on Kevin. And since I wasn't making progress with him or the remainder of the class, I felt my spirit and confidence fizzle. I wasn't a teacher at all.

An experience at Back-to-School Night in late September solidified my spiral into self-pity. I had been advised by colleagues to talk freely with all of the parents and to encourage those families who desired more of my time to schedule conferences. The night was to be one in which the families observed and mingled. I donned a hyper-professional attitude, conscious of how young I appeared and how inexperienced I was. I allowed the students to give tours. I briefly spoke of my teaching creed and explained how some of my new techniques were derivatives of that. I implored families to be an active part of their children's education as the primary teachers. I had just finished my last sentence when a set of parents cornered me, literally. They explained how they were dissatisfied with the education their daughter had thus far received at the school and how they were considering removing their children. They questioned my credentials and threatened to hold me responsible if their daughter was not performing at grade level by the end of the year. Fearful of saying something inappropriate, I explained that I would employ different methods until I found something that suited their daughter, who was desperately behind, but that progress would come only if she received attention from them at home in addition to class activities. They left in a huff, and I left in tears.

My students loved me. My principal supported me. My observers applauded me. My housemates soothed me. My family comforted me. People outside of my classroom could not understand why I grew so dissatisfied and despondent, because we appeared to be doing very well. But they were not a part of that class, and they were not responsible for improving the lives of those students. I failed to love, support, applaud, soothe, or comfort myself, so their hollow words never touched the malignant ache. I could not appreciate small accomplishments because I envisioned only magnificent needs. I fought with moral vigor to keep from lowering my standards, both for the students and for myself, and succeeded in further burdening myself. Our class was bright and creative. The students loved coming to class and participating in my dramatic teaching style. But they struggled with subtraction and could not write solid sentences. Who did I think I was to enter the classroom and assume that I could teach?

I was grateful for the 15 hours of silence as I drove home for Christmas break, a much-needed retreat with my family. I allowed the crossing of each state line to mark a mental distance away from the stress and failure. I pulled into my driveway, stretched my grateful limbs, and bottled up my thoughts before entering my house—two weeks to "fix" myself and return with enthusiasm. My family embraced me and immediately put me to the cathartic task of decorating for the season. Decking out our tree always fosters giddy memories of Christmas Past. Each ornament holds a story, a sweet escape from my worries. We bought last-minute presents, baked gingerbread and pralines for friends, attended the Christmas Vigil mass, exchanged presents, and reveled in the time together. We talked of my brother's upcoming wedding and the exciting plans for his future. I was far away from school and beginning to relax.

As I am one of six very active family members, our telephone is rarely quiet, so there was nothing unusual about a late-night phone call on the fourth day of Christmas, the day of "calling birds." It was my principal, and I was jolted out of my surroundings and quickly taken back to my life at school. For an instant, I was irritated to have my Walden invaded, but concern suddenly washed over me and re-placed any other thoughts. She sounded uncomfortable and hesitant, and I did not know how to acknowledge such a strange tone.

After fumbling over our greetings, her voice quieted and she said, "Kimberly, there's been an accident, and I thought you should know. Kevin Hittle was taken to the hospital, and it doesn't look good." I grew numb and still. She continued, "He and his mother were driv-ing this afternoon. We're not sure what caused her to go off of the road, but she did. The car flipped and landed on a mailbox. The own-ers had cemented the bricks surrounding the mailbox, so it didn't budge. Kevin was in the passenger's seat and the mailbox pierced his side of the windshield. Mrs. Hittle is in critical condition and looks like she'll recover with some significant breaks and bruises, but Kevin has a less than 5% chance of survival."

My mind froze on an image of Kevin screaming as the car went off the road. I blankly asked the details of where he was and who was with him. I wrote down phone numbers and people to call, but my mind was on that image. My principal spoke reassuringly of miracles and Kevin's gumption, and we agreed that prayer was the best gift we could offer him. She promised to call if anything changed, and I thanked her for calling. As I hung up the receiver, one train of thought emerged violently: But Kevin doesn't like to fight for anything. He gives up too easily. How is he going to fight for his life?

As I tried to sleep that night, I forced myself to remember every bit of my time with Kevin to replace that stagnant image of the acci-dent. I thought of his crazy costumes during Spirit Week. I laughed at his poem about being a girl magnet. I pictured him playing the piano in the music room. I remembered him hugging me at the close of a long school day. I imagined his laugh when he gave me his tasty Christmas present with an apology for taking the bow off to give to his forgiving girlfriend with whom he had reconciled. I thought of him looking around the room to see if anyone was watching as he used his fists to make b's and d's during a writing activity. I pictured his smile and crinkly eyes. And I prayed that for the first time since I had known him, Kevin would willingly work at something ever so difficult.

I prayed the same thing for myself that night. I realized that I was more like Kevin than I thought. I still worked to be a better teacher on the outside, but I was stuck in a state of distrust and disbelief. Although Kevin frustrated me when he gave up, I constantly forgave him and continued to love him. I prayed that I would do something ever so difficult—forgive and love myself. If Kevin dies, I asked myself, what have I done to make his life better? And I smiled, because suddenly multiplication tables and irregular verbs lost a bit of their importance. Kevin and I had shared many moments of laughter. We had read together, marveled at the outcomes of science experiments together, created stories together. We had spent many afternoons talking about his parents' divorce and his fears for the future in a world that made no sense without that commitment. I had not hurt him, as I so often felt I had. I had simply added another level of love, and as an inexperienced teacher, I had offered him creativity and dedication, if not expertise. Neither of us had truly failed. We both just needed medicinal direction, time, and self-trust.

Kevin survived the night, and the doctors increased his 5% hold on life to 10%. Time granted gift after gift, because with each hour, Kevin's body grew stronger, and after two weeks, he was moved out of intensive care. He was in a waking coma—becoming responsive, making noises, even smiling—but was not truly conscious. His brain was still too swollen to assess how much damage had been done or to perform surgery on any damaged parts. But he was alive, and he had defeated gruesome odds to be so. He had fought the first obstacle and won. The doctors were joyous. His family was elated. The school community was inspired. I was proud.

During the first day back, I had agreed with my principal to hold a prayer service for our class. We gathered on the steps of the altar and delicately explained Kevin's state to a group of wide-eyed children. It seemed so unnatural. The children asked dozens of questions, good and just ones. Since we didn't know the degree of Kevin's recovery, we prepared the students for the worst and prayed for the best. Brandon uniquely prayed for Kevin's siblings, in gratitude for their not having lost a brother. Some of the students remained contemplative during the day, while others seemed to absorb the information as commonplace. No reaction was like another. We made a huge poster and tissue-paper flowers to deliver to Kevin later that day. After school, parents asked equally good questions and sent along cards, gifts, and prayers for Kevin and his family. The school wanted him to know how much we needed him.

But as I walked into the lobby of the hospital that evening, I grew very scared. I didn't know if I could face Kevin or his family. I had felt guilty during the day, wishing that Kevin were well but secretly grateful for how much smoother the day progressed without him. Ideas for how I could have better helped him to learn darted among the corners of my mind, and I grew heavy thinking of how artificial I was, claiming to be a teacher but not having taught him. I regretted taking even the minimal personal time I had taken to exercise, write, or talk with friends, thinking that perhaps five minutes more could have changed his academic life.

I may have felt that I failed him in the classroom, but I could not choose to fail him now and walk away from an opportunity to see him. I rode the elevator to his floor, walked slowly to his door, and gently rapped at the wood. On the door was a certificate from the nurses for the "Funniest Patient." Same old Kevin. A voice invited me in, and I glanced at the back of a young body awkwardly wearing only a diaper. I looked up to see Kevin's dad watching him sleep on one bed while Kevin's mother rested on another. With a broken pelvis and rib, she struggled to stand despite my urging to remain comfortable. She stood on the other side of Kevin and woke him with the explanation that he had company. He rolled over to reveal the tubes in his mouth and nose. He was groggy, and I quietly insisted that we let him sleep. But Kevin, himself, preferred the stimulation. We taped the poster to the wall facing his bed and handed him the gifts and cards. His blurry eyes followed all of our actions. I stayed only long enough to wish the family my best, assure them of our tremendous school support, and squeeze a smile out of Kevin. I cried all the way home.

Days passed; school grew hectic; Kevin improved. While we tackled geography and geometry, Kevin tackled walking and talking. We used balls in physical education. Kevin used balls in physical therapy. We all worked on basic skills, his physical and ours academic. Kevin even returned part-time during the final quarter to increase his stamina and personal interaction with children. He was amazing. In his moments of immense need, he discovered that he could satisfy himself, and he did. He taught himself. Maybe I had a small part in that, but I suspect more that I was simply graced to be an observer.

I was struck by a much-needed epiphany during the last week of school, after Kevin had given me an infamous smile and hug and Brandon had excelled at a math center. These children are flexible and malleable and intrinsically inclined toward happiness. In this year of incredible humility and self-deprecation, I have been ironi-cally arrogant. I presumed that, in my time with these students, I needed to "fix" them, and if I failed them, their lives would forever be dampened by my incapacity to do so. But I have been just one small factor in their precious growth; I am solely responsible for neither their accomplishments nor their shortcomings. What I have been un-able to give them, they will find from the people and events in their futures. I cannot save them, only serve them. And I did that with the fullness of my being and ability.

My awe for the beauty of my students, particularly Kevin and Brandon in their peaceful resilience, inspired me to write a letter to each of the teachers who had guided me in my own quest for knowl-edge. I closed each letter with the following:

> Thank you. Thank you for the millions of times I should have thanked you and did not. Thank you for the voices and actions of your stu-dents, who spread the impact of your talents, even if your names are never used. Thank you for the endless ways I have been touched by who you are and what you do, since the two are inseparable. Thank you for tapping that spirit in me to teach, so that I, too, could ex-perience those rare, brilliant moments when you see that you are having a positive influence on a child. Thank you, too, even for those more numerous challenging moments when you must resign your doubts to faith that the fruits of your work may never be seen. May we all be patient in our blindness.

### Author Biography

*I taught fourth grade in the same school for three years, where I also acted as assistant principal for one year. I am currently working at the National Catholic Educational Association in Washington, D.C., where I serve Catholic secondary schools in the United States.*

# chapter seven

# April Fools' Day

## Daniel's Story

*Daniel, who taught middle school math and science, experienced some of the most common challenges of first-year teaching. Some of his teaching was outside of his area of content expertise, making the extensive planning required for his teaching very difficult. He also found himself at odds with parents over some issues. What was most striking, however, was that no one of the problems faced by Daniel was overwhelming. Even so, the number of challenges was almost overwhelming, and his story reflects just how daunting many little hassles can be for a first-year teacher.*

## QUESTIONS FOR REFLECTION WHILE READING DANIEL'S STORY

1. How was discipline a challenge for Daniel?
2. How would you have handled the misbehavior in Daniel's class?
3. What student motivation challenges did Daniel face?
4. What types of individual differences increased teaching challenges in Daniel's class, and did he handle them well?

5. How far-reaching do you think the impact of the school's shortage of financial resources was on Daniel's class and his teaching?
6. What were the challenges facing Daniel with respect to teacher-student interaction?
7. How did nonteaching demands challenge Daniel?
8. What was challenging about Daniel's relations with colleagues?
9. What were the challenges facing Daniel in planning?
10. What were the challenges facing Daniel with respect to classroom instruction?
11. What knowledge of teaching and the curriculum did Daniel lack?
12. How was Daniel's relationship with his principal challenging?
13. How was Daniel's personal life affected by his job?
14. What unconstructive attitudes and perceptions did Daniel have?
15. How did gender or sexual issues challenge Daniel?

# THE STORY

I heard the two voices gradually growing louder in the back of the classroom. Even though I was only in my first month of teaching, I sensed that the two boys were getting ready to argue. Before I could make my way to the last two seats where Austin and Kyle sat, one of their voices grabbed the attention of the entire class. "Kyle, you don't know what you are talking about. I saw it on TV last week." Kyle was ready to yell back at Austin, but he had been watching me approach from the front of the room. Austin, his back toward me, was unaware that I was standing behind him and continued, "Let's ask Mr. Thomas. He'll know." The surprise in his face showed clearly as he turned and saw that I was already there, ready to answer his question. My face must have shown some surprise as well, because I was not expecting to be part of the argument Austin and Kyle were having. Indeed I was so surprised that I forgot to get mad at the two seventh-grade boys for distracting the class from their science work. After Austin regained himself, he asked, "Mr. Thomas, isn't it true that there are times when Pluto is not the farthest planet from the sun?"

Suddenly, the urge to correct these two for letting the entire class get off task resurfaced. "Is that what we are working on right now?" I asked with a bit of sarcasm in my voice. "I thought we were working on the review questions for chapter 2. I don't think we get to the planets until chapter 10." I tried to put the sternest expression I could on my face. "Is it okay if we all get back to work now?"

"Yes, sir," both Austin and Kyle answered.

Relieved, I concluded the episode. "Thank you."

The class returned to working in cooperative groups and seemed to get a lot out of that day's lesson. But the relief I felt after that class was not from having successfully diffused an argument or keeping my students on task, both skills I had learned in my education classes. I was relieved because I had avoided showing my ignorance. I thought Pluto was always the farthest planet from the sun, but now I was not sure. Part of me was worried. When next would I have to keep hidden the fact that I did not have the answer to a student's question?

My anxiety about knowing enough about the material I was teaching began two months before I ever started. I believed I was to teach middle school math and science. What ignited my worries was a letter sent to me by the principal of my future school. It read that she was very much looking forward to my arrival in August. The letter went on to describe the school. The facts it contained had already been told to me by people who were familiar with the school. It was located in the heart of the downtown of a large city. It was a poor school. There were only 120 students total in kindergarten through eighth grade. That meant an average of 13 students per grade. This low enrollment was the main cause of the school's financial problems. The school had a very small faculty and staff, with just enough teachers to cover all the grades and classes. The surprise came when I read that I would be teaching seventh- and eighth-grade math, eighth-grade earth science, seventh-grade literature, seventh-grade social studies, and a few physical education classes. I was stunned. Literature, social studies, and physical education were not what I was supposed to teach. I thought that I was headed to a poor, inner-city school to teach only math and science. For some reason I had believed that although the school was short on money and teachers, I wouldn't have to teach subjects I wasn't trained to teach.

So when I arrived, I was on guard against showing how little I knew. The school itself was much as I had expected. It was old, but in good shape. There were a few dead cockroaches around, but at least they were dead and not scurrying around my classroom. When

I arrived, the school was quiet and a general feeling of serenity permeated the building. Miss Smythe, the 14-year teacher who was to be my mentor teacher, warned me that the calmness would not last. Her warning brought me back to the reality that school was starting in a week and that I needed to learn about the subjects that I would be teaching.

With my week to prepare I attacked literature and social studies. I had to prepare for five different classes each day, not counting physical education, but I decided to focus on the two subjects about which I felt most insecure. For my literature class, I had a textbook that contained short stories, plays, poetry, a condensed novel, and a large number of lessons on such topics as theme, characterization, and plot. Happily I realized that I remembered much of what the book covered. I was grateful to my high school English teachers for doing such a good job. My confidence was renewed, and I resolved to read all of the short stories before the school year began. My first literary lessons would pertain to these short stories, and we would deal with the plays, poetry, and condensed novel later in the year. I was also pleasantly shocked as I investigated the social studies textbook I was to use. The material about geography was not complicated at all. With a little reading for both classes, I would be ready to start teaching.

During the first week of school, my optimism about how well I knew the material proved well founded. On the Friday of that week, I stood in the back of the classroom as the students worked quietly on their math homework. I thought to myself that I was all alone with these children. No one was supervising me as I taught, yet the kids were on task. That was the moment when I understood that the students believed that since I was the teacher, I knew what I was talking about. For the most part, I did. I had worked hard to prepare what I had been unsure of previously, and I knew the material. The anxiety I had felt for the two months since learning I would have to teach material other than math and science seemed like a joke to me that Friday. I would do fine.

Even though my confidence about the material increased after that first week of school, my cockiness left as I realized that there was a lot more to teaching than just knowing the subject matter. In graduate school, I had taken classes such as classroom management, child psychology, and foundations of education. My professors had armed me with many lessons on how to be a master teacher. Themes that were repeated, and that I therefore believed were the most important, included the following: During class time, you want as few distractions as possible. Establish a routine to get students on task. Discipline children quietly and sensitively, rather than calling them out in front of the whole class. When I encountered situations my professors had foreseen, I felt I handled them well. It was the situations that I had never been warned about that began to present challenges to me during my second week as a teacher.

Washington Elementary is located in the heart of a historic district in a city known for its natural beauty. Trolleys full of tourists rolled by our school throughout the day. These tourists had no effect on my day until it was time for dismissal. At three o'clock, all of the children from the school were released onto one of the green squares for which the city is well-known. After the crossing guard led the students from the school to the grassy square, the children wanted to run around and play. The city officials and the principal, however, believed it looked bad if the students were beating down the grass, stepping on the flowers, peeling bark from the trees, or dropping candy wrappers into the fountain in the center of the square, so they could see the paper float around on the rippling water. I thought it looked bad as well, but I was frustrated day after day by asking the students to stay on the walkway, watch out for the flowers, and sit down on a bench to wait for a ride home. The parents were no help either. They stopped their cars anywhere possible and called for their children, as young as five years old, to run across the street to meet them. Often, the result was that the crossing guard and teachers told the students to do one thing and the parents directly contradicted us. My education classes had not prepared me for the complications of student dismissal.

Nor did I learn in my education classes how to walk children back and forth from the park. Washington Elementary sat on a small block of property. There was no room for a gymnasium or a playground. Recess meant going a couple of blocks to a city park with two sets of swings, one teeter-totter, and a small wooden structure with a slide on which the students could play. On the way to the park, the students were understandably excited. But, as their teacher, I did not want to look as if I had no control. Each day, I tried to slow them down and quiet them as we walked to the park. On the way back to school, our roles were reversed, and the children would walk at a snail's pace. Upon our arrival at school, the principal would always want to know why we were late and threaten to shorten recess. The students would groan and then get quiet. Next day, though, it was the same routine.

Besides these run-of-the-mill problems, unexpected difficulties arose almost every day. One day, a seventh-grade girl named Lauren didn't feel well. I asked if she wanted to lie on the couch outside of the secretary's office. Lauren said she would rather just put her head down. As I taught math, I occasionally walked by her desk to make sure she was doing all right. I was happy to see that she was sleeping soundly, and I hoped that when she awoke she would feel better. Instead, when she awoke 40 minutes into class, she leaned over the side of her desk and vomited. Another day, a boy leaned against the wall while he waited in line outside of the cafeteria. Miss Smythe walked by and told Dylan not to lean against the wall while in line. He straightened up as she walked past him, but he slumped back against the wall after she passed into the cafeteria. Then, he began to tap on the door to the kindergarten room, which was next to him. He did not know that I had heard Miss Smythe's instructions or that I could see him. As I approached Dylan to correct his behavior, Miss Karen, the kindergarten teacher, pulled open her door. She looked at me with annoyance and asked if I could please keep the students from disturbing her class. I was embarrassed and angry at Dylan; I wanted to scream at him right there. Instead, I sent him to the end of the line. For the next week, I kept my eye on him. Whenever Dylan did the slightest thing wrong, such as take too long in the bathroom, forget his homework, or even whisper in class, I yelled at him in front of the rest of the students.

I knew that Lauren could not help getting sick. Also, I understood that Dylan's misbehavior was not overly serious. All the little things though, from the long hours of preparation and the difficulty in the lunch line, to the headache at dismissal and cleaning up after sick students, were wearing me down. I was becoming tense and was taking it out on the students. By the end of October, I was a mean teacher.

I knew I had to do something if I wanted to survive as a teacher. From the discussions I had with my housemates, who were also new teachers, I concluded I had two main difficulties. The first was that there was no way I could be well prepared for all five of my classes each day. The second was that I was letting every little detail of the school day distract me. I was so concerned with trivia, such as how long the students were in the bathroom, that I became frustrated. I decided that either I would meet these two challenges or get out of teaching.

I thought the problem of preparation would be the harder challenge to face, since I had already come to the conclusion that there were not enough hours in the day to accomplish everything that I needed to accomplish. Even on days when I had been as prepared as I thought possible, something unexpected happened and threw me for a loop. My plan of attack actually turned out to be simple: I decided to relax and do the best I could while remaining sane. I wanted to go into school each day prepared, but I also wanted to have a social life. I began to focus each night on a different subject. For that subject I would plan for 30 to 45 minutes. If the subject were math or science, it might not even take that long, since I knew these subjects well. After planning the best lesson I could, I would assure myself that I was ready to teach the other subjects by checking that I knew what pages I would cover, what activities I would use, and what homework I would assign. It was very easy for me to tell if I had prepared enough for the next day. If I was worried about the next day when I went to sleep, then I had not put enough time into my plans. Any night I felt relaxed and was able to forget about school, I was sure I was ready. This system of preparation worked well for me and allowed me to focus on my second problem.

My days were filled with not only trying to teach the students, but also watching for every little thing that they did wrong. I was trying to control them too much. I came up with a new approach; if a student did something that did not hurt themselves, others, the school, or the city, then I would not get angry about that action. This helped me keep my cool when I saw students leaning against the walls. If they weren't ripping down the artwork hanging on the walls when they leaned against them, I let it slide. After school I gave up having them sit in one place at dismissal and instead kept my eye out for littering, flower stomping, and anything that brought the kids too close to the street. I was feeling better about the job I was doing overall, and I attribute the positive change to the fact that I learned to relax both when I was planning and when I was teaching.

Still, there were days that were far from perfect. One day, about a week before Christmas break, the students were very active. I was teaching math to the eighth grade, and on this day we were playing Math Jeopardy. A student chose from one of the six categories and then went to the board to answer a question in that category. The harder the problem, the more points the student earned for a correct answer. The students were into the game, and their competitive sides were kicking in. The one drawback to taking the game so seriously was that the students with poorer math skills felt tremendous pressure when they were at the board. One such student, Joshua, came to the board and chose a 10-point problem. His team felt confident because 10-point problems were the easiest a student could select. Unfortunately, Joshua missed the problem because he mixed up the sign on the answer. I could see that he felt badly about missing the question. When his team groaned at his mistake, I chastised them by deducting 10 points from their score for being poor teammates. This only caused them to groan more loudly, and I deducted 20 more points. Joshua's team was no longer winning. They viewed this as both Joshua's fault and my fault. Half the class was now mad, and I was on edge because of the entire situation. As I continued the game, I kept an ear on Joshua's team to hear if they said anything inappropriate. Whenever I heard a negative comment from a member of that team, I became angrier and angrier. Then, just as I was ready to explode, the girl with the worst attitude in the class called out, "Mr. Thomas, do you have a girlfriend?" I was caught offguard by the question and for some reason actually answered her.

"No, Jillian, I don't."

"Well, you need to get one," she retorted.

The class was stunned into silence. I was stunned also. I could never imagine saying that to a teacher when I was in school. My shock changed to anger when I understood that she was saying that I was in a bad mood because I didn't have a girlfriend, rather than because the class was behaving so poorly. Jillian was quickly on her way to the office to see the principal, and the rest of the day, I snapped at every student who breathed too heavily. Despite my intentions, I just could not relax that day.

Months passed, and I was still overreacting to the small things. One day at the playground, a seventh-grade girl chased a ball into the street. No cars were coming, but the way she recklessly flew onto the road scared me. The girl, Nicole, nodded politely as I informed her that next time she should retrieve the ball more cautiously. After I finished correcting her behavior, she turned to her friends, clicked her tongue in disgust, and said, "How old does he think I am?"

"Excuse me?" I interjected. "I didn't hear what you said, Nicole."

"Well, that's 'cause I wasn't talking to you, Mr. Thomas."

I do not remember what was said after that. I only remember being right up in Nicole's face and yelling. At first, she yelled back. Eventually though, she stopped trying to win the argument and began to cry. The whole episode had started because I was concerned for Nicole's safety. In the end, I had once again overreacted. The next day I wondered why I hadn't relaxed and let Nicole's comment to her friends go unanswered. One thing I did know was that if I developed the ability to make it through situations such as that one without ruining my day, I would be closer to becoming the teacher I wanted to be.

One method I used to reduce the number of unexpected problems, and therefore reduce my stress, was to develop routines in each class. For instance, in geography, we started a new lesson each Monday by discussing a geographical region of the world. The students told me what they knew and what they wanted to know about that region. On Tuesdays and Wednesdays we read the information about the region that the textbook provided. On Thursdays we discussed any current events that were occurring in the region we were studying and then played a review game to prepare for the quiz that came on Fridays. Following the quiz, we would do an activity that was more fun than the typical social studies class, such as watch an educational program, listen to music with positive messages, or discuss issues that affected the students' lives. Every week the students knew what was coming, and I knew how to plan the lessons. By developing routines, I reduced the chances of awkward situations that were difficult to handle.

As I was experiencing success with weekly routines, I found that my reactions to the little stuff also improved. I handled things particularly well on April 1. When I woke up that morning, I wondered to myself if my students would be into playing April Fools' pranks. The thought passed and did not resurface until I was teaching eighth-grade math. Ten minutes into class, I went to get my teacher's edition out of my backpack so we could correct the homework. My backpack was not on the chair next to the desk where I always placed it. Immediately I suspected an April Fools' joke, but I refrained from demanding my bag back. I knew that I could correct the homework without the answers from the book. After all, I was a college graduate with a degree in mathematics. The easiest thing to do was to call the students to the board three at a time and allow them to work the problems out for the other students to see and for me to check if the answers were correct. As the students worked at the board, I did not walk around the class and search for my bag. Rather, I sat at an empty desk and continued class. After we were done correcting, I checked my lesson plans to see what the next lesson was in the book. We were solving equations with very basic fractions in them. Again I was confident that I could handle the material without my text, so I went ahead and taught the lesson. A few times, I made examples that didn't work out as nicely as I had aimed for, but with 10 minutes left in class, the students started the homework assignment.

With two minutes left and the students still working well on their homework, some doubt entered my mind. Maybe the students had not taken my bag. Maybe I had left it in the teachers' lounge. I didn't remember putting it down on the chair at the start of class. Did I forget it? No, I convinced myself. I wouldn't come to class without that bag hanging from one shoulder.

"Okay, you have about a minute left," I announced, checking my watch. "Please finish this for homework. And by the way, no one goes to lunch until my bag is back on the chair where I put it at the start of class." The bell rang and the students stood to leave. "Sit!" I commanded. They didn't sit, they just stood where they were. "Sit!" I repeated.

If they hadn't sat down after my second order I would have believed that they didn't know what I was talking about, but they all grudgingly returned to their seats. Terence was the first to play innocent. "What's going on Mr. T.?"

I answered very calmly, "I want my bag back on this chair. When it is there, we go to lunch." A groan escaped collectively from the students. A few complained openly, but since it was only a few, I was now positive that the entire class knew my bag had been taken. No one else even bothered to play dumb and ask what bag, or suggest that I forgot it that day.

Three minutes past the bell the grumbling began among the students. My confidence rose because they were bickering among themselves and not at me. Then their hope shot up as there was a knock at the door. It opened to reveal Miss Smythe. Half the class called to her at the same time, "Miss Smythe, tell him to let us go to lunch! It's not fair! I'm hungry!"

I didn't know what to say. Part of me felt as if I had sunk to the level of an eighth grader, because I was on this power trip and keeping them from their hot dogs. Miss Smythe, though, looked out at the class and asked why they weren't allowed to go. They explained. She suggested, in a very matter-of-fact manner, that maybe if my backpack were returned, they would get to eat. This time the whole class groaned.

"Mr. Thomas," she turned to me, "may I borrow Terence? Sr. Elizabeth wants to see him."

"Of course," I answered with a thankful smile on my face.

Terence jumped out of his seat and headed for the door. He wore a smile just as I did. As he left the classroom, Miss Smythe added,

"Don't worry, I'll send him back before he gets a chance to eat." The class laughed as the sound of Terence begging Miss Smythe came back through the closing door. I knew Terence would be back without lunch. Miss Smythe always backed up her words. I understood that it was time to back up my own.

When Terence did reenter the class, he was patting his stomach to show that he had eaten. "Man, those hot dogs are good!" he exclaimed. "I had my two and then ate one of yours, Rob!"

"What! You're crazy, fool!" Rob shook his head as he talked. "We know Miss Smythe didn't let you eat." Rob was right. Not a single person believed that Terence had eaten.

Sensing he was not going to convince anyone he was full of hot dogs, Terence switched his tactics. As he sat down, he revealed, "Mr. Thomas, I may not have eaten, but I do know where your bag is." There was a sense of relief in the class. "It was outside near the dumpster and some wino picked it up." Half the class began laughing, and I smiled some myself. It was a wornout backpack. I had used it all four years in college, and it had been beaten up pretty well. A wino carrying it down the street would look quite fitting. Terence continued, "I tried to get it back, but, man, he stunk!"

The class laughed again, but the tide was turning. Twenty minutes had gone by. Lunch was halfway over. Some of the students were concerned because some days not enough food was ordered, and the last people in line might not get what they wanted. Murmuring among the students increased, and soon all eyes were on Terence. He cracked. "Okay, it's back there. Under my jacket." His finger pointed to the hooks that lined the back wall. The class sighed their relief and stood to go.

"Sit!" I demanded louder than before. They sat. "I said you can go when my bag is back where you found it." I looked at the chair next to the teacher's desk. There was silence in the room. Clearly there was nothing left but pride. Terence was too proud to be so defeated that he would actually have to walk the bag up to the front of the room and return it. I was feeling too proud to settle for anything else. Members of the class urged Terence to get the bag, and he went to the back of the classroom. Dejectedly, Terence reached under his coat and pulled my bag from the hook. With his head down, he walked quickly to the front of the room, dropped my backpack on the chair, and headed straight for the door. "Thank you!" I called after him, and the class rushed out the door.

### Author Biography

*I am glad that no matter what happens the rest of my life I will never have to be a first-year teacher again. That may sound bad, but my first year of teaching was not easy. Even though I had taken education classes before I started teaching, there was nothing that could have prepared me for what teaching is like. Happily, I survived, and following two years at Washington Elementary, I moved to Texas, in order to teach high school math. My school in Texas is much like Washington Elementary. The school is poor, and at times it has struggled to remain open; however, I have enjoyed nearly every day of teaching algebra and calculus. I attribute my current satisfaction to the lessons I learned that first year as a teacher. Those lessons included how to plan efficiently, how to deal fairly with others, and how to stay calm when things go wrong—and the fact that at certain times, Neptune is farther from the sun than Pluto.*

# chapter eight

# Is One Enough?

## Michael's Story

*Michael, who taught middle school English, struggled with how to relate to, interact with, and affect students positively. He had his fair share of special-needs students, which led to much reflection, including the thinking he did in anticipation of and during parent-teacher conferences.*

## QUESTIONS FOR REFLECTION WHILE READING MICHAEL'S STORY

1. How was discipline a challenge for Michael?
2. How would you have handled the misbehavior in Michael's class?
3. What types of individual differences increased teaching challenges for Michael, and did he handle them well?
4. What about relations with parents was challenging for Michael?
5. What were the challenges facing Michael with respect to classroom interaction?
6. What were the challenges facing Michael with respect to classroom instruction?

7. How did unconstructive attitudes and perceptions make Michael's first year more challenging?

# THE STORY

> Anyway, what am I looking for? Why did I really enter teaching? If I'm to continue, I should look for signs that I was meant to be teaching junior high at this place and time.

These were the first words I wrote in a teacher's journal I received from my parents at Christmas. Halfway through my initial year of teaching, Mom and Dad thought it was time for me to write down some reflections. After all, you only have one first year of teaching. Reading the experiences of other teachers in first-year books helped, but if I could not reflect on my own journey, how would I discern whether teaching was right for me? In addition, my students journaled as part of our literature class. I repeatedly announced how they would cherish such writings when they grew old, and I decided to practice what I was preaching.

It was difficult to journal at times. When I was exhausted at the end of a day, often I was tempted to scrap journaling. Even so, I took pen to paper and felt it to be a calming activity. Without it, my experiences would merely be in my memory, and memory fades.

I always had a lot of material. Stories, positive and negative, filled the pages. The more tumultuous the semester grew, the more engaging the narrative. My journal entries from the spring semester of my first year read like the confessions of the commander of the *Titanic*. No matter what I did, I sensed I was still going down.

Nonetheless, sometimes there was good reason to remain hopeful.

> Got this letter on Friday. Six of the girls in my class won awards in a young poets' contest. . . . My new wisdom for the day says I should act like I make a difference because I do. My mentor teacher says I do. Maybe this contest result confirms it. Why can't I always believe this?

In many journal entries, I recorded something I did right and then questioned whether it was enough. Sometimes nothing joyful existed to remove doubt. Feeling good about myself depended upon believing I had touched the life of one student on a given day.

I felt tremendous responsibility as a first-year teacher. I often wondered whether I could make a difference with even one kid. Interrogatives encircled me. What is a difference? How do I make it? Who do I start with?

And most importantly, is one enough?

> My girlfriend gave me cards of daily wisdom. Today's advice was, "We make a living by what we get, but we make a life by what we give." I guess that's one of the main reasons I got involved with teaching. I truly believed that principle. I'm trying to make a life by giving all I have each day at school. It's tiring as hell and usually never seems to be worth it, but keeping this idea in mind is important.

I felt a duty to do something that seemed right. What could be more noble than teaching? Things could be done. People could be helped. One thing was for sure: Doing nothing equaled nothing happening.

Thus, I traveled to St. Joseph's, immediately looking to make a difference. It was almost comical. I expected my mere presence to set the school on a course to becoming one of the top educational institutions in the land. I was arrogant and naive, projecting that attitude: "I'm here now, whom do I help first?" The students at St. Joseph's School seemed to respond, "How do we break him down?" The students were accustomed to a transient faculty, mainly due to living in a town with a military base. Teachers were hired each year to replace others who left after only a year or two. The students were practiced at not tolerating new teachers. This proved especially true in the eighth-grade class, with the majority of students biding their time until high school. The small class had difficulty accepting me, especially since I was replacing a popular language arts teacher.

The students posed lots of questions: "Why don't you do it the way last year's teacher did?" "Why can't we just have the same kind of tests we had last year?" "Why am I getting a C in your class when I got an A in English last year?" I wanted to scream, "I am not like your past teacher. I am who I am." I could not understand why acceptance was so tough to come by. Didn't these kids know I was here to help them? Why was I not being appreciated?

My self-esteem declined. I was clearly not doing things well. I told the seventh grade that their test scores "sucked," swore in class once, and occasionally told students to shut up. My inexperience shined through, and I was quickly disliked by many students. Part of the problem stemmed from being unapproachable. I had told myself that kids have enough friends, and it does not matter if they like you. I came to realize after awhile that it is better to be approachable. Unapproachable people do not make a difference.

I did not know, however, how to be approachable and yet keep an appropriate, professional distance. My class was supposed to be both enjoyable and disciplined at once. I struggled with the teacher-student relationship, usually favoring the side of a tough disciplinarian rather than of an approachable, caring professional teacher. It was exactly where I didn't want to go.

> I say I don't care if I'm liked, but I'm just lying to myself. It melts my heart when a student says something nice about me. I wish all my students could get to know me and see that I'm not such a bad guy.

I then entered the phase of trying not to care about what happened in the classroom. My immense frustration at not being immediately gratified caused me to constantly debate about whether I was harming the educational future of these students. As my self-esteem decreased, I tried to act as if I did not care. What does it matter if they learn this stuff in my class? They will learn it somewhere else. Who cares if I don't like these students? They don't like me.

It took three different students in the dreaded eighth grade to set me straight.

Justin represented a challenge that teachers encounter on a regular basis. He was a special-needs kid trying to make it in a mainstream classroom. He struggled with emotional problems and often acted out. An outcast, he constantly sought attention from classmates. His behavior led to ugly confrontations with St. Joseph's teachers.

Having no training in special education, I proved no match for Justin. He got under my skin. Justin did many little things, such as call out or give ridiculous answers to a question. These annoying actions left me asking why I had entered a situation where Justin and I made each other's lives miserable.

I did not know how to deal with Justin's disability, and my high expectations caused him and me much frustration. I decided to have a conference with his family.

> *Parent-Teacher Conference.* One of the worst inventions of the 20th century. Right up there next to the pizza drive-thru. Justin's grandpa decided to tell me his grandson is playing mind games with me. Of course, I cannot respond to this, having to be civil, being a teacher and all. So I just sit back and take it, and it hurts. I take it with the hope that his grandson makes it in the end and overcomes his

messed-up life. This job teaches you a lot about accepting a situation. You realize you can't do much about it. My feelings were especially hurt because it made grandpa feel better to hurt them. Come June, as long as Justin has a diploma in his hand, it doesn't matter.

Justin eventually walked away with his diploma, but my relationship with him declined as school drew to a close. Prior to graduation, he swore at me during class. By the end of the year, however, I had learned his tricks and usually handled them more discreetly. The swearing cost him the eighth-grade graduation trip. I hoped that he would learn that his behavior had consequences.

> Justin has to swear at me today just because he cannot live by the rules. I feel as if I've failed him all year. I don't think he's learned a thing in my class all year and that is really depressing. . . . Sometimes in all this I forget this is my first year and I'm not always prepared to deal with these things as well as I could. But that's a copout. I care too much to make excuses like that.

It would have been nice to have a moment with Justin when I understood all the frustration was worth it, a moment that signaled a difference had been made, but sometimes you don't get that moment, I guess.

As Justin left me searching for that unattainable moment, Ron provided the moment that would be my first-year turning point. Even if I could not be approachable or a friend, I needed respect from the eighth graders.

> Just about to go to bed, but realized I couldn't put this day to rest before jotting down some thoughts. Today could have been the lowest I have felt. Who gave Ron the right to throw books and temper tantrums and swear at me in class? I don't even know how to relate to that. It would be easier to get rid of him, but it's not going to happen. Must deal with it.

Before the outburst, Ron had been fairly quiet in my eighth-grade English class. He sought attention, but again, I did not know how to handle his ensuing behavior problems. Ron copied homework and cheated on tests. He was careful not to be caught red-handed, for he did not like confronting authority. In his mind, this was his life. No one was going to tell him how to run it.

Especially not a first-year teacher.

Until our February confrontation, challenges of authority did not arise. I worried myself with other students while Ron got away with a lot. On the fateful occasion, I noticed his homework was incomplete, and he erupted like a volcano. Throwing a book skyward, Ron knocked a ceiling tile out of place and then cussed me out. That was it. The make-or-break moment. My heart raced. My palms were sweaty. Nonetheless, I calmly told Ron to go to the office. It worked. Ron received a three-day suspension for the incident.

I decided to call Ron's mom and see how he was doing. I don't know why, but it seemed like the right thing to do. It may have meant swallowing my pride, but my pride went out the window quite awhile ago. She told me I was the first teacher to ever call and see how he was doing and that she was sorry for his actions. He would apologize to me after the suspension. Hearing her just thank me for seeing how she and Ron were doing, made me feel more at peace. Maybe if there's one thing I can teach Ron this year, it's the power of forgiveness.

That simple phone call created peace down the road. Ron did apologize three days later. He did not become a stellar student but now understood I was not out to get him. In light of my call, I imagine his mom reminded Ron that there are teachers who care about you no matter what. Upon his return, I allowed him the space he needed, and he behaved much better for the rest of the year.

Ron's mom thanked me profusely at graduation. During our mock eighth-grade year-end awards ceremony, Ron received the accolade of "Most Creative Use of a Ceiling Tile," and he, the entire class, and I had a good laugh. The award symbolized how far my relationship with Ron—and the rest of the class—had come. The situation never answered my ultimate question, but it left me with the powerful knowledge that I could improve.

Still, it would have been nice knowing I truly made a difference with one student.

Things happen when you least expect them.

"This class is a joke. Nobody takes it seriously." With those words from Mary, I now had fodder for tonight's journal entry. I refrained from telling Mary I have a hard time taking her seriously. When Mary starts to speak for others besides herself, look out!

If there was a popular book to be found in my class, you needed to look no farther than Mary's hand. My English class could not compete with a recent novel by some mass-market author. Mary read voraciously during homeroom, at recess, and in class. While accepting that I was no competition for Stephen King or John Grisham, I felt Mary needed to pay attention in class to one day enjoy the success of these very authors. Even if Mary thought the class was a joke, her report card grades indicated she needed help in English. She also needed a challenge.

When Mary did push herself, the sky was the limit. With an idea from my housemate, the next day I approached Mary to ask her to meet after school once a week. We would discuss her book of the week. I told her that I wanted to know her opinions about the plot, feelings toward the characters, and ideas about what could have been different. In exchange for her time and thoughts, Mary would receive extra credit.

Mary was taken aback by the invitation, although she gladly agreed to it. During those last two months of school, we analyzed books, and I provided all the extra credit she wanted. More importantly, I began to see Mary as an individual, not just someone taking up desk space. We talked about her hopes for high school, difficulties at home, and problems within the eighth grade.

Finally, I got to enter the life of a student. It felt incredible to make such a connection. Teaching literature and grammar was great, but with Mary I came to realize how to make the elusive difference. I needed to go the extra distance and develop trust with students. With a little luck, the students then open their hearts.

Mary poured hers out in a letter at graduation.

> I want to thank you for pushing me to learn and enjoy learning. You didn't let me slack off. You always made me feel that making myself learn is a great reward. I appreciate you making me feel that my reading is important because most people say it's just wasting time.
>
> You are a good teacher.
> Mary

My experience with Mary helped make my last journal entry more hopeful.

> I asked myself at the start what I was looking for. It will take awhile to sort through the wreckage and see if any good was done. It probably was in some cases, but in good conscience, I don't know if that applies to the majority. The real question remains, however: "Is one really enough?" If the answer is yes, well, then I guess I did find it. Deep down, I now know the answer is yes.

### Author Biography

*After finishing two years at St. Joseph's, I took some time off to sort through my experience there. What I concluded was that putting teaching aside for now would be best. A little distance was needed to see if I missed it and to discern whether I could dedicate myself to this vocation in the future.*

*Having majored in journalism, I often felt like I was going against the grain by teaching. Writing is my passion, and I am currently exploring career opportunities in that field. Right now, I am an editor for a legal publisher and also freelancing for a local newspaper. It is good work, but solitary work. In truth, my best day in journalism will never match what could be accomplished in the classroom.*

*Therein lies my conundrum. Ultimately, I will have to decide just how much to sacrifice if teaching is to define my life. For now that question has no answer.*

# chapter nine

# A Different World

## Chris's Story

*Chris taught eighth-grade U.S. history his first year. That year, he not only had to discover the ways of his new school but the ways of an unfamiliar culture. His reputation and career were put on the line when young female students made aggressive advances toward him, but he was able to come through unscathed by making himself less accessible to his students. Throughout the year, he also struggled and made progress with more typical challenges, such as increasing student motivation and establishing discipline.*

## QUESTIONS FOR REFLECTION WHILE READING CHRIS'S STORY

1. How was discipline a challenge for Chris?
2. How would you have handled the misbehavior in Chris's class?
3. What student motivation challenges did Chris face, and how did he try to increase motivation in his class?
4. What about relations with parents was challenging for Chris?

5. What were the challenges facing Chris with respect to teacher-student interaction?
6. What was challenging about Chris's relations with colleagues?
7. What knowledge of teaching and the curriculum did Chris lack?
8. What conflicts did Chris have with school culture?
9. How did diversity issues challenge Chris?
10. What was the impact of Chris's job on his personal life?
11. How did gender or sexual issues challenge Chris? What would you do if you were in his situation?

# THE STORY

The most vivid memory I have of elementary school is the last day of sixth grade. Just before we were to be dismissed for the summer, Mr. Fields spoke to us. He congratulated us on a good school year and for making it through elementary school. He then warned us unsuspecting adolescents of the trials and tribulations that possibly lay ahead in junior high. "I wouldn't go through it again for all the money in the world," he said. "The worst two years of my life." He told us of the insecurities he felt, the temptations he faced, and the feelings of unhappiness that plagued him. I paid little attention to his speech, for those things would not happen to me. I was full of confidence after an enjoyable elementary school experience. But come the next fall, it took me only a few weeks to realize the truth of Mr. Fields's words, as I entered a school looking more like a fifth grader than a seventh grader and had classes with girls and some boys who could pass for juniors in high school. Whereas elementary school for me had meant a wealth of friends, stellar grades, and high levels of self-confidence, my seventh- and eighth-grade years were characterized by frequent loneliness, subpar academic performances, low self-confidence, and constant self-doubt. I relished the thought of moving on to high school and leaving the problems of junior high behind. But years later, I would return to the site of my old demons, where insecurity and uncertainty followed me like bullies trying to prey upon a weak target. When I became a teacher, I decided to teach junior high. My reason was simple. I felt that knowing what I did about junior high and having felt the extreme lows that I did during those two years, I could help students face the same problems.

As a first-year teacher at Saint Peter's Academy I taught eighth-grade U.S. history. I encountered many new and interesting experiences and people in my surroundings both inside and outside the classroom. The population of my new city was overwhelmingly Mexican American. It had a seemingly small middle class relative to other cities its size, a large upper class, and a huge impoverished class. Thus, it was very much like Mexico, where families predominantly fall into one of two categories—those who are wealthy and those who are not. Saint Peter's catered to the city's elite families. It was common to find students with at least one parent who was a doctor, lawyer, or businessperson.

Saint Peter's students tended to be extremely competitive about grades; the majority of them aimed to make a 90 average or better. However, there was a premium on memorization and a disinterest in thinking critically. The students worked hard to memorize facts, but they often were frustrated and gave up rather quickly when forced to think hard to find an answer. They also complained about their workload, which sometimes made them seem lazy, although they really were not.

Education courses and student teaching had not prepared me for the unseen aspects of teaching—those challenges that cannot be learned from a textbook or a classroom lecture. One must experience these firsthand and learn by trial and error. I had to deal with the interest of adolescent girls, self-centered attitudes, and disinterest in social science coupled with apparent laziness toward schoolwork.

The biggest surprise during my first week as a teacher was the attitude and actions of my female students toward me. They were very direct in their comments and would say things like, "You're cute" or ask me if I had a girlfriend. When they heard that I did, they would respond, "That's too bad. You could do better here." At first—and I am embarrassed to admit this—the attention was extremely flattering. In fact, I even enjoyed it, given the lack of attention I received when I was in junior high school. Yet, some of the more direct comments embarrassed me.

One girl who took a liking to me tried to make my life as a teacher as difficult as possible. She purposely would not follow my directions, rolled her eyes in disgust when I gave an assignment, and muttered inaudible words under her breath when she passed me. For a couple of weeks I wondered what I had done wrong in attempting to reach this student. This was a great source of frustration until the counselor came to me to talk about the student's behavior. "She is doing this to get your attention," the counselor informed me. "These girls are used to dating much older men, sometimes seven, eight, or even nine years older." Men who are my age and older, I realized.

I quickly learned that not only were the girls I encountered not shy about being around older men, they were very aggressive. I found that they were also quick to be affectionate in a physical way, such as greeting with a kiss on the cheek or a hug (a cultural norm, but one that made a young male teacher ill at ease) or a touch on the arm. Furthermore, parents did not dissuade their daughters from such behavior. Dating much older men seemed to be accepted by both my students and their parents. For example, I coached a 16-year-old girl on the tennis team who was dating a 27-year-old man. And, just out of college, I was only about eight years older than my students.

There was a group of girls—about six or seven—who came to my room every day before school, during lunch, and after school. It was my policy to keep my door open at all times. I arrived at school early in the morning, ate lunch in my room, and remained in my classroom for about 30 minutes after school. I did this so that students could talk to me about any number of issues or concerns, including grades, home-work, or anything else they felt like talking about. This allowed me to get to know my students better on an individual basis. Initially, I had no reservations about the frequency with which the girls visited the room. There were always others students in the room (male and female) and the conversations were interesting; I learned about them and their families, and they learned about me. However, certain incidents started to occur that made me uneasy. First, the counselor came to visit me. "You may have a little bit of a problem on your hands," she told me. "Cindy wants to have a relationship with you—now. I know you have not done anything wrong because her friends have told me, but she went home crying the other night saying, 'Mr. Johnson will never see me as a woman, but as Cindy, some little girl that he taught. He's going to forget all about me when he leaves.'" The counselor told me that Cindy was angry that I had a girlfriend and was constantly referring to her in angry tones and with inappropriate language. Cindy also began to give me trouble in the classroom. She started to talk back, make sar-castic comments, and roll her eyes when I gave directions.

Then, there was a second disturbing incident. I lived with several other new teachers, and it was our policy to keep the location of our house a secret. We did not want students coming over to the house. One of my housemates and I were leaving church one Sunday, and we noticed a group of girls in the car behind us. We thought nothing of it when they followed for a mile; however, as we drew closer to our home, we realized that they were following us to our house. We turned into several streets, hoping to throw them off our trail. Thinking we had successfully lost them, we proceeded home only to find them right behind us as we turned into our street. They circled the neighborhood a few times and honked as they passed. Other students later told me that the girls would park in front of our house late at night, sit in the car, and try to catch a glimpse of us through the windows.

Undoubtedly, the biggest problem I faced with these girls occurred when a parent spoke about my actions to her colleagues at another school. One of my housemates taught at the Catholic elementary school nearby, a school that also employed two of the mothers of my students. My housemate warned, "Chris, you better watch out. I know you're not doing anything wrong, but some of those parents have been talking. I overheard Mrs. Richards in the faculty lounge saying how the girls had a crush on you. She said that maybe you were leading these girls on by allowing them in your room all the time and talking to them so much. She also said one of the girls caught you undressing in your room before practice."

"That's a lie," I countered, flustered and angry. "I had a t-shirt on, and I was putting another over it."

"Well, that's what her daughter said," offered my housemate.

Not wanting to be the center of more teacher lounge conversation at another school, I reacted by not allowing students in my room before or after school, and I started eating my lunch in the faculty lounge. I rarely talked to that group of girls anymore. I knew it was a harsh reaction, but I did not want any more false accusations floating around. The girls soon realized what had happened, and it led to increased tension in the classroom. On separate occasions, a couple of them left the room crying. Throughout the rest of the year, there was uneasiness between us. I never conveyed the anger, frustration, and embarrassment I felt. At the time, I did not know of a better way to handle this situation. I thought I could at least keep my good reputation intact by eliminating all informal contact.

In general, students at Saint Peter's come from upper-middle-class or wealthy families. This allows the students a wealth of experiences and resources. Many are extremely well traveled. Furthermore, most students possess enviable wardrobes, and those who are of driving age have nice cars. One does not have to look far to spot the Mercedes, BMWs, or other expensive cars in the parking lot. I would venture to say that the majority, or close to the majority, of Saint

Peter's households employ maids. How does this translate into problems within the classroom? Because of their home lives, some of the students are accustomed to getting what they desire without working. I remember having an eighth-grade student who drove herself to school every day in a brand-new red Mazda Miata, while I did not even have my own car at the time. Perhaps, this is endemic to present-day society in general where material possessions are more affordable. Whatever the case, I found that often my students were reluctant to work hard in class. Many of them gave up rather quickly if they could not find an answer immediately. At times, I would hear endless complaining about how hard an assignment was, that "it was too difficult" or "impossible." When asking for assistance, students attempted to get me to answer the question for them rather than help them find the answer. My students were excellent at memorizing facts, but when it came to more difficult assignments, such as critical thinking or essays, their performances were often subpar.

Because I came from much humbler beginnings than they, their reactions frustrated me. I often let my frustration get the better of me. Laziness causes me to become angry very quickly, and I sometimes snapped at students when they seemed lazy. Complaints and grumbling frequently led to conferences with students after school. I had never before been surrounded by so many people who wanted to get by with doing the absolute minimum required of them (and sometimes not even that). Conflicts arose throughout the year with students I perceived as unmotivated.

I also came to believe that the background of the students contributed to their self-centered and selfish attitudes. I was shocked by how students spoke to and treated one another and faculty members. Students laughed at the incorrect answers and misfortunes of their peers. Some students had no qualms about talking back to me or retorting in sarcastic tones. On many occasions, I heard profanity in the classroom. Perhaps this was due to my young age and inexperience as a teacher, and in this way they were testing me. As a result, fostering respect toward others became a major goal of mine, motivated by two incidents in particular.

The first incident occurred in homeroom. My homeroom was an unruly group. They liked to talk a lot, and I lectured on "proper homeroom behavior." One day, I stopped passing out papers to the class because the students would not stop talking. I just stood in front of class and waited for them to quiet down and pay attention. Finally, recognizing that they might be late for their next classes, the students quieted down and I began to distribute the papers. Under her breath, one girl muttered, "This is stupid." I noted what she said but did not say anything to her. The bell rang before I was finished passing out the papers, and the class started to file out, but I told them that they would stay until I was finished. The same girl rolled her eyes and again muttered under her breath, "This is stupid, he should pass out the papers quicker. I don't know why he's being this way." I finished passing out the papers, and as Michelle reached the door, I told her that she needed to stop by my desk for a short conference. I told her that I did not appreciate her comments, and I would appreciate it if she did not make such comments in the future. She rolled her eyes again. That was it. Unable to control my frustration, I gave her a lecture, not yelling or raising my voice, but speaking in a confrontational tone. "I don't know who you think you are," I started, "but I am not going to accept that type of behavior in this classroom. Next time you feel like rolling your eyes, you can go to the office and roll them until your parents come to pick you up at the end of the day. You have way too much attitude for an eighth-grade girl. You walk around here thinking you are some sort of princess and show disrespect not only toward me, but your classmates as well. I don't know how you are allowed to act at home, but in this class things will change. Do you understand?"

Looking away, she answered with a quiet "Yeah."

"No," I pressed on, "do you understand me?" giving her the hardest, angriest look I could muster.

"Yes, sir."

At the time I felt good about the encounter, thinking that the girl deserved the talking to, though it was confrontational. Instead, it only made her more withdrawn and resistant to me in the classroom. I knew I had made a mistake, but pride would not allow me to admit it.

The second incident of disrespect that raised my ire occurred in the lunchroom. My supervision assignment designated me to monitor the junior high lunch. Essentially what I did was to play parent to these students, making sure they were not too noisy, reminding them to push in their chairs when leaving, and prompting them to throw away their trash. After my first few periods as lunch supervisor, I noticed that very few of the students did throw away their trash or push in their chairs, even after my continual reminders. They would wait until I looked away and would sneak out. When I caught students and told them to go back and throw away their trash and push in their chairs, I frequently received looks that seemed to say to me, "How dare you tell me to do such a thing as push in my chair or throw out trash!" For the first couple of weeks, I stayed and helped the janitors clean up the mess. Then, grasping how ridiculous this was, day in and day out, I started a new policy. Those who did not pick up their trash or who had a messy table would help me clean up the entire cafeteria the next day. One day, one of the students was leaving and I noticed that his table was very messy: soft drinks spilled, ketchup on the table, and trays left at the seats. I told this boy and the group of boys with him to pick up the trash. They assured me they would, but as I turned to remind others of their duties, this group of boys slipped out the door. The next day, I informed them that they would help me clean the cafeteria that day.

Not surprisingly, they were angry. "Why do I have to do that?" asked one.

"Because you left a mess yesterday," I replied. "You didn't pick up your mess."

"Yes, I did."

"No, you didn't, and don't lie to me. I watched you."

"That's the janitors' job anyway," he claimed. "I'm not going to clean up."

"Yeah, you are," I informed him. "In fact, because of the way you've talked to me, the fact that you tried to lie to me, and since you don't think that cleaning up after yourself is your job, you can help me the next two days. I clean up after lots of people in this cafeteria and if I'm not too good to do it, then you aren't either."

As he walked away, he said, "My maid cleans up after me. I shouldn't have to clean up in the cafeteria."

The next day there were messages on my phone from two angry parents who said that I had treated the boys unfairly and that they should not have to clean up the cafeteria. They contended that lots of other students had left a mess and questioned why I singled out their boys. The dean of discipline backed me up and told the parents that the boys would also serve detention.

I also addressed the attitude problem in class. After growing increasingly frustrated with the overall attitude in class, I informed the students that they need not bring their books for the next week; we would not be learning history. Instead, we would work on how we behave, how we treat one another and the teacher, and how our attitudes toward school need to change. That night I developed a mini-unit that targeted the problem behaviors in the classroom. The first day, I asked the class why it was necessary to discuss behavior and attitudes in the classroom. Surprisingly, the students were quite candid. They knew why

I was angry, and their insights were similar to mine. Next, I told them that I wanted a better attitude in class. There were reasons why they were in Catholic school. If they simply attended the school to receive a formal education, they were in the wrong place. They could obtain "just an education" in a public school. Here, I informed them, we live by a set of values. More is expected here. Your formal education in math, science, and English should take a back seat to religious education. One attends Catholic school to receive a religious education, not a secular one. Thus, their priority should be to learn and practice the faith. I reminded them how lucky they were. Many families want to send their children to Catholic schools to receive a religious education. Many cannot afford to. Others have no options. As an elementary, junior high, and high school student I could not attend Catholic schools, though my parents wanted to send me. Finally, I told them that I did not care if they became history experts—that was additional. What really mattered is that we strive to become better people (myself included).

For homework that night, I asked for a page-and-a-half essay on why they attended Saint Peter's Academy. The next day, we discussed this in class. Sadly, only a few mentioned that they wanted a religious education. Most indicated that they attended the school because family members had or because the public schools were either "no good" or too violent. Over the next two days, we constructed a class constitution, we engaged in further conversation about how we should behave and what they should receive from a Catholic education, and I read to them. I ordered a book entitled *There Are No Children Here*, a story about the plight of two impoverished youth in the housing projects of Chicago. I read this book to show my students how fortunate they were. Many of the students were touched by the story (a few cried). The mini-unit worked. The next week, I saw a positive change in their behavior that continued through the end of the year.

In addition to inappropriate flirtations and student disrespect, I encountered another major challenge during my first year of teaching: My students were not interested in what I was teaching. Students questioned why they had to learn history ("It's boring"). Homework was often not completed. Even students who never missed homework in other classes failed to turn in history homework to me.

"Why do we have to learn about dead people and things that happened hundreds of years before we were born? We don't have to know this later on. How is history going to help us?"

Why was history regarded with such disdain? Saint Peter's students tend to show more proficiency in courses such as math, science, business, and computers, and in classes related to these disciplines. Their parents seem to be concerned mainly with their children's financial success and push their children to perform especially well in these courses. They seem less interested in English, Spanish, social science, and even religion courses. I remember having a conference with a parent after the first report cards of the year were issued. She noticed that her son had received a much lower grade in history than in math. Yet, her comment to me was, "I want to see him pull that science grade up. That's what we want to see him work hard in—in science and math." Such experiences were a huge source of frustration for me.

Overcoming student indifference to history required an injection of creativity into my everyday instruction. I quickly realized that I needed to make history fun for the students. I made some changes in how I conducted class. I became an entertainer, running class, at times, like a game show. Long-winded lectures and note-taking sessions gave way to increased amounts of group work and class discussion. I became more energetic and enthusiastic, telling students that eighth-grade history would be the best class they ever took. I only lectured for between 10 and 15 minutes and only for two to three days a week. Class consisted of three or four activities a day. I used humor; it became a constant in the classroom. We often started class with journaling about current events. I drew parallels between events that transpired hundreds of years ago and contemporary issues. We talked about movies, music, and television programs that had historical significance and others that did not. Because of my relatively young age, I listened to the same music as my students, which not only impressed them but also gave us some common ground for discussions. I read from a book entitled *Presidential Anecdotes*, which contained amusing stories of U.S. presidents. The students especially liked to hear of Andrew Jackson's wildness, Lyndon B. Johnson's crudeness, and Ronald Reagan's jokes. Finally, I made the class more student centered. One of my favorite activities was assigning students dialogues. I gave them some background on a certain event in U.S. history, and the students would construct a dialogue that might have taken place between two historical figures. For extra credit, I allowed students to perform their dialogue in front of class. With these types of activities, I found students enjoyed class more (they commented on how much more fun they were having). They participated more, their grades were higher, and I noticed myself having more fun in class.

I also think that students found history a boring subject because it is a heavily reading- and writing-based course. In today's MTV and video game age, youngsters want immediate satisfaction and results. History requires time: time to read, to write, and to think critically about questions being posed and events that have transpired. The culture of students today is much different from that of students only 10 years ago. I would say that the ability to focus one's attention is diminishing and I blame this on television, Nintendo, Sega, and other forms of entertainment that allow one to flip through an endless number of channels if uninterested or switch to another game after the current one has become boring or outdated. Consequently, reading and writing suffer. I relayed an anecdote to my students about when I was perhaps their age or younger, and my family would go shopping at the mall. I would go directly to the bookstore and read, sitting there for perhaps an hour or two and either finishing or almost finishing a book. My students looked at me amazed. Why would I do such a boring thing (in a mall)? Sadly, I think such occurrences are a thing of the past. Instant gratification is desired, and if something is not immediately fun, attention is lost.

These first-year challenges taught me a great deal. In fact, I often tell people that I probably learned more than the students did. The first year of teaching was an interesting one, thoroughly enjoyable and always unpredictable. Before I entered teaching, I knew that I wanted to help kids through some of the most formative years of life, the beginning of adolescence. I also knew that I loved the kids. A couple of years later, although my philosophy of teaching has changed a great deal, my motivation remains the same—I love the kids. Teaching can definitely be likened to a roller coaster—we all have our good days and those when we struggle. Yet the positives far outweigh the negatives. I can think of fewer gratifying experiences than having half a dozen students follow me around at lunchtime asking me about my family, friends, hometown, college, and, of course, girlfriends. Undoubtedly there is a selfish element to teaching. I enjoy the students' attention, and I in turn give them back enthusiasm and have genuine feelings for them all. Those challenges I have encountered in the classroom have forced me to look at myself very closely and identify those strengths and weaknesses that I possess both as a teacher and as a person. They have taught me patience, justice, and above all the ability to care for others. After all, when I talk with others about my students I always refer to them as "my kids." People often say, "You look too young to have children." I quickly correct myself and tell them I mean my students. Yet in many ways they are my kids, and I treat them accordingly. Perhaps, this is why dealing with first-year challenges is so difficult and at many times frustrating.

I have learned a great deal about the teaching profession in the last year. Sadly, some of what I learned was negative, although a great deal was positive. I learned that too many teachers enter the profession because they think it is an easy way to make money and have summers off. Too many count the days until retirement, and still others complain endlessly in the faculty lounge about students. Yet, the most important thing I learned (although I think I knew this before) is that a great teacher affects lives maybe more than just about any other person, with the exception of parents. I guess in overcoming my challenges one of my goals was to positively affect at least one life.

### Author Biography

*When I became a teacher, I knew that I wanted to teach for just a couple of years and move on to another profession. I enjoyed teaching a great deal, but there are still other things I would like to do, perhaps go into business or return to school and enter a doctoral program in Latin American history or politics. I would like to remain in education in some capacity because there are many problem areas that need to be addressed and because education has afforded me so many opportunities. With the exception of my parents, education has made me, to a large extent, the person I am and provided some incredible experiences for me.*

*chapter eleven*

# Learning the Hard Way

## Kelly's Story

*Kelly, who taught freshman religion her first year, faced many of the most common and serious challenges a first-year teacher can confront. She did not find herself in agreement with the administration of her school on some important issues and felt estranged from many of the other faculty. Discipline was a major issue for her, as was interacting with special-needs students. Often, the challenges she faced were everyday hassles, but she also had some more memorable negative experiences, including one interaction with a parent that made her feel very badly about herself as a teacher.*

## QUESTIONS FOR REFLECTION WHILE READING KELLY'S STORY

1. How was discipline a challenge for Kelly?
2. How would you have handled the misbehavior in Kelly's class?
3. What student motivation challenges did Kelly face, and how did she try to increase motivation in her class?
4. What types of individual differences increased teaching challenges in Kelly's class?

5. What about relations with parents was challenging for Kelly?
6. What were the challenges facing Kelly with respect to classroom interaction?
7. How did nonteaching demands challenge Kelly?
8. What was challenging about Kelly's relations with colleagues?
9. What were the challenges facing Kelly in planning?
10. What were the challenges facing Kelly with respect to classroom instruction?
11. What knowledge of teaching and the curriculum did Kelly lack?
12. What conflicts did Kelly have with school culture?
13. How was Kelly's relationship with her principal challenging?
14. How was Kelly's personal life affected by her job?
15. What unconstructive attitudes and perceptions did Kelly have?

# THE STORY

My first year of teaching was begun as a labor of love and hope, endured through determination and grace. Ultimately, I will always remember it as a time of some of the most intense change, challenge, and growth in my life. You couldn't pay me to go back and relive that first year, though I would be a different, and I believe a lesser, person, had I not experienced all it had to teach me.

In hindsight, I can see that nothing could have readied me for what lay ahead. No course or theory could have paved a smooth way through that first tumultuous year. I would soon learn that only the work, and the students, would teach me how to do it. As the bell rang on that first already hot August morning and my homeroom sat expectantly before me, neither the students nor the teacher knew quite what was in store.

Though just a decade before it had come dangerously near to closing its doors due to lack of funds, when I arrived at my new school, enrollment was high, school spirit was strong, and the campus was on the verge of a new growth spurt. As the only Catholic secondary school in a vast diocese, it drew from a diverse population. The parking lot was packed with the more affluent students' Jeeps and Mustangs, yet at the same time many other students were bussed in daily. Racially, the students were a diverse group—though predominantly white, African, Caribbean, Latino, Asian, and Indian American students made up a strong minority. In contrast, the religious background was homogenous, for more than 75% of the 1,300 students came from Catholic homes.

Marian was bigger than any high school I had ever attended or visited, and its size produced a sense of potential chaos, with control maintained by strict rules and supervision for both students and faculty. The uniform the students wore was conservative and rigid, and this outward control was reflected, continued, and expected in classroom conduct. Student deviation from the school and individual faculty rules was met with detentions after school and visits to the serious, deep-voiced dean of discipline. As for faculty, we were required to turn in lesson plans each week and work under the supervision of the curriculum advisor. Since I was a novice teacher, my performance in the classroom would be observed and evaluated more than six times each semester.

All of these factors—the school's size and financial strength; the students' ethnic and economic diversity and shared Judeo-Christian belief system; and the overall strict code of behavior—made for an academically rigorous and athletically competitive institution. However, sports could often seem to challenge or overshadow the importance of coursework, and though school spirit was relatively strong, a sense of community was not. The large and largely ununified faculty felt itself caught between often unwieldy students and an adversarial administration. As I entered the faculty ranks, I soon perceived the underlying attitude of us against them.

# First Impressions

I was thankful that I had only one course to plan: freshman religion. I taught six sections of this class on Christian morality and Church doctrine. Although I would have liked to teach English, which had been my major in college, freshman religion would give me good and much-needed experience at presenting material in a straightforward manner. More importantly, I hoped it would afford me the opportunity to really talk with and get to know my 150 students on a spiritual level.

To help me get started, before the school year began Marian provided me with a mentor to help guide my instruction. At first I found Helen, who had taught the same course for the past 15 years, to be an understanding advisor and supporter. As I had been encouraged to do, I borrowed from her well-structured lesson plans, following her lead by teaching the same units in the same order, and using a similar testing format to reinforce the material. As I matched her pace and met with her on a regular basis to ask for advice, in those first months Helen helped me to deal with the academic challenge of presenting the terminology and concepts within my preset curriculum.

However, as is true for most teachers, my responsibilities did not end when I left the classroom. All of the teachers at Marian were required to help out with at least one extracurricular club or sport. I, along with a veteran faculty member, was in charge of running the school's concession stand. We maintained a club of dedicated girls who worked at all the home football and basketball games. This required that we spend anywhere from one to seven hours a week scheduling workers, holding club meetings, and selling popcorn and candy to our loyal fans. Although I enjoyed getting to know the girls and interacting with them in a casual setting, the time that it took away from my social life and preparation time was difficult to part with.

The first day of school was one of the most anxiously anticipated days of my life to that date. Some aspects stay vividly in my mind. For example, I remember not sleeping the night before. And I remember planning my first-day speech as carefully as my first-day outfit, both designed to convince my students that I knew what I was doing. Of course, I also remember this feeling of certainty evaporate as my first class sat staring expectantly up at me at the front of the room. I was paralyzed by fear, daunted by the seemingly simple task of surviving the next 40 minutes, let alone five more classes in a row. I don't remember much from that point on; I only know that I managed on a sort of automatic pilot. The stunned and nervous freshmen were scared silent, and I survived my first day of teaching high school.

At the end of the day, after the final bell rang and I sank with relief into one of the students' uncomfortable chairs, I could do nothing but marvel. It was unfathomable that the administration had enough faith in me to hand these kids over to my care, no questions asked. Unlike my friends who had pursued jobs in the business world, there would be no training period for me. I would not have to work my way up through the ranks to finally prove myself worthy and capable of the title "teacher." It was my first day on the job, and I was the boss.

In those first few days and weeks, I was overwhelmed by the responsibility of overseeing what 150 kids learned each day. While only eight years older than my students, I was the captain of the ship, utterly in command of the direction we would travel, the pace we would take. So why did I feel like we were on a makeshift raft being carried along by a powerful, unpredictable current? I knew that I was supposed to be in control, so why did I feel so powerless?

As I drove to school each morning, I grew more and more anxious as I neared the campus. Even on days when my lesson plans were done and papers graded, I knew the day would hold untold conflicts. They couldn't be avoided, only met and dealt with. At any given moment a student might talk back, act out, or question my authority in any number of ways. My worries stemmed from an utter lack of confidence that I would know how to handle, diffuse, or manage the situations that would arise in my classroom.

I felt a chasm open up between my students and myself. They could and were expected to slip up, to fumble, but I felt that it was my job to have all the answers to their questions, the perfect response to any challenge of my authority. If I wasn't ready to teach that day, I couldn't just skip or postpone class. The kids might stay home sick or forget their homework, but if I didn't have a lesson plan, I had no excuse, no recourse. If they found out that I didn't know it all, their confidence in me would plummet and I would be exposed as the fraud I felt myself to be. I was a kid in adult's clothing.

Though I felt like an imposter in the classroom, I was equally uncomfortable in the teacher's lounge. Almost all the other faculty members were at least 20 years older, many with kids my own age, and yet I was expected to call them by their first names. Could they really ever consider me to be one of their colleagues? I was as awed by them as most of their students were, and I felt all self-assurance drain away under their veteran gazes.

# COMMUNITY

At school I felt left out. I wasn't 14 like the students, and I wasn't 40 like most of the faculty; it seemed I didn't fit in anywhere. Thankfully I could return home at the end of the day and find three housemates who were the same age and dealing with the same issues. We stayed up until two in the morning pulling together resources for the next day. We had grading parties and laughed at stories of how idealistic lesson plans, brilliant in theory, had gone terribly awry in practice. And we listened to each other's problems and commiserated in a way that only other first-year teachers could.

I don't know how I would have survived without this companionship. They buoyed me up when I felt I couldn't drag myself out of bed and challenged me to laugh at and learn from my failures. At our best, we provided a surrogate family and a sounding board for one another.

One of the times we often sought to bolster one another's flagging spirits was at the dinner table. Soon after school began, we noticed that our dinner conversation tended to focus almost exclusively on the bad experiences in our classrooms that day. It was cathartic and comforting to vent frustration, anger, and disappointment with ourselves and our students. However, these meals threatened to degenerate into unproductive gripe fests if we let them. When we recognized this one evening, we decided to set a ground rule for dinnertime. Each of us had to share at least one good thing that had happened in our lives and classrooms that day, no matter how small or insignificant it seemed in relation to our struggles. In this way we encouraged each other to keep our attitudes positive and our hopes up. Knowing that I would have to tell my housemates about it, I began opening myself up to every good experience in my classroom, noting them, and remembering them.

However, there were a few drawbacks to this living arrangement. Put four people together, each submerged in and struggling with the same demanding career, and the air becomes so charged with talk and thoughts of teaching that there can be room for nothing else. Upon returning from a tough day at school, when all I wanted to do was escape, the sight of someone else's grade book wouldn't let me forget it. And the loneliness I experienced at school could not be fully alleviated at home. While we grew to love each other, each of us was missing home and grieving, in a way, for our old friends, family, and the security and lighthearted lifestyle of our undergrad days.

## LESSONS LEARNED THE HARD WAY

Thomas Carlyle once wrote, "Experience is the best of school masters, only the school fees are heavy." My experience as a first-year teacher was full of challenges. Each day presented me with a new lesson in how to deal with obstacles, create opportunities, celebrate small victories, and forgive my failings. Sometimes I was a quick study, but more often I felt myself running into the same brick walls again and again.

The goal I had set for myself was clear in its simplicity, though ultimately unachievable in its scope. All I wanted to do was engage my students' minds and hearts. What could be so difficult about that? Like most first-year teachers, I had the best of intentions. There was only one problem. I was dealing with free agents, all of whom had their own agendas for the 40 minutes we would spend together each day.

Once I settled into the routines and rhythms of high school, my three main stumbling blocks soon took shape.

The first was the one aspect of teaching I'd feared the most: *discipline.* Of course I'd heard the old adage, "Don't smile until Christmas." Maybe if I could have done that, some of my kids would not have pushed me as far as they did, or tried to. However, it was simply not in my character to try to rule with an iron fist, to impose order through fear.

All my education courses had reassured me that if I would just make my lesson plans entertaining and relevant, the students would sit rapt and on task. This made perfect sense to me. After all, while I hadn't loved every minute of high school, I always enjoyed learning and found it relatively easy to pay attention and live by my teachers' rules. If I was fair and fun, open and accepting, why wouldn't my kids comply?

Well, my education classes hadn't taught me one important truth. Teenagers are like horses; they can smell fear. While I wasn't quite afraid of my students, I lacked the confidence that I could rein them in when they decided to get out of hand. I soon discovered that no matter how riveting the lesson plan, it was often much more fun and challenging to try and make Miss Caplan lose it.

Five of my six classes had a pretty even share of good and bad days. In each there were one or two students who presented behavior problems by acting out or talking back. Sometimes they succeeded in winning the others over to the dark side, but by making calls home, taking the time to talk one-on-one after class, and handing out occasional punishments, I could restrain the ringleaders, if only for the time being. With vigilance, I could maintain some semblance of order without raising my voice or making constant threats. Somehow we managed to arrive at an unspoken truce, and learning generally went on uninterrupted.

And then there was that sixth class.

In hindsight, these students were not actually any more unruly than the kids in my other classes, at least not on an individual basis. However, as a group, they created a negative chemistry that was strangely powerful. Six extremely immature kids, the instigators, had been in school together since third grade. They had been torturing teachers for years, and I was no match for that kind of history and momentum. Religion class was just another arena in which they tried to outdo one another's obnoxious, rebellious attitudes and actions. And even the students who would have otherwise been respectful and compliant could not resist their pull.

My first mistake was to underestimate exactly how dedicated these kids were to disturbing my class and my peace of mind. For much too long I persisted in believing that they could be won over by sincere pleas for good behavior and by mercifully benign punishments. When it became clear that they weren't about to obey out of an innate respect for me or out of concern for their grades, I instituted a series of classroom management plans.

The first was a three-strike system. If I had to reprimand anyone three times in one class, they would earn an automatic detention. This worked for a few weeks and provided me with a little more control. However, like all discipline plans, it was effective only to the extent that it was consistently applied. This particular system required such constant, conscious effort on my part that it became an impediment to learning. With so many students acting out at once, I spent the entire class writing down names and assigning "strikes," abdicating my role of educator for that of umpire.

When this system failed, the next, much more drastic, one was simply to throw students out of class until they could behave. An ex-army drill sergeant taught history in the room next to mine, and toward the end of the year and my patience, I resorted to sending difficult students to him, even though I knew that this was a tacit admission that I could not deal with them myself. I knew that they feared him and hoped this would deter them from misbehaving. While this plan of action was far from ideal, it was a last-ditch effort on my behalf to redeem my class and reach out to the students who needed me and wanted to learn.

My second and much more devastating mistake was in taking their behavior personally. Instead of seeing the truth—that their demands for attention and control were about *them*, about satisfying *their* needs—I mistakenly believed that they really had it in for *me*. As a young teacher, I couldn't know that they were rebelling against the instructor, the authority figure, whoever he or she happened to be. Though at the time they seemed to hate me, now I can see that they really hated what I represented. I embodied the rules, the demands of responsibility, and a refusal to accept that they were as bad as they wanted to believe themselves to be.

In the final analysis, I committed the cardinal sin of discipline. I allowed the class to turn into a battleground. After exhausting my store of patience and threats of detentions and referrals, I simply dug in and fought. Every day, from bell to bell, we battled for control. The moment they walked in, we picked up the war from the point we'd left off the day before. On the last day of school, three of the students were still so disrespectful that I gave them each a detention to be served on the first day of summer vacation. While their friends went to the beach, they came to school to serve it. I don't think this taught them any lasting lesson or gave me the last laugh, but it symbolized to me that I would not give in and abide unacceptable behavior. I had vowed that even though they would not capitulate, neither would I.

Of course, war in the classroom, like any war, is unwinnable. We all survived, though none of us thrived. In the end, I finally saw that to them, it had been a game. They simply enjoyed pushing my buttons. If instead of taking it to heart I had refused to join their game, they might have simply lost interest in playing.

Within this war zone I discovered my second major challenge as a first-year teacher: the student with *special needs*. While the rest of the class raged out of control, one student sat quietly in his chair, hands folded on his desk, a stoic, blank look in his eyes. Brian wasn't just quiet; he wasn't merely shy. Rather, when I could take my watchful eye off the rest of the class long enough to notice, I could almost see the prison he was locked within.

I know that I neglected Brian, and there were many reasons for that. First of all, he did all of his work, on time and, if perfunctorily, at least to completion. And on top of that, he never spoke out of turn—never spoke at all, in fact. At first, I misdiagnosed him as simply introverted. I thought that if I spoke a kind, encouraging word here and there and then left him to emerge from his shell when he felt comfortable, he would do so.

Yet as absorbed as I was by the misbehavior that plagued the class, even I couldn't miss the warning signs that indicated Brian wasn't just an introvert. When I called on him to answer even the simplest question in class, his voice shook with something more than nerves and schoolboy anxiety. And, while he did his homework and took notes dutifully in class, Brian's test scores were surprisingly low. As I handed back quizzes and tests, he swallowed his frustration, burying it deep inside him where he kept all of his other emotions. Only a flash of anger would brighten his eyes for a moment, before the dull glaze returned.

In retrospect I can see that I simply didn't want to pay attention to Brian, and it certainly seemed that any and all attention from the outside world was unwanted. He didn't speak to anyone voluntarily, not me, and not even his classmates. When he was forced to answer one of my questions or those of other students, he was short and rude, and his responses had a definite air of superiority and coolness.

In a parent conference his mother expressed her own concern that he seemed antisocial and had a way of putting off his peers. After much diplomatic questioning, she finally asked me point blank, "Does my son have *any* friends?" I had to admit to her that as far as I could tell, he did not. After the silence of their telephone at home—no one ever called her son—and his disinterest in school activities like football games and dances, this did not come as a surprise to her. However, I could see the pain in her face as she was confronted with confirmation of the truth she had been suspecting and dreading for some time.

Brian's unhappiness was almost palpable, but I was so busy tending to the kids that weren't behaving themselves that I had little time to focus on a student who was. The breaking point came when I assigned a group project. I had hoped that a little cooperative learning would appeal to the students, who seemed intent on talking incessantly to one another anyway. I chose the groups carefully, separating the troublemakers and trying to pair them with the few relatively responsible students I had left. Brian, the quietest and most serious student, was grouped with a ringleader and a student I knew to be marginally learning disabled. He would take on the role that most "good" kids end up playing to help the teacher maintain order; he would be a buffer.

Both my hopes and my intentions were good. After all, maybe Brian would open up in this small group, practice socializing, and find a level on which he could interact. And maybe the other two students would buckle down to business and follow Brian's studious example. Or, as I would soon see, maybe this would be the proverbial straw that broke the camel's back.

The day came for the groups to present their projects. Before class began, Brian approached me and whispered simply, "We can't give our presentation. It's not done." I asked him why, but all he could do was repeat again and again, "We can't do it." Having watched his group members goof off the day before, I now felt my frustration rise.

"Why is this the first I've heard of this? I told everyone yesterday that it was up to all of you to insure that each individual within the group completed his or her task. You've had plenty of time, and I can't make an exception after your group members clearly ignored my warning. Do the best that you can," was all I could weakly offer as a consolation. I was tired of being taken advantage of by the entire class, and I knew that an extension would seem to reward laziness to the other groups who had taken advantage of the class time and worked hard and well to get their projects done on time.

I took volunteers until there were no more and finally was forced to call on Brian's group to come to the podium. The other two members brazenly admitted that they had nothing to show for themselves, as I had anticipated. My face flushed with anger and after questioning them brusquely, reminding them that their lack of preparation would hurt the whole group's grade, I asked Brian to present his part of the project. Suddenly I, and everyone else in the class, saw the tears blurring his vision. As he attempted to speak, he blinked them back until they ran down his face. His voice shook with humiliation and despair, stammering out a few lines before he shut down completely and could not go on.

Quickly, I tried to distract the class's attention by moving on to their homework assignment. Brian, once seated, continued to cry silently. His cloudy eyes stared out of his red, pinched face, fixed on a blank point in space before him.

That afternoon I spoke with Brian's mother a second time.

"Brian told me what happened in class today, and that he is being penalized for other students' mistakes," she accused.

I tried to explain the object of the cooperative learning assignment, which my education courses had promised would unify the class and encourage them to take ownership of the educational process. "I just felt that it would be unfair to make an exception for Brian and his group members after the time they were given to complete their work," I offered.

"Well, I would think you would take Brian's special needs into consideration," she protested. "I don't know why you would have put him in a group of such rebellious students when he struggles with so much himself."

"What exactly are his special needs?" I asked in confusion.

"I didn't want to have to spell it out for you," she replied, "but Brian has attention deficit/hyperactivity disorder and also suffers from narcolepsy. The combination makes treatment difficult, as you can imagine, but his doctors seem to have it under control."

I was speechless. Here this child had been sitting in my classroom for months, and this was the first I had heard of these health concerns that seriously affected his ability to learn and interact in class. All of a sudden, the glazed look in his eyes took on a whole new meaning. I had never heard of a student being both hyperactive and narcoleptic at the same time, and I could only imagine the medication his mother indicated was necessary to balance the two.

"Of course, Brian deserves special consideration," I conceded, and I quickly terminated the conversation, promising that the other boys' refusal to cooperate would not affect Brian's grade.

What I didn't ask was, "Why didn't anyone tell me?" Due to my lack of information, I had inadvertently caused Brian untold humiliation and anxiety. I knew how cruel and callous I must have seemed to him, and I resented his parents and the school for keeping me in the dark. The real question was why no one at Marian had told me of the odds this boy was up against. The only answer I could fathom was that he had just slipped through the cracks at a school with almost 400 freshmen and only one freshman counselor.

For the rest of the year I worked to deal with the challenges of including Brian in the class yet also understanding his unique concerns. I tried to give him as much individual attention as possible, and I fought an uphill battle to convince him that he could trust me. Knowing part of its cause, I found it much easier to endure Brian's icy demeanor and help the other students to accept him and refuse to be put off by his defense mechanisms. However, until the last day of school I struggled to walk the fine line of accommodating his emotional and learning differences while not allowing him to use his disabilities to manipulate me and excuse him from doing the work of which he was capable.

My third challenge as a novice teacher also surfaced in my dealings with Brian and returned later that year: *parental criticism.* My final test in accepting, evaluating, and withstanding this came on the last day of school.

Earlier that day, as my notorious sixth period was finishing up their final exam, the three most poorly behaved students made their last stand of rebellion. They had finished the test and were getting noisier by the second. When they went so far as to wad up their review sheets and begin hurling them across the room at one another, I decided that even though it would be easier to ignore this, I had to take action. Other kids looked up from their exams with irritated and worried faces. With feigned calm, I wrote each of the instigators a detention to be served the next day, which also happened to be the first day of summer vacation.

Needless to say, they were aghast, though they each vowed they would not serve their punishment. After class I made what I thought would be three very difficult calls home to three disgruntled parents.

To my surprise, the first two parents I called, both of whom I had been in contact with numerous times to get support in controlling their kids, were sincerely concerned and apologetic for their boys' behavior. Each of them assured me that their sons would be at school to work off their transgressions, and one of the parents even thanked me for my vigilance and attention to her son's attitude and behavior.

After meeting with such reassurance and gratitude from these parents, I dialed the third number expecting much the same reaction. I confidently explained the situation to Alex's father, awaiting a supportive response. The one that I got could not have been more surprising.

After I had informed him of Alex's actions and their consequences, he replied, "Well, Miss Caplan, I think you should know that I have talked to several parents about you. Everyone says that you are a terrible teacher. You have absolutely no business being in the classroom, and the other parents agree."

My cheeks burned with shame. I couldn't believe the ease with which this man delivered such direct, unmitigated criticism, especially after all the time I had taken with his son. Had I had this conversation any earlier in the year, I most likely would have burst into tears and quit the profession for good. My own feelings of inadequacy rose up within me to agree with him, but another, smaller, part of me refused to believe his cruel accusations. I knew that I had made plenty of mistakes in my first year of teaching, but I did not deserve this total rejection.

"I'm sorry to hear that," I finally replied with what I hoped was composure. "Could you explain exactly what you mean? This is the first I have heard about it, and I would really appreciate any constructive criticism you could offer. If I have failed you or your son, I would like to know how so that I can be sure not to make the same mistakes in the future."

He was taken aback, obviously hoping to just attack me and re-turn to his business. "I really don't think that would do any good," he began. "You don't listen to reason. All I can say is you simply are not a good teacher."

I wanted to get off the phone more than anything, but I couldn't let him make such slanderous comments without giving me the chance to evaluate their merit or defend myself. "Please, I am absolutely sin-cere and would appreciate the input," I replied.

Reluctantly he tried to provide examples, though he could only name a few. He suggested that I gave the kids only negative reinforce-ment, which I knew to be only partly true, and he made a few more generalizations about my inexperience and immaturity as a teacher.

"I *am* inexperienced," I responded, "and your son's class has been particularly challenging for me. Can you give me any advice as to how I could have handled them better?"

He was delighted to offer his parenting advice and by the end of the conversation even told me that he had hope for me and that he was glad I could be so open-minded.

As I hung up the phone I felt as if the wind had been knocked out of me. I was hurt and embarrassed, but I also sensed a tinge of pleasure for refusing to allow the discussion to end on a totally neg-ative note. While I knew that there probably were other parents that agreed with this father, it was utterly irrational to think that they all believed I was a total failure. In fact, within the last week of school I had received several notes expressing parental thanks for the love with which I had treated my students. Back in my classroom, cards and gifts from kids who had enjoyed me and had thrived under my care sat waiting for me on my desk.

I looked dazedly around the teacher's lounge, hoping that no one had heard my responses and guessed at what this father had said. Thankfully, the only person who had taken notice was a kind veteran teacher with whom I was friends.

"Who was that?" she asked gently.

I told her and then summarized what had transpired. She rolled her eyes. "Alex failed my pre-algebra class, too, and made everyone else miserable in the process," she said. "In fact, he failed Spanish and English, too. His parents told the administration that they blame the school and that they're withdrawing him from Marian."

She smiled and patted me on the back, concluding, "I wouldn't take it personally if I were you."

I tried not to, but the words cut deep. I have never forgotten that one parent's scathing remarks, and I have had to work hard to accept the grains of truth in them and discard the rest. It was this difficult, final lesson in both humility and self-confidence that ended my first year of teaching.

## Looking back

Of every experience, both trying and rewarding, Ecclesiastes reminds us: "This too shall pass." In my first year at Marian I turned to these words often not only for solace and support, but also for a reminder of how precious and irreplaceable my time in the classroom was. Like each student seated before me, each day was unique, demanding a specific and often unknown response from me. On our worst days we persevered; on our best days we connected and laughed and even learned from each other. And though the trials recede into the past, a strong, true sense of my personal victories and the warm memories of my students remain.

Often I am tempted to look back on my first year of teaching and focus only on the many ways I failed. However, I need only look at the valentines and notes, pictures and letters, that my students gave me, and that I still treasure, to realize how much I won.

It was Thomas Merton who once said, "If you have love, you will do all things well." I have to disagree. Every first-year teacher knows that love helps, but passion and good intentions alone don't produce success. However, though love for your students doesn't guarantee an easy year together, it does ensure that all the mistakes that you make along the way can be forgiven.

### Author Biography

*I now have been teaching for six years. After spending two years at Marian, I married and relocated. I currently teach junior composition at a Catholic high school. Life in the classroom has gotten easier and more fulfilling every year.*

# The Courage to Do What Is Right

## Dennis's Story

*During his first year, Dennis taught high school social studies and coached basketball. He spread himself thin at the beginning of the year by taking on too many extracurricular duties, but he soon realized that his teaching and personal life were suffering as a consequence. He worked hard on his planning and his unconstructive attitudes in order to strike a healthier balance.*

## QUESTIONS FOR REFLECTION WHILE READING DENNIS'S STORY

1. How was discipline a challenge for Dennis?
2. What types of individual differences were challenges to Dennis in the classroom and on the court? Did he handle them well?
3. What about relations with parents was challenging for Dennis?
4. What were the challenges facing Dennis with respect to classroom interaction?
5. How did nonteaching demands challenge Dennis?
6. What was challenging about Dennis's relations with colleagues?

7. What were the challenges facing Dennis in planning?
8. How well did mentoring serve Dennis?
9. How was Dennis's personal life affected by his job?
10. How did unconstructive attitudes and perceptions make Dennis's first year more challenging?

# THE STORY

During my first year of teaching, my seemingly altruistic decision to become a teacher would lead to a deeply personal journey of self-growth. Teaching became as much about my growth as it was about my students'. I had to grow as a person in order to develop the courage to do what I knew to be right. Several challenging experiences during my first year of teaching forced me to reexamine who I was and imbued in me the courage to act. My ideas and beliefs concerning personal limits, objectivity, and identity, which I had thought would never change, were taken from their places in my heart and soul and put up for reconsideration. While this reconsideration and reexamination of self was a laborious and challenging process, it has resulted in greater self-knowledge as well as a more comprehensive development of the ideas and beliefs I hold sacred.

One belief that I held sacrosanct before I entered teaching was that I should always give completely of myself to any organization I represented. When I walked through the doors during my first weeks of teaching, I was intent on doing anything and everything to make my school better. Given my initial disposition, an encounter I had with a certain teacher would prove to be both disturbing and prophetic. The teacher, a 30-year teaching veteran who is an extremely talented physics instructor, was reacting to a conversation that I was having with another faculty member in which I was naively explaining that I wanted to be involved in many of the school's extracurricular activities. "That's not exactly the smartest thing to do," she warned.

Often, I entered the school and saw how many different activities could benefit from my assistance. I immediately became active in numerous extracurricular activities that consumed a tremendous amount of time and energy. I remember in one 36-hour span I taught, coached basketball, chaperoned the debate team, and took the Praxis teaching examinations. I also managed to drive approximately 450 miles. It was a very interesting two days. I woke up at 6:00 A.M. on Friday and went to school until 11:00 that morning. At 11:00, I drove the debate team to a tournament three hours away. After getting the debate team situated and waiting for my relief to arrive, I drove back to school in a fierce storm and coached basketball until 11:00 that night. I went to bed at 1:00 A.M. and awoke the next morning at 5:00 to drive an hour to take the National Teacher Examinations. After completing the examinations, I then drove four hours to the debate tournament to watch our team in the finals and then drove them home. I arrived back at school at about 1:00 A.M. I was so tired, I just wanted to find my car and go home. Unfortunately, I forgot that I had given another teacher permission to take my car home. Delirious with exhaustion, I called the police to report that my car had been stolen. Only after the officer had filled out the stolen car report, at approximately 4:00 A.M., did I remember that another faculty member had taken my car. Perhaps the whole weekend wouldn't have been ruined if on Sunday I did not have to go to basketball practice, plan for the week, and grade more than 100 exams.

While the whole year was not as hectic, most of my free time was consumed by school activities: teaching, coaching, and other extracurricular activities. What I didn't at first realize was that all of these additional responsibilities were detracting from my teaching. With respect to the aforementioned weekend, I not only did poorly on my Praxis tests, I failed to get all of my grading done, and my lesson plans for the week were bland at best.

Such adventures were also wearing on me physically. My physical decline was given additional credence in a teacher appreciation note in which a student expressed concern about my physical welfare. The student said that while he appreciated all that I did, it looked like I had lost weight and that I began to resemble a raccoon because the circles under my eyes were so dark. He also said I was less energetic in class and that my class wasn't as "fun." The degeneration of my physical appearance was also confirmed by my mother's attempts to impose a regimen of sleep and forced feedings during the Christmas holiday.

After the letter from my student and my mother's nurturing, I began to realize that I had limits. While I thoroughly enjoyed all of my activities, I realized that if I didn't take care of myself and continued to push well beyond what I was capable of accomplishing, I would burn myself out and be of no use to the students. This was a painful lesson for me to learn, that there is only so much that one person can do. I realized that I am not invincible and can indeed be overwhelmed. Coming to terms with my limitations was a necessary part of my maturation process. This is not to say that I began to "settle" or do less for my school and students. Instead, I realized that if I try to do everything for everybody in the school, I end up serving nobody well. The physics teacher tried to tell me this, that I must know myself and learn my limitations so that I can take on the appropriate amount of activities and teaching burdens to assure that my students realize success. This teacher, my mother, and the student were telling me that spreading myself too thin would be detrimental to myself and the welfare of my students. Accepting the reality that, at a certain point, I was doing less to serve my students by taking on more responsibilities was a difficult concept to realize and then act upon. Even when I was tired and knew I had too much to do, I would never act to remedy the situation. It took a near breakdown and outside intervention for me to develop the courage to change.

For the remainder of the year and the following year, I would sometimes decline requests for assistance. My ability to tell somebody no actually made me a better teacher. However it was more than saying no; I had developed the ability to budget my time and set limits on how much I could and would do. I no longer brought four hours of work home each school night. I tried to give myself one free day each weekend to do something that was not related to school. I scheduled appointments, meetings, and activities at times that were good for me and for the people I was trying to help. I just got better at taking care of myself while I was taking care of others. Because of these changes, I was able to devote more time to my classes, and I sensed my students were learning more and enjoying my class.

Understanding my capabilities as a teacher was not limited to the amount of physical energy I possessed, it also concerned how I utilized these capabilities to impact my students. One of my school's guidance counselors would always tell me that I wouldn't make it in teaching if I didn't have favorite students. He said that my favorite students would get me through the rough times in teaching. I would defiantly retort that "I do not nor will I ever have favorite students." The counselor would then just smile at me as I grew more and more flustered, because he and I knew that he was right, even if I was not ready to acknowledge this reality. Subconsciously, I liked certain students more than others. Did this mean that I helped them more than my other students? Such a thought troubled me. But equally as disturbing was the eventual realization that I actually was doing less for the students I liked by not being objective with them.

At the beginning of my final hour on my first day of teaching, a student bounded into my classroom and promptly introduced herself. She announced that social studies was her favorite subject and that since I was teaching her this subject, I would be her favorite teacher. She was intelligent and caring, and she exuded energy. For the first two weeks of school, this student was nothing short of spectacular. Her work was of superior quality and her personality was engaging. She was my favorite student. I would call on this student frequently in class not only for the content of her response but also for the energy with which she answered. Even so, she also had the habit of not becoming quiet when asked to do so and distracting other students. In class discussion, she would frequently dominate the discussion and fail to stop talking when other students had ideas to express. During projects, she would take the lead to such an extent that the other students would sometimes feel intimidated and therefore fail to participate. She would walk into class and disrupt others as she made her way to her seat. These are but a few behaviors that began to occur on a more frequent basis as the year progressed; however, I considered these to be minor vices that I could overlook since I thought she contributed so much to the class. How could I discipline somebody whose work I would often use as an example of what to do for the other students? Objectively, she did not miss a point in the first four weeks of class, while many of my other students were struggling.

While this student had discovered the key to success in my class, she also soon discovered that I really didn't discipline her when she disturbed others. Day after day, week after week, and month after month, the disruptive behavior continued to worsen. It was at this point that I came to the painful realization that I had done my favorite student a disservice. Because she was so intelligent and energetic, I thought I could treat her as an adult; however, I realized that she, like the rest of my students, had the needs of an adolescent. It was painful to realize that one of the students whom I cared for the most was the one whom I had given the least.

As a result of this painful realization, I vowed that I would care for this student in the manner that she needed and deserved. This began by disciplining her when she interrupted other students. I would also not allow her to dominate classroom discussions and began to call on other students for answers. Finally, I began to seek out other examples of exemplary work in addition to this girl's as models for my students. This method of attention was quite different from what she had become accustomed to in my class, and, as a result, she initially felt a great deal of animosity toward me. In fact, for the last three weeks of school she refused to talk to me outside of class and would respond tersely in class when asked a question. This was a second painful realization that I endured. Inside, it killed me that this student was no longer friendly toward me and that she would often remain silent. As I cleaned up my room on one of the final Fridays of the year, there was an ache in my stomach because one of the students that I admired most would be leaving my class on such bad terms. As I directed traffic on that day, I saw this student driving toward me. Given our relationship of the past month, I would not have been surprised if she was intent on driving her car within inches of me to express her disapproval of the treatment she had been receiving. As she approached, I was thankful when she slowed down and handed me a letter. She also thanked me for a wonderful year and promised to keep in contact. In the letter she apologized for her behavior and thanked me once again for teaching her.

Two weeks after school, I wrote this student a letter in which I thanked her for being a wonderful student and apologized for not better serving her throughout the year. This student had forced me to expand and redefine my understanding of objectivity. When I became a teacher, I had to learn that caring was not only saying yes, it was saying no. Caring wasn't necessarily doing things for others, it was helping others to do for themselves. Caring wasn't necessarily saying what a student wanted to hear, it was saying what a student needed to hear. And finally, if you truly care for your students, your actions and words might result in their not immediately caring for you. Even when I came to this realization, I had to muster additional courage to overcome the fear of not being liked

Sometimes, it is extremely challenging to remain objective when the actions and words of students and parents are anything but objective. Parents want and see the best in their children. No parent actually told me that they thought their child would be the next Einstein or Michael Jordan, but some of their actions during my first two years of teaching led me to conclude that they believed this to be the case. Athletics can be a wonderful vehicle for children to experience success. However, athletics can also expose the limitations of a child. Some parents cannot handle the reality that their daughters and sons have limitations and are not the next Mia Hamm or Michael Jordan. They place unrealistic goals on their child and blame the coaches for not enabling their child to reach these goals.

During my first year of teaching, the placement of blame on coaching led me to adopt a bunker mentality in dealing with parents. I came to believe that some of the parents and athletes were out to get me. I became suspicious and reclusive. I took the parental criticism personally. I didn't understand that I shouldn't take such comments personally because the issue is personal for the parents. The parents were only doing what they thought was in the best interest of their children. Parents were going to be subjective, and it was up to me to remain objective and professional.

I developed the ability to remain objective and to empathize with the parents only after some painful experiences. During a sports convocation at our high school, I went up to the parents of a junior who was on the basketball team that I coached the previous season. I complimented the parents on how hard their child had been working in the off season and how much I thought he had improved. The father responded by telling me that if his son didn't start varsity next year there would be hell to pay. The parent continued on about how his son had been a star at the junior varsity level and how he couldn't understand why he didn't start for the varsity. He said that as the junior varsity coach it was my duty to make the head coach play his son. After 15 minutes of this profanity-laced tirade, I left the conversation deeply upset. At home that evening, thousands of questions raced through my head. How dare a parent talk to me that way! Was the parent blind, did he not see the difference between the two levels of competition and realize that his son was not ready for the higher level? If one parent is talking this way, what are the other parents saying about me?

After talking about this situation with our head basketball coach, teachers, and administrators, I came to realize that I made too much of the parent's protestations. The parent was mostly just defending his son. While he was mistaken about his son's ability level, I should not have taken his comments so personally. I came to realize that it was important to remain objective and professional. I had to understand the perspective of the parents and be empathetic, even if I did not agree with their assessment of a certain situation.

The need to remain objective and professional is crucial for coaches. Only then can you focus your energies and the athletes' attention on what is most important. When coaches are objective and professional, children can learn that success can be achieved on any team, even on teams without winning records. Our high school basketball team was 6–20 my first year and 7–21 the second year. On the surface a difference of one win might seem to indicate a relatively equal lack of success. However, I was more objective and professional in my second year of coaching and could focus my energy toward helping the team realize the true measures of success. When I look back on the two records, I feel that the team accomplished a great deal more in the second year because of the lessons we learned, even though we won only one more game. Our team had been able to play to our potential and do so as a team. Even after the same father once again accused me and others of not giving his son a chance to succeed and made his son quit the team in my second year as coach, I was able to deal with the matter and not let it affect how I viewed the other players or parents.

I am thankful that I was eventually able to separate these initial occurrences from other interactions with parents and players, because I later had to deal with another upset player who was considering quitting because he had not been playing. He was not the best player on the team, but he was one of the hardest workers. He told me that he was upset because he didn't think that he was being given a chance to play. Even when the player became upset, I was able to react objectively and professionally throughout the situation. This player then began to develop to the point where he saw significant action on the varsity team toward the end of a very long and hard year. By the end of the year, he was a catalyst on a team that needed a lift.

I also realized the utility of this lesson beyond the coaching arena. For a teacher, it is also absolutely necessary to remain objective and professional at all times. In class or on the field, a teacher must realize that parents are not always the most impartial judges of their children. In spite of this reality, it is the job of the teacher to work with the parents and for the children with the utmost professionalism and objectivity.

### Author Biography

*After teaching high school for two years, I gained deep appreciation for what the vocation of teaching can do for teachers and students. To that end, I am currently working at the University of Notre Dame for the Alliance for Catholic Education (ACE). ACE trains committed and motivated young educators to serve in our country's most underserved elementary and secondary schools. I am also helping other institutions of higher education to create their own ACE programs. Finally, I am working with the community to develop mentoring and tutoring programs with Notre Dame students and local K–12 students.*

*chapter twelve*

# Another Window on Beginning Teaching

## What Challenged You Today?

All the stories or case studies of beginning teaching presented thus far in this volume were developed by having teachers reflect on their first year of teaching as a whole. Such an approach results in reports of some of the most memorable challenges, with the danger that it may not produce much insight about everyday challenges. Thus, as reflected in this chapter, we took a different tactic in the development of cases about beginning teaching in this chapter. We called beginning teachers in the evening and asked them to report the challenges they had confronted on the day of the call. We wanted to call each participating teacher four times on separate weeks over the course of the spring of 1999. On average, however, we succeeded in making contact with each teacher three times. By calling in the spring, we were obtaining data after the teachers had opportunity to settle into their settings. During each of the phone interviews, six questions were asked: What challenges/frustrations/problems did you face today as a teacher? How serious was each challenge? How frequently is this challenge experienced? What do you think caused this challenge? How did you attempt to resolve it? Were your resolution attempts successful?

What follows in this chapter are summaries of the responses made by first- and then second-year teachers. As a preview, what are presented here are reports of many small hassles, but ones that often are

not easily resolved. More positively, these cases include many examples of creative problem solving, in which the beginning teachers often
think well on their feet. What is also obvious from reading these cases
is that there are challenges every single day for the beginning teacher.
It is also clear that there has been much learning on the job, with several teachers commenting on how they were doing things differently
at the end of the year compared to their first days in school. There is
much in these cases about how young teachers must learn to interact with others—most often the students, but also other teachers, administrators, and parents. It is notable that the first- and second-year
teachers who were interviewed all had daily challenges. If teaching
gets easier during the second year, it still remains challenging day in
and day out.

Within the first- and second-year samples, the cases are ordered
by teaching level, from primary-level teachers through high school.
A few important generalizations that follow from these cases are taken
up in a concluding discussion section.

# FIRST-YEAR TEACHERS

## Abby

Abby taught full-day kindergarten in a rural southwestern community. The students she served were predominantly Mexican American
and lower to lower middle class, so her proficiency in Spanish was a
great asset to her and her students. Although she worked with needy
children, it was not so much the children that challenged Abby.
Instead, she was most challenged by issues pertaining to time and
classroom management. When she was having difficulty with student
behavior or attention, Abby felt that she could change the structure
of the classroom and school day to take advantage of her students'
strengths.

*Week 1*

On the day of the first phone call, time management particularly challenged Abby because she felt she did not have enough time in the
day to get through all the subject areas she wanted to cover and still
have time for centers. This had been happening to her more and more

frequently in the second half of the school year. Today was the second day in a row she did not have time to fit everything in. Although Abby found this quite frustrating, she was determined not to let it phase her and to go with the flow that day. Abby considered a primary cause of her challenge with time management to be changes to her students' schedule. She had been tapering down their nap time to prepare them for first grade, but they were having trouble adjusting and it left some of the students groggy. Furthermore, their computer teacher was holding them longer than normal. In the end, Abby still had about the same amount of time to work with her students, but the daily routine that they had practiced during the first half of the school year was thrown off by the new and unexpected alterations. This made transitions throughout the day longer and more difficult.

To add to the challenge of not being able to fit everything in the day, her students were having trouble paying attention and concentrating because they were excited about a big field trip the next day. Field trips and the disturbances they created were infrequent happenings, so Abby again tried not to let it phase her, considering it a passing inconvenience. She was certain, however, that her students' difficulty with attention and concentration was only magnified by the huge amount of anticipation the children had built up over the past month waiting for the big day to arrive.

Abby resolved her time management challenge by planning to postpone one subject area until the next day when students returned from the field trip. After cutting out that one subject, they managed to cover everything else. Abby felt she was very successful because they still had center time, and, although they were a little rushed, her students learned the concepts she taught.

*Week 2*

The biggest challenge Abby had on the day of the second call was with managing her centers: Her students were not putting effort into the activities they had right before center time, students at the block center were hitting and telling on each other, students were out of control in the playhouse, and they were not cooperating with cleaning up after center time. These issues were new that week, and she did not feel they were too serious. Overall, Abby felt good about the day and was sure she would be able to work things out. While having centers was very important to Abby because she felt they offered her students a chance to practice socializing and to be autonomous, she did not want her students' schoolwork to be sacrificed. Abby also felt that some of her centers were very familiar to her students from preschool. They liked them so much they would rush through their work just to get to them. Abby reacted by having students redo their work if they did not put enough effort or thought into it. She also made the decision to reorganize her centers. She changed the schedule so students would not be doing work that required a lot of attention right before centers and would still have time for cleanup afterward. Abby closed the block center, where the worst behavior and the biggest mess were, enticing the students away from the blocks and playhouse with Easter-oriented activities.

## Week 3

During the third call, Abby reported that changing the scheduling of her centers had worked well. Now, Abby was challenged by nap time again. The students were now down to only a half-hour nap, but half of her students were ready not to nap at all. These students could not fall asleep, so they wanted trips to the bathroom and water fountain. Abby was frustrated because the noise and movements they made bothered those who still needed to sleep. This challenge had been increasing in frequency. Every day, more and more students did not want to nap. Abby found this challenge to be particularly stressful.

Abby formulated a plan to allow students to choose two books to read during nap time. They selected the books before nap time so they did not disturb others by going back and forth to the bookshelf. Abby was hopeful that this resolution would help her to keep the non-nappers meaningfully occupied and the nappers undisturbed.

## Week 4

On the day of the final call to Abby, she was challenged because of mandated assessments required of her students. She was required to assess her students' knowledge of the alphabet, sounds, shapes, and math concepts six times a year. What she found most challenging about these assessments was keeping all her other students busy and quiet while she worked with an individual student. This challenge was not as stressful for her, however, as it had been earlier in the year, when she had been less experienced. Abby had already found that trying to assess students in small groups was not an effective solution, because such young children were likely to be distracted by each other, to copy, and to yell out answers. Thus, to make sure she was accurately assessing each student, Abby had decided to do her assessments one-on-one, which took 30 to 45 minutes per student.

To make it a little easier for her to keep the other students occupied while she did assessments, Abby chose to do assessments when a third of her students were with the computer teacher. She also had the students doing independent work but was careful not to pull a student out of something he or she was particularly interested in to do an assessment; this was Abby's proactive plan to prevent students from rushing through the assessment just so they could go back to working on more interesting activities. Abby found that her strategies for dealing with the challenge of these assessments was effective. They were going much smoother than they had in the beginning of the year, but she was also resigned to the fact that assessment time was always going to be somewhat of a challenge.

*Discussion*

Abby faced a number of challenges that were related to management: Finding the time to cover everything she wanted to cover was challenging, as was managing student behavior during centers, nap time, and assessments. More positively, Abby did not find any of these difficulties overwhelming, because she had a great sense of perspective. Abby realized she was becoming better at dealing with the challenges she faced and that doing some fast thinking on her feet could allow her to reactively deal with them. She was also very reflective at the end of the day about how she could organize and manage her time and classroom in ways that would allow her to prevent similar challenges from recurring. To her credit, Abby was sensitive both to the developmental constraints on her kindergartners' abilities and understanding and to her students' potential for improvement when given the appropriate environment and opportunities.

## Casey

Casey taught first grade in the urban South. Her students were primarily African American and lower to lower middle class. This was a particularly needy population that had students with many challenging individual differences for Casey to address in the course of managing her school day. Nonetheless, her challenges were compounded by the fact that this needy population was being served by a poorly funded school that lacked a full-time principal and a supportive working environment.

*Week 1*

On the day of the first call, an emotionally depressed student had challenged Casey. This student's depression caused him to act out in ways that disrupted the whole class. Casey attributed his depression and behavior problems to his status as a low achiever; he most often acted out and was upset when he felt he was not succeeding. These patterns had been so consistent that Casey had become used to the student's disruptions and no longer found them to be as serious a challenge as she had earlier in the school year.

Casey had a couple of strategies for dealing with this disruptive student: She would threaten to call his mother (and she did actually call her several times throughout the year), she would send him out of the room, and she would explain to the other students that it was important not to get him riled up. She had some good communications with his mother and found it helpful if a student had supportive parents who were willing to try to create some consistency between the expectations and consequences at school and those at home. Casey also felt that her strategies were successful because sometimes they worked to calm the student down. Furthermore, he had shown improvement over the year, as he had become less violent and better able to control himself.

*Week 2*

At the time of the second call, Casey reported that her day with the students had been a good one in general. There was, however, an uproar within the faculty over the firing of another teacher at the school. She and the other teachers had felt that they had been kept in the dark by the administration about the whole incident and the surrounding circumstances. All that they knew they had learned through the grapevine: The parents of a student had threatened to file charges against this teacher unless he or she was let go. The other teachers felt that the administration, in succumbing to the parents' threats, was not behind this teacher, and they were left with a sense that the firing was unjustified. Overall, Casey found this to be a very serious challenge because it lowered the morale of the teachers, who were afraid that something like that could happen to them as well.

There had been a lot of problems with the parents of the older students in this K–8 school; many of the older students had supposedly made up stories to get their teachers into trouble. Although this never happened to Casey, the negative atmosphere it created surrounded her. She believed this challenge was the result of a weak administrative staff and the lack of experienced teachers in the school. There were no strong disciplinary procedures established in the school, and teachers could not even send students down to the office when they got in trouble because the principal was seldom there, for he was also the principal of another school. To make matters worse, most of the teachers in the school were first-year teachers and were not returning next year. Casey coped that day with the uncertainty by trying to find out from other teachers just what had happened. In the end, though, it was just a lot of talk. The teachers still felt unsupported and left that day with no official report from the administration about the situation. Casey was hopeful that things would improve next year when they were to get a new principal just for their school. She felt that she would benefit from the opportunity for more interaction with a principal because she felt nervous around the current one since she never had the time to build a rapport with him.

## Week 3

On the day of the final call to Casey, she had been facing the challenge of recapturing classroom routines and student focus after a four-day weekend at the end of the school year. She was having difficulty coming up with end-of-the-year activities to keep students engaged, while her students were being extra talkative and were having trouble shifting back into a structured school schedule. Adding to the general chaos, one student also tried to steal another student's Air Jordan sneakers. Such difficult transitions back into routine were pretty normal after vacations, and Casey was more frustrated than anything else. The one student's attempted theft, however, signaled a more serious escalation of his behavior. He had previously been caught stealing only small toys like yo-yos.

Casey attributed the disruption in her classroom routines that day to a few causes: the students simply had been out of the routine for too long, they were confused because they were following a Tuesday schedule when they expected a Monday schedule on the first day back to school, and some eighth graders who were helping out in the class were also distracting. She tried to get things back under control by reiterating the rules and emphasizing that they knew how to behave and that school was not over yet. Ingeniously, she got the stolen sneakers back to their rightful owner without too much additional disruption and, most importantly, without drawing too much negative attention to the situation or the culprit. When the owner of the sneakers told her they had been stolen, Casey assured him that he had probably just misplaced them. She then had her students look in their book bags to make sure they had not been put away in the wrong bag. One student tried to sneak his bag out of the classroom, but she caught him and had him open his bag just like everyone else. The sneakers turned up in his bag, but he claimed that he did not know how they got there. She returned the sneakers to their owner and devoted no more time to the incident during the school day, although she did call the offending student's mother later to tell her what had happened. In all, Casey felt she was rather successful that day because she had remained cool and had diverted some of the even more potentially disruptive situations from getting out of hand.

## Discussion

Casey faced challenges in classroom management that she felt were enflamed by issues ranging from student depression to student theft. She also felt challenged when her routines were disrupted but was well practiced at reacting to these different situations. She, however, did struggle with developing proactive changes to her routines that would create an environment in which she would have to react less. Her working environment, which fostered an air of distrust about an already absentee administration, probably made it very difficult for her to receive the mentoring she needed to take that next step.

## Pam

Pam taught second grade in a needy urban community.

## Week 1

During her first interview, Pam reflected on how her students were often absent and often late for class. She felt that these absences were a big deal, noting that the students doing the worst in her classes were the ones who were absent. Pam was having trouble figuring out how to help the absentees make up what they missed, for the rest of the class was moving far ahead of them.

Pam recognized that some of the problem was that many of her students were in single-parent families. If the parent was ill, there was no one to bring the youngster to school. Then there were the parents who just did not seem to care about whether their kids were in school or made it to school on time. It was not that Pam was not trying to get through to parents. She sent formal reports home to all parents every Monday, with personal notes added to the communications sent to the parents of absentees. Typically, these personal notes were requests for the parent to meet with her.

Although one parent responded positively to the feedback Pam gave her, there were at least three other parents who were very frustrating because they were unresponsive. Although Pam recognized that it was difficult for some of the parents to find the time to come in for a conference, she found herself discouraged by the lack of response.

## Week 2

In the second phone call, Pam talked about a situation involving the classroom next door, a first-grade classroom with quite a few hyper kids. Sometimes when a first grader got out of hand, the first-grade teacher sent the offending child over to Pam's second grade as a discipline measure. Usually, it was one student at a time who made the trip to the second-grade classroom, but there were occasions when it was two or three first graders who came to visit.

Pam coped with this problem by involving the visitor in the ongoing work in her class. She also coped by visiting the first-grade classroom more often to make certain that the class was in line. On one occasion, when things were out of control in the first-grade class, Pam called the principal and a few parents of misbehaving children.

None of the attempted resolutions had been very successful. The principal was more concerned with keeping the students in school and with avoiding offending the parents. In fact, the principal would rather have the misbehaving first-grade students out of the first-grade class for half the day—and thus, in Pam's room—than risk upsetting the parents.

## Week 3

On the day of the Week 3 call, a parent brought in goodies for a class party without consulting with Pam first. Having faced the same problem several times previously during the year, this was not a big deal for her. Pam's resolution of the short-term problem was to let the party proceed, wrapping up a lesson more quickly than she would have otherwise. Her long-term resolution of the problem was to write a note to herself to make certain that next year she made very clear to parents at the beginning of the year that all special goodies and associated class parties be cleared with her in advance.

## Week 4

As the end of the year approached, Pam was trying to figure out how to end. She really had no idea how to do so. She was spending some time going through textbooks on teaching to see what suggestions might be there. At the time of the Week 4 phone call, however, Pam did not have a plan for bringing closure to the second-grade year for her students.

## Discussion

Getting students to come to school was a huge problem for Pam, one that included difficult interactions with some parents. So was having to deal with the discipline problems in another classroom, a challenge that probably affected her relationship with the other teacher and certainly affected her relationships with parents and her principal. Some parent actions, such as the unscheduled birthday party, caused Pam to be rethinking how she would deal with parents in the future. Pam also had her share of planning problems as a new teacher, reflected by her concerns about how best to wrap up the year.

## Laura

Laura taught a variety of subjects and grade levels at a suburban K–8 school in the South, including third- through fifth-grade computers, sixth-grade math and science, and eighth-grade religion. Her students were solidly middle class and ethnically diverse. She faced a number of challenges, ranging from problems with substitutes and classroom observers to troubled students and end-of-the-year excitement.

## Week 1

On the day of the first call to Laura, she had just returned to school after being out sick for two days. Laura estimated that she was sick about once a month, making this quite a frequent challenge for her. To make things worse, the substitute teacher did not follow the plans she had left. Laura found this to be a fairly serious problem because it made her students worried about being caught up and prepared for tests. The entire situation was trying to Laura's patience, but she assured her students that she would go over all the information they had missed as well as push back the date of the test. Such flexibility mitigated the disruptions caused by her absence.

## Week 2

The end of the school year was fast approaching at the time of the second call to Laura, and that only served to exacerbate the other challenges she faced that day. Her students were talkative and did not want to pay attention. Additionally, a number of students were not consistently doing their homework. She also had one student who had been unprepared in another teacher's class that day; in that class he had done his work with a colored pencil and not a regular one.

Such inattentiveness had begun in the last few weeks, and Laura blamed it on the nice weather and the students being tired of school. She dealt with it by talking with the class about the end of the year: They had things they still needed to learn, and she had things to teach, even though she would rather be outside too. Laura explained that if they did their best to pay attention, she would try to keep class fun by continuing to allow them to have the privileges of working together and doing projects outdoors. This did not work, and thus, Laura decided that the next time she was confronted with student inattention, there would be more direct and immediate consequences.

In contrast, the homework problem had consistently occurred once or twice a week throughout the school year. Laura was not sure what caused this, but she did not think that the situation was as serious as it could be. The students were able to do their homework well when they chose to do it. She would have been more concerned if they never did any at all or if what they did was poorly done. She tried to get them to do their homework by mentioning that the zeros they received affected their grade. But Laura was at a loss because this strategy had not been working and students continued not to do all of their homework.

Once or twice a week, a habitually unprepared student challenged Laura. He was a very disorganized student, and his mother indicated he had learning disabilities. While Laura had heard that he had not been prepared in another class, he came prepared to participate on the day of the Week 2 phone call. That was a plus for the day.

A paper airplane thrown by one of her students during an outdoor aerodynamics lesson accidentally hit an older student from another teacher's class. The student who had been hit, however, did not perceive it as an accident, so he took the plane and would not give it back. He was very argumentative with Laura when she tried to persuade him that it had not been thrown at him on purpose and that he should return the plane. The student who was hit was frequently at the center of disagreements, but Laura did not usually have to interact with him because he was not in any of her classes. What she did know about this student was that he had a tough life, and he had not learned appropriate ways of handling conflict. Furthermore, he displayed a classic characteristic of bullies in that he tended to project his own aggressive intentions onto others' actions (i.e., he assumed any action negatively affecting him was intended by the offending person). Laura dealt with this situation by having a quick talk with this student about doing what she and other teachers ask right away. He did give the plane back, but she was painfully aware that, while her intervention succeeded in diffusing the immediate situation, nothing she had said or done was going to help him or even prevent such behavior in the future.

### Week 3

On the day of the third call, Laura had been dealing with a challenge resulting from a field trip she had attended the Friday before. She had left lesson plans for the substitute who filled in for her, but she had forgotten to leave the test the substitute was supposed to give. The substitute, however, was able to work with Laura's mentor teacher to put together another test for the students. When Laura returned on Monday, her students were upset that they had not taken the "right" test and wanted to take the original test that she had prepared for them. This challenge was not a very serious one. She just told the students that they had all done very well on the substitute's test, so there was no need to take another one.

This mix-up had helped Laura come to the realization that the problems she had been having off and on with other substitutes were actually her own fault. She had a tendency to be forgetful when she had too much on her mind, and the plans that she would leave were sometimes not detailed enough or were not left in a place where the substitute could easily find them. A positive on the day of the Week 3 phone call was that Laura's mentor teacher had been a great help in deciding what supplies she should get for the next school year, and this helped to relieve more of Laura's stress. Her mentor's experience and support were invaluable to Laura throughout her first year of teaching.

*Week 4*

On the day of the Week 4 call to Laura, she had to switch her class to a different room because another teacher wanted to do an art project in her regularly scheduled classroom. In her school, the teachers had to share rooms, and this most often caused problems at the beginning of the year before the schedule was really set. The room change made her students unsettled, and this developed into a more serious challenge because Laura's principal arrived unannounced with a new teacher to observe her next lesson. While such observations occurred quite a bit, they did not often happen when her students were so wound up.

The first lesson that was observed went fine. The second lesson was disrupted when a number of students had to leave for band. The students who remained just did not get on track.

*Discussion*

Although challenged, Laura was a very reflective beginning teacher. She recognized her successes and failures and then considered what led to them. It helped as well that she had a good mentor teacher.

## Denise

Denise taught a number of different elementary-level subjects at a rural K–8 school on the Texas-Mexican border, including fourth- through sixth-grade science, fourth- and fifth-grade math, and fourth-grade religion, computers, and art. Most of her classes were mixed grade levels. The school serves a number of needy students, many of them Mexicans who cross the border daily to attend school in the United States.

*Week 1*

On the day of the first call to Denise, she had not been in the classroom. Instead, she had attended a conference on computer technology. She reported having had no challenges related to her continuing education as a teacher or her absence from the classroom on that day.

## Week 2

On the day of the second call to Denise, she had been struggling with disciplining two of her male students. They were not respecting adults, and this was very frustrating for Denise. She felt that she had not been strict enough at the beginning of the year, and she was now finding it hard to recover toward the end of the year. This was a serious challenge only because their disrespect was so frequent. Denise surmised that their behavior was due to a number of factors on their side, including spring fever, street smarts about how far they could push things, and a lack of self-discipline, and on her part a need to provide more structure for students who did not have much self-discipline.

Denise had been dealing with the misbehavior of these two students lately by pulling them aside and having one-on-one talks about self-discipline with them. She had been trying a lot to scaffold their use of self-regulatory behaviors. She often asked, "How can I help you to learn to control yourself?" And she gave them the opportunity to take ownership of the decisions they made. Denise gave them options for what they could do differently and what the consequences would be if they did not control themselves. Her students responded well to this because they appreciated the questions she asked and liked making the decisions. While she did not have to send them to the principal much, she sometimes did not feel that her strategies were entirely successful because frequently she still had to talk to them about their behavior.

## Week 3

On the day of the final call to Denise, a male and a female student had a yelling fight. It was actually quite a serious situation because the female student started crying and the male student showed no remorse. The whole class was disrupted. Denise sent the offending students to the principal's office.

Denise knew that sending the students to the principal's office alone was not going to settle the situation, so she spoke to both the female and the male student separately and then together. Earlier in the year, Denise would have brought the students together to talk over their disagreement right away, but she had found that one would usually be more timid and feel intimidated in that situation. With a little more experience, Denise had discovered that it was much more productive to give each student a chance to say what he or she wanted to say to her first and then have them talk to each other while she acted as a mediator. Ultimately, on this day, the two students were able to work things out.

*Discussion*

Denise's most important observation was that her students' behavior problems related back to how she began the school year. She let her students get away with too many things in the beginning, and now the students were walking all over her. She had begun developing an effective repertoire of strategies for instilling self-regulation and ownership of the classroom rules. There were now clear consequences for misbehavior. By incorporating these strategies from the very start of her next school year, Denise expected to prevent many of the behavior problems she experienced during the first year of teaching.

## Raina

Raina was completing her first year of teaching at the middle school level in a K–8 school on the Texas-Mexican border. She taught language arts, with her extensive background in Spanish very useful in teaching at a border town school. The school serves a largely middle-class clientele.

*Week 1*

The challenge that was on Raina's mind at the time of the Week 1 phone call involved a student who was to serve an in-school suspension. Raina was reflecting on the situation, in part, because she was concerned that students behave; she felt that unless they did, they would not perform to the best of their ability. The issue with which she wrestled was just what work to assign for the detention. Although it was the first time she had to deal with a punishment for this particular student, it was the eighth time during the year that an in-school detention assignment had been required of her.

Raina did not want to send the message implicitly that language arts work was a punishment, and she risked doing that by making a language arts assignment part of the detention. That said, an assignment was necessary, because there was no way that Raina wanted to convey that an in-school suspension was a holiday from language arts. She did not want to assign just busywork. The difficulty in deciding

what to assign was increased by the fact that the student was scheduled to give a presentation in class the next day during the detention
period. The presentation would have to be rescheduled. At the time of
the Week 1 phone call, Raina still had not resolved the problem.

*Week 2*

The most pressing challenge the day of the second phone call to Raina
involved two sixth-grade girls who were in one of her classes. These
girls were distressed because of rumors going around about them.
One of them had a crush on a boy a year older, and some of the boy's
friends were suggesting that there was an explicit sexual relationship
between her and the boy in question. In particular, the two girls had
learned that a number of boys had been talking in the boys' bathroom about what they imagined had been going on between the boy
and girl. The two girls came to Raina expecting her to do something
in response to the situation, but Raina was not sure at all about how
to proceed. This was the first time such an incident had occurred.

Raina was very concerned, for she was very aware that she was
teaching in a Catholic school. Such teasing and sexual innuendo are
not supposed to happen in Catholic schools, at least in principle.
Raina felt a duty not to ignore such misbehavior.

How did she react to this challenge? First, she asked another
teacher to watch her class, giving them an assignment. She then pulled
some of the offending seventh-grade boys out of their classes for 30
to 60 seconds, asking each of them a single question: "What did you
hear in the bathroom?" This provided a good deal of information.
Nonetheless, Raina still did not know how to react. She was concerned
at this point that it might be a very serious incident, involving many
of the seventh-grade boys. Also, she felt very tired on this particular
day, which increased her concern that she might blow it if she tried to
solve the problem on her own. Thus, she turned to the mentor teacher
who had been working with her throughout her first year of teaching.
In addition to knowing the policies of the schools, the mentor also
knew the potential offending students and their families.

Raina's mentor identified a couple of the seventh-grade boys who
would be especially good informants; both Raina and the mentor
probed these youngsters for additional information. What emerged
from the conversation was that the real perpetrators were some sixth-
grade boys who were trying to establish their manliness in the context
of a boys' room discussion, although it was not clear exactly which of

the sixth-grade boys had spread the rumors that offended the two girls who had come to Raina. So Raina and her mentor then talked to all the sixth-grade boys, making the point that rumors of sexual interactions were not appropriate for discussion at school—or at all. Raina felt that it was good for the sixth-grade boys to hear this discussion, a discussion that focused on how upset the two girls were about the rumors. Raina also felt that it was better that all of the sixth-grade boys hear the discussion rather than just the few who were responsible for this particular incident. Did it work? Well, time would tell.

## Week 3

In the week of the third phone call to Raina, students in one of her classes were preparing a full-costume production of *Romeo and Juliet*. With the performance day tomorrow, the kids were excited. It was hard to keep them focused and quiet. The problem was accentuated because the class in question tended to be social and boisterous anyway. Also, the physical setting of the classroom was altered, with the back wall of the room a backdrop for the play and much of the room now transformed into a stage.

Raina tried to keep order by appealing to the students for cooperation. She did not want to put a damper on the event by getting angry, although she did have to raise her voice a couple of times to keep the group under control. In general, Raina felt her approach worked.

## Week 4

Because of a special event in the school (a field trip that only some students took), only a fraction of Raina's students were in class on the day of the fourth phone call. This special event was a reward for students who had not gotten in trouble the entire year, who had not earned a demerit. Hence, staying back at school was a punishment of sorts for the students who remained in class. Raina felt she was in a bind.

First, many of the infractions that earned the demerits had happened months before. Raina could think of no good reason to remind the students of some petty infraction (e.g., chewing gum, wearing more than one ring) that should have been long forgotten. Even so, she had qualms about permitting anything really fun on a day that was supposed to be part of these students' punishment.

Second, Raina also did not feel there was much she could do in class without penalizing all the students who were absent. Her solution was to spend some time with individual students who needed help with particular issues. Also, even though staying back in school on this day was supposed to be part of a punishment, Raina let the students have some extra recess time. One additional downside to the scheduling of this special event was that Raina really needed to have some extra time to videotape the student production of *Romeo and Juliet*. Losing this day to the special event probably meant that not all of the scenes would get taped.

## Discussion

Raina reported challenges involving discipline and mild student mis-behaviors. She was also learning that discipline interacts with plan-ning, for she had to modify her instruction on particular days because of discipline processes (e.g., rescheduling one student's presentation, rethinking when and how to tape *Romeo and Juliet*, figuring out what to do with the students whose demerits kept them at school rather than on the field trip). Although Raina did not always resolve com-pletely the challenges she faced on these days, none of the challenges seemed overwhelming. On all four days sampled, there were events that called for flexibility and on-the-spot reactions, and Raina rose to those occasions.

## Chelsea

Chelsea taught seventh-grade science in a southern junior-senior high school, a suburban school with a diverse student body. She worked with African American and Anglo-American students from a whole range of economic backgrounds. She faced some very different chal-lenges related to instructional planning and religion, a first field trip, and a struggling student. A common theme among them was that Chelsea was quite adept at keeping potentially serious challenges from getting out of control by going with the flow and finding a way to shine a positive light on her students' successes as well as her own mistakes.

## Week 1

On the day of the first call to Chelsea, she had a challenge related to a hands-on science demonstration. Her curriculum had suggested having students manipulate and experiment with raw chicken wings to get a better understanding of anatomy and of how muscles, ligaments, bones, and joints function during movement. Chelsea had decided to use Kentucky Fried Chicken because she thought the students would find it less repulsive and would also be able to eat it afterward. Her idea was a creative one, but it caused her problems that she had not anticipated. Most of the students in the Catholic school in which she taught were Catholic, while Chelsea was not. She had set this science demonstration up on a Friday during Lent, without realizing the students were not supposed to eat meat then. Chelsea's students were quick to point this out to her and spent 10 minutes debating whether or not they could eat it. Chelsea did not feel she had the background to moderate this discussion, so she brought in an expert, a priest at the school, to talk with them about the meaning and value of the tradition.

In the end, they did the science exercise but did not eat the chicken. Although Chelsea had feared that this challenge might cause a mutiny, the students were less upset about not being able to eat the chicken than they might have been because their class was right after lunch. She had also been very successful in turning this challenge into a learning experience about faith for her students. Chelsea's problem was caused by a cultural difference between her and her students. Although familiar with the Catholic faith, she did not know all of its traditions. Luckily, the sort of challenge she had that day was extremely rare. Her own Protestant background, her sense of faith, her use of prayer, and her values were not extremely different from those of her students, so Chelsea was able to incorporate faith into her time with her students almost every day. She opened class with a prayer and fostered discussions about how the science they were learning interacted with their beliefs, especially during debates about cloning and creationism. Chelsea felt that she handled her challenge very well that day because her students were able to get two lessons in one.

## Week 2

Chelsea's first field trip was the day of the second call. She and a class went to the pathology department at a local hospital to see examples of healthy organs compared to organs affected by smoking, drinking, and bad eating habits. Chelsea did not know exactly what to expect at the field trip site, because the visit was to be directed by hospital staff. As the sole adult responsible for more than 30 students, Chelsea worried about keeping track of the students. Might an extra student sneak along for the trip without a permission slip? What if she lost a student while away from campus? Chelsea felt that her challenges on this day were due to all the uncertainties involved in any first-time experience. More positively, Chelsea was very successful in dealing with the challenges of the trip. Her students had a good time, and they seemed to learn a lot. The most satisfying part of the field trip was when Chelsea read the evaluations that her students wrote. One student stated, "After seeing the lungs of a smoker, I will never smoke another cigarette." She felt her job for the day was a success. The field trip went so well that she impressed her principal, who usually discourages field trips, enough to permit another teacher to take her students on the same trip.

*Week 3*

The final call to Chelsea occurred on a day that was not very stressful for her. One of Chelsea's struggling students did really well on a quiz that day. She chose to celebrate his success and used the opportunity to build his sense of self-efficacy. Chelsea called the student's parents to report the good news, making the student very proud.

*Discussion*

Implicit in all of the examples provided by Chelsea was the challenge of motivating students. To meet this challenge, she provided interesting hands-on activities, such as the use of fried chicken for a science demonstration. Chelsea highlighted the relevance of what was being studied, such as when she brought her students to a pathology lab to see people doing science-related jobs. Chelsea provided positive feedback to students rather than dwelling on what they did wrong.

## Luke

Luke taught eighth-grade social studies and religion in a southern junior-senior high school. He worked with African American and Anglo-American students from a whole range of economic backgrounds at this suburban school.

## Week 1

The first call to Luke occurred toward the end of the school year when everything was winding down and his students could not seem to pay attention at all. This challenge had been getting progressively worse over the last four weeks. Luke attributed his students' inattention to nice weather and student anticipation. The students could tell that they were getting to the end of units because they had begun reviewing. They were also looking forward to an awards ceremony and picnic, as well as a field day and field trip. Luke had to cut down on having his students do group work, although he preferred it, because the students were too noisy. Instead, he had them doing quiet seatwork. Luke had also given a number of quizzes to his students in order to motivate them to continue paying attention in class. He noted that this strategy had been working in most cases, for he had only a couple of students who persisted in not paying attention.

## Week 2

The Week 2 call to Luke occurred on field day, during which he had to break up a fight between seventh and eighth graders over a race. This was not a situation that he had to deal with very often, but he did handle it appropriately and effectively. First, Luke did not use physical contact to break up the fight. Luke knew that teachers should not intervene physically, unless all other options have been exhausted, because they can be injured, sued, or fired. When Luke saw students circling around the fight, he ran over to them and asked what was happening. His presence caused them to stop fighting immediately. Some students who had been watching told Luke who was involved, and he then asked all of the non-participants to leave. This was a good next step to prevent others from being hurt. He might also then have asked them to get another teacher to help him, but since the fighting had already subsided, Luke did not find that necessary. Luke then had the students involved in the fight move away from each other. He first took the two seventh graders involved aside and tried to calm them down and then did the same with the two eighth graders. He told them all to stay away from each other for the rest of the day. Finally, he reported to his principal what had happened. Luke felt that he had been very successful because there were no injuries and no additional skirmishes after he intervened.

*Discussion*

Luke's teaching illustrated how external motivators, like quiz grades, can actually be effective tools for enlisting student attention when internal motivators, like group work, no longer work. Luke also knew what to do when confronting a student fight, which is a frequent schoolyard misbehavior.

## Timothy

Timothy taught high school math in a solidly middle-class community and school. He had had a demanding first year, with discipline being a major issue in his classes. Timothy taught six periods a day. On most days, at least one class gave him problems.

*Week 1*

During the first interview, Timothy spent most of his time talking about the persistent discipline problems in his classes. He talked about some classes in which students did other homework while he tried to teach math, with as much as half the class not paying attention. Often, it was hard to keep teaching because the students were not only inattentive, they were also noisy, distracting other students. His first interview was filled with these concerns because on that day he had had a lot of inattentive students.

During the interview, Timothy reflected on a criticism that he had heard from fellow teachers: He was "too nice." Timothy knew that he permitted more talking than other teachers did and that he rarely yelled at the students. He knew the students saw him as "too patient," and some of them took advantage of his calm demeanor. He had let things get out of hand at the beginning of the year, and he was never able to regain control once it was lost.

Today, and throughout the year, he had tried to deal with the problem by talking to offending students one-on-one. He also contacted a few parents. He had had some success with such tactics, although admittedly it only worked with some students. One student, in particular, was on his mind this week, a girl with ADD who seemed to want to achieve but just could not overcome her attention deficit.

## Week 2

On the day of the second phone call to Timothy, his classes were dedicated to reviewing for tests tomorrow. Thus, the inattention today was especially frustrating, because it would affect tomorrow's test performance. Although he rarely yelled, Timothy yelled today. He also gave out quite a few detentions. He noticed that both the yelling and detentions helped some, with students quieting after being punished or witnessing another student being punished.

## Week 3

In the Week 3 interview, Timothy said that because of state exams, the schedule was reworked so that students would be available for two-hour blocks of testing. The result was that those students not being tested today had two-hour class blocks. If Timothy had trouble holding the students' attention for one hour, it was much harder to do so for two hours. He coped with the situation by varying the routine and breaking up the class time. He lectured for awhile and then broke the class into cooperative problem-solving groups for about a half hour. The groups came back together to ask questions and to work problems at the board. Then, Timothy lectured a little more, followed again by cooperative grouping. Several youngsters who were really rowdy were informed that they would have to stay after class, which seemed to deter others.

## Week 4

Timothy gave a test in two classes the day of the Week 4 interview. Although there had been in-class review for several days, quite a few kids said they were not prepared and balked at taking the test. They were trying to get the test canceled today in favor of another day of review. After some discussion, both classes quieted down and took the test on this day. It was clear to Timothy from the students' test performances, however, that many were not ready, that many had put off studying, expecting that they could get an extra day of review.

## Discussion

Student inattention was a persistent problem for Timothy, one that was apparent on the four days sampled and throughout the year. His difficulties with discipline led to criticisms from other teachers, undoubtedly creating challenges in his relations with other teachers. One result of the behavior problems was that Timothy often had to be punitive with students. He also had to plan classes carefully so as not to make the situation worse. Then, of course, he had to stick to his plan even when students resisted it, as they did in trying to persuade him to delay a test.

## Mark

Mark taught high school physical science and biology in a needy urban community. The teaching and vacation schedule at Mark's school was somewhat unique to accommodate a 12-month school schedule.

*Week 1*

At the time of the Week 1 call, Mark had just come back from an extended weekend vacation and missed two days of classes. Mark was uncertain about what the substitute teacher had actually covered and thus was not certain what he should be teaching and reteaching. He was particularly thrown by the first class in the morning, because going into it, he thought he knew what the substitute had covered. By allowing the first class to ask questions, he was able to figure out what the students had covered and what they had not covered, what the students had learned and what they had not learned. By the second and third periods, he realized that he needed to probe the students some in order to find out where the class was.

The class seemed more talkative than usual on this day, perhaps reflecting that the year's end was nearing. In fact, Mark had to tell most of his classes to stop talking two or three times on this day. Students recognized that they were near the ends of their textbooks, and there was not much more information that would be covered. The final exam had taken on an importance in students' minds, with some students deciding that if they did all right on the final, it would not matter how they did on the tests before the final. Some students seemed to think that they could cram for the final and do well, not recognizing the connection between what they learned now and the ease of preparing for the final and the likelihood of doing well on the final.

In general, at the end of the day, Mark felt he had coped reasonably well with the problems he faced. He had managed to teach the lessons he thought his students needed; he had kept the classes under control.

## Week 2

The day we checked during Week 2, Mark had little basis for complaint. He had given a test in his classes, with the only hassle coming after students finished the test. After concluding it, while waiting for others to finish, students were to be working on a review guide for the final. Quite a few kids talked instead, in part because many students had done well enough during the term to earn exemption from the final. Hence, there was no point in worrying about the review guide. In the past, when students talked after completing a test, Mark took points off their test score. Today, he just informed the students they were out of line, which was sufficient to stop the talking, at least, even if the students did not put any effort into the review exercise.

## Week 3

Again, when we checked with Mark in Week 3, he had had a good day. All of his classes were dedicated to reviewing for the final. The biggest hassle for him was that some students were inattentive during the review—those most in need of help to do well on the final. Three students, in particular, irritated him because they really needed help, and today's inattention was consistent with a history of inattention for them. One of them seemed to have a total lack of interest in learning, not studying for Mark's class or any other class that he was aware of. The second seemed more interested in learning but was not concerned with grades. The third had a complete lack of respect for Mark. She had misbehaved in his class all year long.

Mark's approach with the inattentive students was to tell them to focus on the review and be more attentive. He also tried to get them involved in the review by asking each of them questions. None of this seemed to work. After class, he had a discussion with the one girl most in danger of failing. He was satisfied that she at least knew how serious her situation was and did agree to see him next Monday, the day before the final, for any last-minute questions she might have.

*Discussion*

Although Mark had some planning issues (e.g., what to teach after he returned from a vacation, finding ways to get students to study for the final appropriately), most of his problems were concerned with mild misbehavior, particularly student talking and inattention. Although Mark certainly did a good enough job in managing students' behavior, he was finding out that not all problems can be solved completely (e.g., the student who was most at risk for failing could be helped a little but not a lot).

## SECOND-YEAR TEACHERS

### Nell

Nell was a kindergarten teacher serving in a suburban school, although it is a suburb with many economically disadvantaged families.

*Week 1*

At the time of the Week 1 call, Nell's biggest challenge of the day was attendance. There were quite a few kids missing from class, consistent with high absenteeism by some students throughout the year. Of her 30 students, 6 tended to miss one or more days of school each week. Some of these students were at risk for not advancing to first grade because of failure to attend for the minimum number of days required by the state for passing kindergarten. Nell had been frustrated because some of the parents felt they could keep their children home from school even when they were not sick. Nell's way of coping with the problem was to call the parents of each of the absent students and ask why the child was not in school. With a few of the parents, this resulted in embarrassment on their part, and they then got the youngster to school. Others either did not answer the phone or did not bring the student to school.

*Week 2*

The day of the Week 2 phone call had been hectic for Nell. At the last minute, there were many changes in the daily schedule by the school administration. As a result, many of the plans that Nell had for the day could not be carried out. Thus, instead of reading the story she planned to read, Nell read a shorter story to the class. Although Nell sensed the students needed a recess at midafternoon, it was not possible to provide one. Nell was accustomed to disruptions, for the administration of her school often made last-minute changes with the expectation that the teachers would adjust. At the end of the day, Nell felt that she had managed to squeeze into the revised schedule most of her goals for the day.

## Week 3

The Week 3 phone call came on the day of the practice for the kindergarten graduation. The graduation practice had been stressful for Nell because the students were very excited. They were very animated, not wanting to stand still for long. The kids also forgot the words to the songs they had been practicing for graduation.

One way that she dealt with the students' excitement and energy was to give them an extra recess. This worked somewhat, with the students able to focus more on the rehearsal after running around outside. Even so, with the graduation tomorrow, Nell was not at all certain that her students were well prepared for the ceremony.

## Discussion

Nell had some behavior problems (i.e., students skipping school, inattention at the graduation rehearsal). These were in the context of and caused by, in part, challenging relationships with parents. That is, some of her parents just were not supporting school attendance the way that Nell thought they should support school attendance. Planning issues were prominent with Nell as well, challenges that were heightened by the actions of other adults in the school community. With the administration changing daily schedules without advance notice, planning often had to be flexibly adjusted.

## Rebecca

Rebecca taught second grade in an urban school, one serving many children living in poverty.

## Week 1

The Week 1 call came on Monday evening. Rebecca had been away from school the preceding Friday, and the students were excited to have her back. The students also were wound up because of a birthday party for one of the girls in the class. As Rebecca reflected on the excitement of the day, she recognized that life in her classroom was much better now than at the beginning of the year. The class had been very immature at the beginning of the year, with lots of fights, tattling, and nasty remarks directed at others. It took awhile for this class to learn how to cooperate with one another. In addition, earlier in the year, a huge challenge for the class was to assimilate a student who had transferred from another school, a boy who was very aggressive and liked to fight back given the slightest provocation. The excitement today was nothing compared to the problems earlier in the year.

## Week 2

The day of the Week 2 call was filled with distractions. Rebecca's replacement for next year visited the class. (Rebecca was not returning to the school, having decided to accept a teaching job elsewhere.) The students simultaneously were excited to meet the new teacher and expressed remorse about Rebecca's impending departure. The student in the class who had been most frustrating to Rebecca acted out during the day, and the class was generally chattier even after the visitor left. Two fifth graders, who were the only members of their class that had not gone on a field trip away from the school, were also visitors in Rebecca's room. She put them to work disassembling a section of the room that had been dedicated to the rainforest theme that was the centerpiece of science and social studies instruction for the past few weeks. The fifth graders were hard for the second-grade students to ignore, as they moved in and out of the room. Between interacting with the new teacher, supervising the fifth graders, and dealing with the extra talkativeness, Rebecca had to stop instruction more often than usual, reminding students not to yell, asking them repeatedly to keep the talking down, and reminding students that they were to show the new teacher the academic work they were doing. By the end of the day, she was threatening to take away recess time if the students did not behave better. The result of all the distractions was that Rebecca did not get through all of the material she intended to cover.

As Rebecca reflected on the day, she realized, however, that the students had been much more talkative at the beginning of the year than now, although there was still the occasional bad day, like today.

Also, when she introduced consequences for talking (i.e., loss of recess), the students did quiet down. In fact, by the end of the day, the class was working hard without the talking and distraction that had occurred in the morning and early afternoon.

*Week 3*

On the day of the Week 3 phone call, Rebecca was challenged by a student who talked back to her repeatedly. It was the same most frustrating student who had acted out the week before when the new teacher visited. He always seemed to need to get in the last word, a behavior that was especially marked today. An assembly provided an opportunity for him to show off and be a little rowdy. The misbehavior today was particularly disappointing because he had been very good last week, except on the day the new teacher visited. Rebecca had thought she was making some progress with him.

As Rebecca reflected on the boy's day, she realized that he had been more of a little annoyance today than a major problem. Rebecca has a conduct contract with this particular student, with a chart on his desk that he must put a check on whenever he gets out of line. Five checks and he must leave the room. He only got to four today, so at least he stayed in the room. Also, he seemed to respond when she gave him a stern look. Rebecca recalled as well that the boy's mother was cooperating with her to encourage better behavior. That the mother was backing her up put extra authority behind the warning, "Do we need to go to the office?"

*Week 4*

The only real frustration of the day of the Week 4 phone call was with keeping the students on task. Rebecca kept the class happy, in part, by showing a movie in the afternoon. At the end of the day, she was generally happy about how the day had gone.

*Discussion*

Rebecca reported some mild behavior problems with the class as a whole, with them often more talkative than she would like. More disturbing was an individual student who challenged Rebecca and whose chronic misbehavior contrasted with the generally improved behavior of the class over the course of the year. Although it helped that the boy's mother was supportive of efforts to bring her son into line, the boy's misbehavior added challenges, including necessitating more communications with the parent and the school office. Teaching colleagues also put demands on Rebecca that day (e.g., the new teacher who visited, the fifth-grade teacher who had Rebecca cover the two fifth-grade students who did not make a field trip), but these proved to be manageable challenges. In general, Rebecca seemed to be able to make adjustments to keep her classroom running smoothly.

## Shelly

Shelly taught third grade in a suburban school that serves primarily lower-middle-class Anglo-Americans. This was also a Title I school, and the reality of many students' financial need created some tensions in her classroom.

*Week 1*

On the day of the first call to Shelly, one of her male students announced that he was going to be picked up from school by a limousine the next day. This touched off an argument in the class about whether that was actually possible. Many students thought it was outrageous and impossible and concluded that he was lying, and others were just upset because they had not been invited along for the ride. Shelly found this to be a minor challenge but reflected that the jealousy created by the situation could have led to a much more serious situation if the students had been older. She felt they were too young to be very conscious of the economic disparity in their classroom. Nevertheless, issues about money did occur about once a month, though usually not on such a grand scale. Her students seemed to be aware of the disparity only when it was particularly salient to them. For instance, students would become upset if they did not have money for candy and others did. If there was a willingness to share the candy, however, much of the tension could be preempted.

Shelly reacted to this curious situation by pulling aside the student who expected the limousine and asking him to try to keep it quiet because other students were jealous. She also pulled aside the student who had called him a liar and explained that it was possible that his classmate was not lying and that he might actually be getting a ride home in a limo, for a limo was within the means of the student's family. She also tried to prevent some of the distractions that might occur the next day by asking that he be sensitive of the other student's feelings if the limousine did not transpire. Shelly had success with this tactic because the commotion in the classroom died down after she spoke with the two students, and she was certain that this issue would only be completely resolved once the limousine actually came. If the limousine failed to show, she knew that there would continue to be tension among her students about whether the boastful student was a liar.

## Week 2

During the second call to Shelly, she talked about the class's field trip to a museum about Native Americans and pioneers. The source of her challenge that day was one of the parent chaperones. This parent had volunteered to go because she felt obligated to support her daughter by being involved with the class, but clearly she did not enjoy the outdoor zoo part of the exhibit. There were five other parents on the trip, and each was managing a small group of students. Because the one mother was so unenthusiastic, Shelly took over her group for her. This was not a very serious challenge, however, because she had another teacher on the trip with her. Shelly was accustomed to difficulties related to parental involvement. She often had parents who came to class but rarely provided constructive support to Shelly and the students. Some would just use the time to baby their child. In this instance, the mother's attitude was a little better after she took a side trip to the gift shop, and the group this parent was to supervise had a good time with Shelly.

## Week 3

Shelly had another field trip the day of the Week 3 call. During this trip to the zoo, some of her students were fighting and being mean to one another. Shelly was able to get the problem under control quickly and easily by yelling out the offending students' names to get their attention. When the students explained themselves, Shelly found that the student who had started it was the same one who had announced he was going to be picked up at school by a limousine a month earlier. The limousine had never come, and ever since then he had been getting into trouble a lot. It was very clear that he had self-confidence problems, and it did not help him that his father, while very indulgent, was not very reliable. Shelly knew that this student was going to continue to have more problems down the road.

*Discussion*

Shelly was lucky to have a good deal of parental participation. Her next challenge was to figure out a way to organize and set guidelines for parental visits to make them constructive, because she realized the importance of the home-school connection for the success of her students.

# Edward

Edward taught middle school–level language arts. He worked in a K–8 school that is in an urban location and primarily serves lower-middle-class Anglo-Americans.

*Week 1*

On the day of the first call to Edward, he had a couple of teacher-parent conferences. The first conference was to be with a mother who was often delinquent in signing report cards and paying the school tuition. She showed no interest in her son's learning or behavior problems. Both she and her husband worked, and while their oldest son was never in any trouble, their youngest seemed to be looking for attention that he did not get at home. He wanted to be the big man on campus and would give teachers and students attitude. He also had a good deal of anger built up and was ready to explode at any minute. The principal and other teachers wanted to meet with this parent as well, but they could never persuade her to come in. Although she had made an appointment to meet with Edward that day, she failed to show up. Edward gave her son detention, which would continue daily until the mother showed up. This was a rare challenge for Edward; most of his students' parents showed a great deal of concern for how their children were doing in school, and some were even valuable resources.

The other conference was with the father of a sixth grader who was not being very responsible. This student rarely did her homework and also did not deliver to her father a letter that she was to bring home. While this father showed up for his conference, he used the time to blame his daughter's teachers rather than to work on a solution to the problem. He spent some time complaining that Edward was the youngest, least experienced teacher in the school. Although this father was a teacher himself, he never thought to create or enforce any consequences with his daughter at home. As a second-year teacher, Edward found that he was able to put less pressure and blame on himself in this sort of situation than he would have during his first year of teaching.

The lack of consistency between the rules, values, and consequences at home and school was a common problem that Edward faced. Edward started trying to give the sixth grader some extra attention, tapping lightly on her desk to help her focus when she started to go off task. Because she was also having trouble handling the amount of homework given to sixth graders, Edward devised a folder for her to take home to her parents with a weekly progress report and whatever homework or notices she had received.

## Week 2

On the day of the Week 2 call to Edward, he reported that he had no major challenges. He did have, however, an annoyance. The female student whose father he had met with on the day of the earlier interview continued to have difficulty being responsible. Edward's attempts to help her were not very successful without support from home, and she continued neglecting her work. Although her father had the idea to send home a homework sheet for him to sign and did sign it, he seemed to disregard the comments Edward made on the sheet. One comment was that the girl should drop softball or at least cut back on practices, especially because she had been recently suspended from softball for missing two assignments in one week. She had just received another bad grade on the day of the Week 2 call, but instead of being motivated to put more time into her homework and studying, she went to help her dad coach the high school softball team. She spent a lot of time with her dad at the high school where he was a teacher and coach. While her participation in sports seemed to boost her low self-esteem a bit, Edward felt that it was definitely detracting from her schoolwork.

Throughout the year, Edward had been learning that it was counterproductive to carry the entire burden of his students' problems.

Therefore, the challenges of this day were not as stressful or serious for him as they would have been earlier in his teaching career. Edward worked hard to do his part, but he realized that it was unrealistic to think that he could fix everything on his own.

*Week 3*

During Week 3, Edward struggled to end the school year on a good note. The students who had followed the rules all year started to act as if the rules did not apply to them anymore. This was not a very serious challenge, however, because they were just doing silly, annoying things rather than actually challenging Edward's authority. They could have been hurt, however, when a football game accelerated from tag to tackle. In the classroom, Edward had to tell one student to stop being distracting to others, including the students in another class; he had been dancing in front of the door to another teacher's class while in line in the hallway. Another teacher down the hall also complained that Edward's students were too loud. Students were calling out more in class, and they were not really trying because they knew that report card grades were already recorded. The administration had mandated that finals be given before the last week of classes so report cards could be distributed on the last day of school.

Edward had tried to make his lessons interesting to keep students' attention, but that did not work. Because there was no detention so close to the end of the year, Edward could no longer use it as a deterrent. Instead, he told his students that he would take hours from their field day if they acted up, and this worked pretty well.

*Discussion*

Edward had some very formidable challenges in his teacher-parent relationships. He realized that whether his efforts to help his students were reinforced or hindered depended on parental support and cooperation. He tried some different tactics to reach out to parents of more troubled students, such as phone calls, conferences, and teacher reports. Yet, for all his efforts, he had little success. During this second year of teaching, however, Edward had enough experience to realize that, in some cases, he alone could do quite a bit for a student. This was a healthy perspective that allowed him to persist in facing the challenges of teaching without becoming demoralized.

## Susan

Susan taught science and mathematics to the sixth, seventh, and eighth grades in a suburban school. Having five different preparations every day proved to be a continuous challenge for her during the year. Susan did much to keep hassles to a minimum, including making certain she went to bed at a decent hour so she would have the energy to be patient with students.

### Week 1

In the first week's phone call, Susan reported that one of her classes had been making models of organic chemicals using marshmallows and raisins. After class, she found marshmallow smeared all over the overhead projector. This was particularly disturbing because the class in question had displayed many behavior problems this year, with vandalism and disrespect of other people's property common in the group.

As Susan reflected on the incident, she recalled some other problems that this particular class had encountered. This class lost a classmate to cancer the year before. Many members of the class still seemed affected by the loss. And another issue was that these students were eighth graders in a K–8 school. As the eldest in the school, they felt that they were above the rules, and they got away with a lot. Their homeroom teacher, for example, permitted chaos during the homeroom period and refused to discipline the students. Disciplining the eighth graders was often difficult.

Susan had the offending class again later in the day. She came down on them hard, scolding the entire group because she did not know which students had been involved in smearing the marshmallows. After the scolding, the students were well behaved for the rest of the class period. Susan felt satisfied that at least she did not let them think they could get away with damage to school property. However, no one ever admitted to the crime, and she did not feel as though the issue was resolved.

### Week 2

The Week 2 call came at the end of a pretty good day. Some of Susan's classes were in final exams. Other classes were preparing for finals. Much of the preparation for finals involved some extra worksheets, which required additional planning for Susan, but she felt the effort was worth it for the benefit of the students. As Susan reflected on her day, she remarked to the phone interviewer, "The more you plan, the better the day goes." She felt she had a good day because she had planned well. As Susan reflected on the days ahead, she recognized that the end of the year demanded little lecturing and more interactive work.

## Week 3

With final exams going on all around her, Susan found herself reflecting on the pressure of the finals experience in the middle school during Week 3. She recognized that the finals made the students review, but she was struck by a student who told her that she could barely sleep the night before a final exam. After much reflection, Susan realized that she did not fully agree with the school's final exam policy. It could put too much pressure on the students. Also, as the very last activity of the year, it did not permit any winding down and reflection time with the students, which seemed especially important to her, since she was leaving the school at the end of the year.

In recent weeks, Susan had also worried about what to put on the final exam. Should she make the exams really cumulative and comprehensive or easier so that they were an experience the students would feel good about? Her resolution was to make her final exams easier this year than they had been during her first year of teaching. Also, she adopted the school policy that exempted some students from the final. She did not require the students who had made high grades throughout the term and had a good overall grade point average to take the exam.

Based on the couple of sets of exams that she had graded already, Susan was pleased that at least there was a nice bell curve to the grading distribution. Even so, she was concerned that for one of the math finals, 5 of her 35 students did not have enough time to finish the test, each leaving about 10 problems undone.

## Discussion

Like all teachers, Susan had to deal with the occasional student misbehavior that was more than talking or inattention. Susan recognized, however, that such misbehaviors are contextualized, for example, she speculated that the marshmallow infraction was perhaps affected by the death of a classmate the year before or by the lack of discipline administered to the class, especially during homeroom period. Planning instruction was constantly on Susan's mind. It was a little more on her mind at the time of the calls because Susan's attitude about final exams was not entirely congruent with the school culture. Susan found ways to deal with the challenges, even though not everything was always resolved as she would have liked.

## Jessica

Jessica taught high school chemistry in an urban setting, in a school with many economically disadvantaged students.

### Week 1

Jessica's biggest frustration on the day of the Week 1 call was with getting her classes to settle down. The weather was warm and very nice, which seemed to increase the students' energy. Jessica felt that the "good weather" effect was especially pronounced in her class because her classroom had one entire wall that was windows; with the sun especially pronounced in the room in the afternoon, the afternoon class was especially aware of the nice weather. Although this really bothered Jessica at the beginning of her last class period, the last-period students did seem to be more involved in the class demonstration activity today than they normally were. When Jessica reflected on this last-period class at its conclusion, she felt that more good than harm came from the students' additional energy due to the weather.

### Week 2

Jessica's biggest frustration on the day of the Week 2 call was with respect to class preparation. She had planned much too much to do on that day and had found there was too little time to do it. In particular, she had a number of demonstrations that needed to be prepared so that they could be carried out safely and with everyone involved. Although Jessica had felt preparation pressure throughout the year, today seemed especially stressful. Jessica realized in several classes that she probably had expected to be able to do more in class than she could do. Her solution was to work patiently at preparing for and teaching class and just get as much done as she could. At the end of the day, Jessica felt that she had gotten through everything essential, although she was not certain that students had learned everything that they needed to learn.

*Week 3*

Jessica's hassle of the day when the Week 3 call was received again involved being prepared for class. On this day she had not only fewer in-class demonstrations than usual but also fewer than she felt she needed. Jessica saw this was a serious problem, for the end of the year was approaching, and to her mind there was much remaining to be covered. She was particularly worried that some of the material that was slated to be on the final might not get covered in class, that some undone demonstrations related to content covered on the final. Part of today's problem reflected that she may have covered material too thoroughly and too slowly earlier in the term, giving more demonstrations than necessary, with the result that she fell behind the school's recommended curriculum in chemistry. Jessica dealt with today's challenge by adapting her lesson to cover essentials. Also, she remembered that she had a demonstration from last year already made up that was pertinent to this day's lesson. She retrieved it from the back room and used it in today's class. Things did not go great, but they went okay.

*Week 4*

On the day of the Week 4 phone call, Jessica had a student in class who refused to listen. This student did not respond when she asked him to calm down—either the first, second, third, or fourth time she asked. In fact, the student was confrontational when Jessica persisted in her efforts to quiet him. The offending student was one of twin brothers, both of whom were in the class. Generally, they tended to dominate much of the class conversation. Although she kept him after school to discuss the incident, she was uncertain the student would behave any better at the next class meeting. Jessica felt that she was more frustrated by this student today than she had been with any other student over the course of the year.

*Discussion*

Although there were some mild behavior problems (e.g., a class talking too much, an individual student who was inattentive), Jessica's biggest problem was with planning. Moreover, her current plans were affected by the yearlong plan, with a great deal left to do at the end of the year, in part because of the thoroughness of her coverage at the beginning of the year. Jessica was flexible enough that she was able to get through her days with a good deal covered, but she was not succeeding in getting everything done that she felt needed to be completed.

## GENERAL DISCUSSION

When the case studies in this chapter are examined, a few issues are salient:
1. Mild misbehavior, such as student talking and inattentiveness, is a frequent challenge for beginning teachers. Some handle it routinely, and although it continues to recur, it is not a big hassle. Others cannot bring it under control, resulting in a long-term and more serious problem.
2. Occasionally, there are more serious misbehaviors that require the teacher to take immediate and sterner action. These almost always take up some class time. Although the teachers all felt that they could not ignore these more serious incidents, we were struck that often the teacher's action did not completely solve the problem, although progress was usually made.
3. Confronting planning challenges and adjusting plans were both commonly reported in the telephone interviews. Moreover, today's plans and adjustments are often affected by what the teacher did previously (e.g., Jessica retrieved last year's demonstration in a pinch, and Susan changed her finals based on her experience the previous year).
4. There are often interactions with other adults associated with the school that provide many possibilities for challenge. Other teachers' actions can affect the beginning teacher's days, as can the whims of an administrator. Parents who are supportive of the teacher and those who are not can demand a teacher's time and attention.

In short, we found plenty of evidence in these case studies that there are some challenges that are very frequent in the classrooms of beginning teachers. What was optimistic about these cases was that the beginning teachers were coping with the daily challenges reasonably well. Yes, there were exceptions. We note, however, that by interviewing teachers at the end of the year or at the end of two years, we were dealing with survivors. In the Notre Dame program, as in all teacher education programs, some teachers do not survive to the end of their first year of teaching. As we reflected on who did not survive, we remembered many serious challenges that led to dismissal of a teacher or resignation from the program. In most such cases, administrators made the decision fairly early in the year that the teacher was not doing a good job. Sometimes the teacher's problem was brought to the attention of the administrator by parents or other teachers. In short, many beginning teachers who are perceived as wholly inadequate to the task of teaching by other adults associated with the school do not make it to the end of their first year of teaching. As we reflect on the relatively mild challenges reported in the case studies in this chapter, it is important to keep in mind that some beginning teachers encountered insurmountable challenges early in their first year of teaching that resulted in their leaving the field before the data reported in this chapter were collected. By the end of the first year, surviving teachers seem to have relatively mild challenges and are able to handle them rather than permitting them to accelerate into unmanageable situations.

# chapter thirteen

# Concluding Reflections

S ince doing the research reported in this book, we have spoken to several groups of young teachers about the challenges of beginning teaching. There is a variety of reactions to the information presented in this volume. When talking to young people near the completion of their first year of teaching, their invariable reaction is that of recognition: They recognize many of the challenges discussed here as ones they experienced or their beginning-teaching peers experienced. Naturally, we find this validation gratifying. When we speak to young teachers with a little more experience, they endorse the conclusion that the second year is less challenging, identifying with the short portraits of second-year teachers, all of whom seemed less hassled than their first-year counterparts. Again, this validates the conclusion that the first year of teaching is a baptism by fire, a growth experience that permits the young teacher to do better in the years ahead. Then, there are the reactions of young people who are about to experience their first year. Their reactions are the most variable, from disbelief that there could be so many challenges to terror at the thought of so many challenges. It is these young people that are our greatest concern, for it is not adaptive either to believe there is nothing to fear or to believe that beginning teaching is an overwhelming experience.

We can safely say to every new teacher that there is no way they will experience every challenge listed in the appendix of chapter 1. That said, every beginning teacher we have studied in our teacher education program reports many challenges during the first year. Being multiply challenged during the initial year of teaching is probably a universal experience. This point is illustrated well by the stories of the teachers in this book and by Table 13-1, in which the many different types of challenges that each of the teachers faced are summarized. By expecting such challenges, the young teacher is prepared to recognize them for what they are—a natural part of professional development. The young teacher definitely should not feel that being challenged is a sign of failure as a beginning teacher!

The teachers whose stories are featured in this book learned a lot from dealing with the challenges they faced, and it is a sign of success when reflective growth occurs because of some challenge! It is made clear in Table 13-1 that these teachers faced challenges in each of the 22 categories of challenge highlighted in this book. Though no one teacher reported challenges in every category, challenges in 7 to 15 of the 22 categories (50% on average) were described by each of the authors of the chapter-long stories about their first year of teaching. The teachers whose stories were derived from the end-of-day interviews reported facing challenges in only 2 to 9 of the categories (23.9% on average) over the course of a mere two to four days. Some of the categories of challenge were represented in the stories more often than were others, as well. Only several categories appeared in more than half the stories, with the most common categories of challenge being disciplining students, dealing with student misbehavior, motivating students, coping with individual differences in students, and planning. On the other hand, more than half of the categories (59.1%) appeared in less than a third of the stories, with the least common of these categories of challenge (addressed in three [12.5%] or fewer of the stories) being resources, nonteaching demands, mentoring/induction, diversity, gender/sexual challenges, and outside community issues.

In coping with challenges every day, beginning teachers come to recognize that their job largely is solving the problems that occur. Such on-the-job problem solving is a high-level professional development experience; it is how young teachers develop into more competent teachers. Even more positively, although the new teacher will face multiple challenges every day, most are solvable. Most are the kinds of problems solved by hundreds of thousands of teachers every day. That is not to take lightly these challenges, however, for there can be so many of them that the young teacher can be overwhelmed. Also, what is a solvable problem for most beginning teachers can be unsolvable for some beginning teacher somewhere. A message for all those who work with beginning teachers is to recognize that the beginning teacher's world is filled with challenges and that, although most of the problems can be solved by the beginning teacher, sometimes a little help is needed and appropriate.

One way that the participants in the Notre Dame program are learning about the challenges they face is by being provided this book. Beginning this summer, all students in the program will have access to an on-line version of the book and will be encouraged to spend time with it. Once the book is published in a print version, it will become required reading in advance of arrival at the program, an introduction about what is to come. We hope that others find this book similarly useful, although we also encourage other programs to develop their own cases that might reflect well the schooling environments where beginning teachers in their programs are serving.

Our philosophical perspective is that school should be student centered. After all, the institution of schooling largely exists to develop students. From that perspective, it is heartening that so many of the issues of beginning teaching reflect student-driven challenges. Many of the challenges reflect that teachers do work with a wide variety of young people, that what teaching is about is working flexibly to accommodate and adapt to the needs of the young people in the teacher's charge. That challenges with individual differences in student characteristics and behaviors were so salient in the data has increased our awareness of the need for a much greater emphasis in teacher education on dealing with diversity and individual differences. As this concluding chapter is being written, we are making plans to reshape the required exceptionality and human development courses in our teacher education program to provide more input to the young teachers in our program about student differences and how to address them.

Even so, as constructivist teacher educators, we know very well that the most complete learning about human differences that matter in teaching will occur as young teachers work with diverse students. Our teacher education program requires two years of actual teaching and hence provides real-life opportunities to experience the full range of students that come to the contemporary schoolhouse. As much as young teachers can learn on their own by actual teaching, there is no

**TABLE 13-1**

*Teachers' Stories as They Address the 22 Categories of Challenge*

Chapter

| Category of Challenge | 4 Amy | 5 Sarah | 6 Kimberley | 7 Daniel | 8 Michael | 9 Chris | 10 Kelly | 11 Dennis | 12 Abby | 12 Casey | 12 Pam | 12 Laura | 12 Denise | 12 Raina | 12 Chelsea | 12 Luke | 12 Timothy | 12 Mark | 12 Nell | 12 Rebecca | 12 Shelly | 12 Edward | 12 Susan | 12 Jessica |
|---|---|---|---|---|---|---|---|---|---|---|---|---|---|---|---|---|---|---|---|---|---|---|---|---|
| 1. Discipline | | ✓ | | ✓ | ✓ | ✓ | ✓ | ✓ | | ✓ | ✓ | | ✓ | ✓ | | | ✓ | ✓ | | | | ✓ | ✓ | ✓ |
| 2. Misbehavior | ✓ | ✓ | | ✓ | ✓ | ✓ | ✓ | | ✓ | ✓ | ✓ | ✓ | ✓ | ✓ | | ✓ | ✓ | ✓ | ✓ | ✓ | ✓ | ✓ | ✓ | ✓ |
| 3. Motivating Students | ✓ | ✓ | ✓ | ✓ | ✓ | ✓ | ✓ | | ✓ | ✓ | | ✓ | | | ✓ | ✓ | | ✓ | | | | ✓ | | |
| 4. Individual Differences | ✓ | ✓ | ✓ | ✓ | ✓ | | ✓ | ✓ | ✓ | ✓ | | ✓ | | | | | ✓ | | | | ✓ | ✓ | | |
| 5. Assessment | | ✓ | | | | | | | ✓ | | | | | | | | ✓ | | | | | | ✓ | ✓ |
| 6. Parents | | | ✓ | | ✓ | ✓ | ✓ | ✓ | | ✓ | ✓ | | | | | | | | ✓ | | ✓ | ✓ | | |
| 7. Classroom Management | | ✓ | | | | | | | ✓ | ✓ | | | | ✓ | ✓ | ✓ | ✓ | | | ✓ | | | | ✓ |
| 8. Resources | ✓ | ✓ | | ✓ | | | | | | | | | | | | | | | | | | | | |
| 9. Teacher–Student Relations | ✓ | ✓ | | ✓ | ✓ | | ✓ | ✓ | | ✓ | | | | | | | ✓ | | | ✓ | | | | |

| | 1 | 2 | 3 | 4 | 5 | 6 | 7 | 8 | 9 | 10 | 11 | 12 | 13 | 14 | 15 | 16 | 17 | 18 | 19 | 20 | 21 | 22 | 23 |
|---|---|---|---|---|---|---|---|---|---|---|---|---|---|---|---|---|---|---|---|---|---|---|---|
| 10. Nonteaching Demands | | | | √ | | | √ | | | | | | | | | | | | | | | | |
| 11. Faculty Relations | | | | √ | | √ | √ | √ | | | √ | √ | | | | | √ | √ | | √ | | √ | √ |
| 12. Planning | √ | √ | √ | √ | | | √ | √ | √ | | √ | √ | | √ | √ | | √ | √ | √ | √ | | | √ |
| 13. Instruction | | √ | | √ | √ | | √ | | | √ | | | | | | | | | | | | | |
| 14. Knowledge Base | √ | √ | √ | √ | | √ | √ | | | | | | | | | | | | | | | | |
| 15. Mentoring/ Induction | √ | | | | | | | √ | | | | | | | | | | | | | | | |
| 16. School Culture | | | | | | √ | √ | | | | | | | | √ | | | | | | | | √ |
| 17. Relations with Principals | | | | √ | | | √ | | | √ | √ | | | | | | | √ | | √ | | | |
| 18. Diversity | √ | | | | | √ | | | | | | | | | | | | | | | | | |
| 19. Personal Life | | | √ | √ | | √ | √ | √ | | | | √ | | | | | | | | | | | √ |
| 20. Attitudes | √ | √ | √ | √ | √ | | √ | √ | | | | | | | | | | | | | | | |
| 21. Gender/ Sexual | | | | √ | | √ | | | | | | | | √ | | | | | | | | | |
| 22. Community | | | | | | | | | | | | | | | | | | | | | | | |

doubt that support from others who have gone before them can be helpful as well. Thus, as this chapter is being written, we are planning to increase the clinical supervision support our teachers receive in the field so that they can have opportunities to reflect with experienced professionals on the student challenges they confront. Part of this supervision will include greater accessibility to a clinical psychologist who can provide professional-level input to young teachers in our program about some of the most challenging students in their classrooms.

Another important insight emerging from the analyses summarized in this book was that even experienced teachers felt there was more they could learn, especially about the increasingly diverse students in U.S. schools. As we think about how to create postlicensure professional development experiences, we are going to keep this need in mind. That is, an important focus of postgraduate professional development should be recognizing individual differences in students and dealing with those differences.

Although we are seeking to expand and improve our supervisory support, the program already has extensive support, largely because every year a number of our teachers will confront some of the most serious challenges that were considered in chapter 2. For example, every year, beginning teachers in our program confront students who engage in extreme behaviors—gunplay resulting in injury, or anorexia, or attempted suicide. Each year, we have had to deal with schools in which corporal punishment is the norm; such punishment is often traumatic for young teachers even to witness incidentally (e.g., hearing loud cracks of a paddling down the hall). Every year, a parent somewhere will hassle a beginning teacher in our program to the point of harassment, for example, attempting to get the young teacher dismissed. A few beginning teachers in the program will have experiences with decidedly unconstructive colleagues who seem determined to make the young teacher's life miserable. Some principals also are inappropriate with beginning teachers, for example, in one instance, publicly making much of the fact that a young woman had done well as an undergraduate at an elite private university in the North, which resulted in some students in the school concluding that her background was mismatched to the southern school she was serving. When these types of serious challenges occur, teachers in our program receive support from the field supervisors as well as additional help from Notre Dame–based personnel, including program directors, counseling psychologists, and faculty with expertise in various aspects of education and schooling. We think that all faculties of education should reflect on what really serious challenges their student teachers confront and how best to support the beginning teachers in their programs to work through very demanding situations. An important message of the analyses summarized in this book is that not all challenges are ones that the beginning teacher can solve on his or her own.

Are we always completely successful in working through problems? Frankly, no, but we can makes things better. For example, one of our first-year teachers was asked to teach in a content area completely mismatched to her training and interests. Although the Notre Dame staff could do nothing to improve the teaching assignment during the first year, we were able to negotiate a much more appropriate teaching assignment for the young woman during her second year in the program. As we reflected on this experience, the Notre Dame staff resolved to make it a priority to impress on schools working with our program that teaching assignments must be appropriate and matched to the talents and interests of the young people who choose to do their teacher education with us. The staff of the Notre Dame program spends a lot of time thinking about the most serious challenges its beginning teachers face, and we believe this is something that every teacher education faculty in the country should take on as an important activity.

Everyone associated with teacher education knows that some young teachers do better than others. Although those who do better seem less challenged by interpersonal relationships at school (i.e., they find students, colleagues, and other adults encountered at school less challenging), it was somewhat surprising to learn that they seem to have more personal problems than do other beginning teachers. They reported worrying more, seemed more hassled in their personal lives, and tended to doubt their own abilities more. We think that some hard thinking might be in order about how to counsel the best and brightest of beginning teachers so that their lives are more satisfying. What can be done to help such teachers manage their time so they have more leisure, more opportunities to have more of a home rather than a house? Can anything be done to decrease their sense that the demands of teaching are overwhelming and to increase their confidence? Can they be taught to be realistic about how much planning is enough, to be more accepting that not all of the material that might be covered necessarily will be covered? Often, the best beginning teachers get overlooked, as field supervisors and faculty do what they can to help beginning teachers who are struggling. An important message in this book is that even the best beginning teachers often can benefit from support, although different types of support than those required by the struggling teacher. The teacher educator community needs to seriously consider what it can do to make beginning teaching as fulfilling as possible for the best of the young teachers, the young people we should most want to encourage to remain in teaching for the long term.

As we reread the stories of beginning teaching that were showcased in this book, we recognize the challenge for us as teacher educators to anticipate the needs of any young teacher. Quite frankly, who could have predicted what happened to any of the young people whose story was told in this volume? One of the greatest challenges for teacher educators in preparing beginning teachers to face the challenges ahead of them is that the problems are so unpredictable.

Yes, it is a good bet that many of the 571 potential challenges of teaching cited in chapter 1 will happen to a new teacher during the first year of teaching, but which ones? Moreover, even if the subset of the 571 challenges that a young teacher was going to face were known in advance, every potential challenge can manifest in a multitude of ways because of factors—such as the unique students, colleagues, administrators, and parents in a given school—that exist in a unique cultural milieu at a unique point in time.

So, as we close this volume, our advice for teacher educators is to do all possible to support young teachers during their initial years of teaching. Our advice to the beginning teacher is to be ready to be challenged. Be confident as well that you are equal to most of the challenges that will confront you, and that much of your job as a teacher is to solve the day-to-day problems that are the 571 potential challenges of teaching reviewed in this volume. Know that there are no canned solutions, but find inspiration in the many stories in this volume of young teachers who were not much different from you, who often served their students and schools well by getting very good at generating solutions to problems on the run. We hope that you noticed, as we did, that many of the young teachers really seemed to have great fun as they invented their teaching as problem solving. They were proud of their accomplishments as they told their tales here, as you will be as you rise to the occasion in the first year or two of your teaching career. You are about to begin a great odyssey, and many of you have it within you to meet its challenges.

# Acknowledgments

WE WOULD LIKE TO THANK the following contributors, who were charitable enough to share the stories of their first year of teaching with all of us:

Bridget Barry
Lizabeth Bradshaw
Sheila Buck
Gina Couri
John Eriksen
Daniel Kelly
Thomas Perez
Dominic Picón
Joseph Villinski